AF270178

PLACE
MATTERS

ORO Editions
Publishers of Architecture, Art, and Design
Gordon Goff: Publisher

www.oroeditions.com
info@oroeditions.com

Published by ORO Editions

Text by Robert McCarter
Foreword by Kenneth Frampton
Afterword by Steven Holl
Managing Editor: Jake Anderson

Book Design by Pablo Mandel and Maureen Hollboll
www.circularstudio.com

Typeset in Avenir

10 9 8 7 6 5 4 3 2 First Edition

ISBN: 978-1-940743-42-4

Color Separations and Printing: ORO Group Ltd.
Printed in China.

ORO Editions makes a continuous effort to minimize the overall
carbon footprint of its publications. As part of this goal, ORO
Editions, in association with Global ReLeaf, arranges to plant trees
to replace those used in the manufacturing of the paper produced
for its books. Global ReLeaf is an international campaign run by
American Forests, one of the world's oldest nonprofit conservation
organizations. Global ReLeaf is American Forests' education and
action program that helps individuals, organizations, agencies, and
corporations improve the local and global environment by planting
and caring for trees.

PLACE MATTERS

THE ARCHITECTURE OF WG CLARK

ROBERT MCCARTER

Contents

The career of the exceptionally talented W. G. Clark testifies to the regrettable provinciality of American regional culture, given the remarkably imaginative competition designs made during his partnership with Charles Menefee that were submitted for significant public works in Pheonix and New Orleans, neither of which would be realized, as well as Charleston, where the South Carolina Aquarium of 1987, sited on a canal that marked the original waterline of the Cooper River, would eventually be realized in revised form after a 13 year interval. An even more chequered fate will befall a more recent competition entry, designed by Clark alone, namely the Clemson Charleston Graduate Center which, despite having been accorded first prize is seemingly not going to be built.

The significance of this loss might be judged from the quality of the Clark and Menefee Middleton Inn, dating from as long ago as 1985 and built adjacent to a national historic landmark known as Middleton Place. What is striking about this work is the way in which a thick service wall, pierced at regular intervals by vaulting access stairs, is poised on top of a rectilinear ridge in such a way as to integrate the three-storey structure into the topography. Here, in the most explicit example of Clark's tectonic and topographic work, we encounter a version of the Kahnian interplay between servant and served, that is to say, between the heavy, opaque, thick-wall service structure bounding the hotel and the light-weight, three storey assembly of the bedrooms themselves, faced with floor to ceiling, wood-framed glazing which culminates in the rhythmic fenestration pattern of the common lodge/lounge at the end of the bedroom wing, fully glazed with the same framing at a larger scale. This syntactical play between heavy and light will also animate the cubic form of his Croffead House of 1989 which will, in effect, initiate the series of modest, two storey houses that are destined make up the bulk of Clark's career to date.

Clark's Lucy Daniels pre-school of 1992 and the modest house that he built for his own occupation in 1996 exemplify, at different scales; a micro-cosmic architecture made up of the articulation of diverse materials drawn from Clark's signature palette of concrete block, steel-framed glazing, glass lenses, exposed timber joists, and structural frames in fair faced concrete, along with built-in storage, tubular steel handrails, timber floors, and, very occasionally, precision brickwork and lightweight "aerial" roofs. Clark's stoic career has been that of a committed, sensitive and exceptionally skilled American architect who truly deserves to be better recognized on his own turf and one hopes that this new publication will finally gain for his highly refined achievements the local audience and support that he so richly deserves.

Ruins of Sheldon Church, Yemassee, South Carolina, 1756.

Place matters to WG Clark. The architecture of WG Clark is inextricably grounded in its place, the Atlantic coastal states of the American South. Over the course of his 50-year career as a modern architect practicing in historic contexts, Clark has constructed a small but significant body of work of unparalleled high quality and experiential richness. Clark's remarkably resolved spatial compositions are formally restrained and contextually appropriate, and while relatively few in number, have nevertheless exerted an outsize influence on architects around the world. Clark's regional grounding, slow and measured pace of design, and modest publicity has provided him with the time-in-place necessary for thinking and making at the very highest level. Like the relatively few works of Louis Kahn and Carlo Scarpa, the works of WG Clark have attained canonical status, and his redefinition of architectural design as being grounded in the history of the discipline, as well as in the particularities of its place, has proved to be of ever-increasing relevance to contemporary practice.

Making place matter begins with the place in which the architect works, extends through the thinking about the making of place involved in architectural design, and culminates in the pre-existing place that is transformed into a new place in the act of constructing a building. Clark is one of the few US architects—like Carlo Scarpa in his lifelong relationship to the Veneto region of Italy—best understood by being introduced in parallel with the place where he works. The peripheral location of Clark's regional practice, the relatively small number of works realized at infrequent intervals, and the formal restraint, and contextual appropriateness the works exhibit have together resulted in the work's receiving little notice from the global centers of publicity. Yet Clark's relative anonymity has never hindered his small local practice from establishing important precedents for the larger discipline of architecture.

As a modern architect working and living in the tightly constrained cultural and natural contexts of the historic city of Charleston, South Carolina, WG Clark evolved a set of ordering principles that would prove to be of critical importance to the larger international discipline of architecture. Clark's work begins and ends with the land, irrespective of whether the site is urban or rural. Clark's reverence for the landscape has given rise to his ethical principle that architecture, while inevitably involving destruction in its realization, should nevertheless always construct a place that honors and respects the innate character of the landscape in which it is built; "The most important quality of architecture is the way it relates to, signifies, and dignifies a setting on earth."[1]

In its relation to physical, natural, and cultural place, Clark's architecture is grounded in its place, his built works having all been realized in South Carolina, North

Carolina, and Virginia, and his practice having been based in two Southern cities: the initial 14 years in Charleston, South Carolina, and the last 30 years in Charlottesville, Virginia. To the increasingly homogenous, universal and placeless conditions of our contemporary "globalized" world, the architecture of Clark stands in counterpoint and opposition, drawing strength from its being grounded in the specifics of its local culture and place.

WG Clark was born in Louisa, Virginia on May 14, 1942. The county seat of Louisa lies in the agricultural lowlands drained by tributaries of the James and York Rivers, 80 miles to the southwest of Washington, DC, and less than 30 miles to the east of Charlottesville, the site of Thomas Jefferson's two great works of architecture, his house at Monticello and the University of Virginia, both of which would exercise a profound influence on Clark's architectural thinking. Growing up close to the land in the agricultural context of rural Virginia, Clark later began his lectures by describing an old mill near his hometown as being an example of building as if place mattered; "One didn't regret its being there because it made more than itself; it made a millpond and a waterfall, creating at once stillness and velocity … There was an unforgettable alliance of land to pond to dam to abutment to building. It was not a building simply imposed on the place; it became the place, and thereby deserved its being—an elegant offering paid for the use of the stream. Its sureness made other buildings appear to be lost and haphazard."[2] Clark holds that the old mill improves its place and intensifies our experience of it, whereas most recent buildings impose themselves on the place and impoverish it. The mill and other vernacular constructions set an ethical standard for Clark's own work, and he believes that new buildings should act to reconcile us with the land, replacing what is inevitably lost in new construction with something that atones for that loss by making the place better after the building is complete than it was before.

Clark attended architecture school at the University of Virginia, receiving a Bachelor of Architecture degree in 1965. During his five years in architecture school, Clark recalls that he learned about Frank Lloyd Wright and Louis Kahn, but that none of the faculty talked about Le Corbusier, whose work he learned about only after graduating. Following his graduation, Clark moved to Richmond, Virginia, where he worked for a year for Rawlings and Wilson Architects, a firm made up largely of University of Virginia alumni, which was later involved in designing several buildings on the University of Virginia campus. Learning of a new school of thought then emerging in Philadelphia, Pennsylvania, Clark moved there in order to take part in what was called the "Philadelphia School" of architecture, which was centered on University of Pennsylvania faculty such as the practicing architects Louis Kahn, Romaldo Giurgola, and Robert Venturi, the landscape architect Ian McHarg, the structural engineer Robert Le Ricolais, the urban planner Edmund Bacon, and America's foremost cultural historian and architectural critic, Lewis Mumford.

The seven years he lived in Philadelphia, from 1966 to 1973, would prove to be profoundly formative for Clark, who recalls; "Philadelphia was important. I moved there shortly after completing school because it was—in 1966—the center of architecture in the U.S. … many good architects were there, part of a very close architectural community. It was an exciting place to be, especially for someone who grew up in a small southern town. We lived in the center of the city, on Quince Street, a narrow cobbled alley/street within view of the PSFS Building and a short walk from other important buildings—and their important lessons."[3] George Howe and William Lescaze's Philadelphia Savings Fund Society (PSFS) Building, built from 1929 to 1932—in the midst of the Great Depression—is considered the first modernist skyscraper,

Farm buildings.

Byrd Mill, Louisa, Virginia.

where, as William Curtis has said, the "inherited typological thinking about the American skyscraper and the emergent vocabulary of the International Style came together in a way that modified each."[4] Of his time in Philadelphia, Clark later noted, "This was my real education—the city, its idealistic founding and its architecture."[5]

"It was an intense time," Clark later recalled, "After work there was often [an architectural design] competition, or night drawing classes at the free Fleisher Art School," this being the same school where, as a youth in the 1910s, Louis Kahn had walked 20 blocks to take the free art classes at what was then called the Graphic Sketch Club. Clark recalls spending his lunch hours with the other young architects at the Joseph Fox bookstore, where half the space of the small shop was devoted to architecture books. While working in Philadelphia, Clark obtained a 52-page reading list of books on urban design assembled by David Crane, a former employee of Marcel Breuer who had recently started the urban design program at the University of Pennsylvania. Clark employed Crane's reading list in his autodidactic "post-graduate" study after work each day. For the young architect, the seven years in Philadelphia were nothing less than "a total immersion into a design world."[6]

After applying to work for Louis Kahn and Romaldo Giurgola, neither of whom were able to offer him a position, Clark worked for the last five years he lived in Philadelphia, from 1968 to 1973, in the office of Venturi & Rauch, where the principal, Robert Venturi, had worked in Kahn's office for several years. During that time Clark recalls drawing the perspectives for the Yale Mathematics Building competition, the New Haven Fire Station, the Purchase Humanities Building, and the Thousand Oaks California competition. During the slower times in the Venturi & Rauch office, Clark drew several section-perspectives showing construction of theaters (including Kahn's Fort Wayne Performing Arts Theater), for George Izenour's book, *Theater Design*, published in 1977. In 1966, the year that Clark had come to Philadelphia, Venturi had published the enormously influential text, *Complexity and Contradiction in Architecture*, in which he argued for the re-engagement with disciplinary history and the particulars of place and cultural context in the design of contemporary architecture.

Clark was especially affected by the quality of the architecture of the city of Philadelphia, and of its historical continuity: "The Philadelphia School referred not only to the strong design ethos of the time, but also to the continuity of architectural excellence from the beginning. To live and work there as a young architect was to become immersed in the excitement of both old and new. A two-mile walk from river to river revealed the work of Robert Mills, Frank Furness, Howe & Lescaze, Mitchell-Giurgola, and Louis Kahn, to name a few. Charleston and Charlottesville [the cities in which Clark would later practice] have their lessons in architecture to be sure, but not the unbroken presence of design spanning the old and the new [as] in Philadelphia."[7]

During the period in which Clark lived in Philadelphia, from 1966 to 1973, Louis Kahn was increasingly recognized as an architect of the first rank, and he was realizing many of the designs for which he is today most famous, including the Kimbell Museum, the Exeter Library, the Indian Institute of Management, the National Capital of Bangladesh, the Fort Wayne Performing Arts Center, and the Yale Center for British Arts, among others. While Clark never worked for Kahn, like many of his generation he was deeply affected by Kahn's work, which redefined modern architecture in three fundamental ways. First, by re-establishing the foundational significance of ancient monuments, the rituals they housed, and the geometries that ordered them, for the design of institutions, Kahn re-grounded contemporary practice in the history of the discipline. Second, by basing his designs on a poetics of action rather than functionally rationalized programs, Kahn's work was critical to the emergence of an experiential interpretation of architecture. Third, by re-establishing the primacy of the art of construction in the design of contemporary buildings, Kahn was critical to the emergence of a "tectonic" interpretation of architecture, based upon construction traditions and innovations rather than stylistic form.

Recalling his time in Philadelphia, Clark notes: "Philadelphia is a city of institutions. Louis Kahn said it was why he loved the place. The Pennsylvania Academy of Art was one of these, housed in Frank Furness's polychromatic riot on Broad Street. The Philadelphia Museum of Art, at the juncture of Fairmont Park and Center City was a favorite weekend place. And it's interesting that parks were so integral to the city from its beginning. What Jefferson taught about the powerful juncture of landscape and architecture at his university was also taught by William Penn with his famous Squares."[8]

After this formative experience in Philadelphia, Clark moved to Charleston, South Carolina, where he established his own architectural practice in 1974. The 14 years in which he lived and practiced in the historic context of Charleston and its surrounding landscape would prove to be essential in establishing Clark's characteristic way of thinking and making architecture. In turn, through constructing appropriate modern buildings within its historic setting, Clark would transform Charleston and the surrounding region as a context for the practice of architecture, and his practice increasingly offered a model for the making of contemporary architecture in historic contexts.

Charleston is a place steeped in American history, having been established in 1670 on the peninsula at the confluence of the Ashley and Cooper Rivers, which form the Charleston Harbor that opens to the Atlantic Ocean. Settled by the British and French Huguenots, Charleston became a major seaport and center for agricultural export of rice and sea island cotton from the surrounding Carolina low country. Charleston was the leading town in the American South from Colonial times to the Civil War, growing wealthy from its active slave economy. More than half of the African slaves brought to the US came through the port of Charleston. South Carolina led the secession of Confederate states in 1860, the first shots of the Civil War were fired in Charleston, and the fall of the Union-held Fort Sumter in 1861 was a major victory for the Confederacy.

Following its devastation at the end of the Civil War, Charleston never recovered its national or region-leading position, but remained the most important city in South Carolina. In 1886 an earthquake destroyed 2,000 buildings in Charleston, and the city has a long history of being struck by hurricanes. During World War II, Charleston became an important naval base, and in recent years tourism has become a major source of income for the city, known for its historic architecture both in the city and in the many surrounding plantations. In 1989 Hurricane Hugo struck Charleston, damaging three-quarters of the homes in the city's historic district, as well as doing extensive damage to the historic gardens and landscapes along the Ashley River.

The culture of building that evolved in historic Charleston involved predominately wood construction for houses, a unique building regulation regarding the siting and orientation of houses, and a distinctive house-type, all developed in answer to the climatic and environmental challenges of the place. As Clark notes, Charleston is a city of houses, with relatively few churches and commercial buildings, so that the residential lot structures the urban grain of the city. The predominant house-type in the city is the side-yard house, called the "Single House" locally, a variation on the Georgian two-room, central hall plan, its volume adapted to the hot, humid climate by being long, tall, and thin – only one room deep. The elongated house runs from the street to the rear of its lot, and the house occupies one-half of the lot, with its garden occupying the other half of the lot. Historic building regulations reinforced the predominance of the side-yard house type, as well as its orientation to the sunlight, by requiring that the domestic gardens be placed either to the west (on east-west streets) or to the south (on north-south streets) of the house itself. Thus on the street front, each lot is half building and half garden, forming a regular pattern of solid and void.

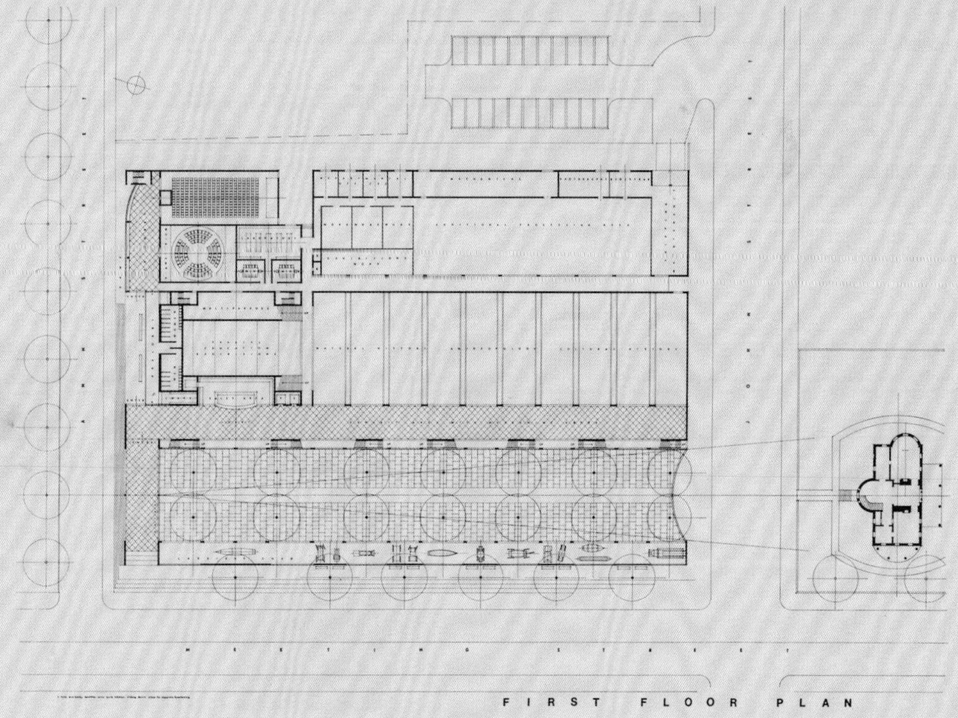

Plan, Charleston Museum competition entry, 1975.

The house and garden, each occupying one-half of the building lot, are locked together by the deep side-yard covered porches (called "piazzas" by Charleston's citizens) that run continuously along the garden façade at each floor level. The porches, opening onto the garden, are the largest "rooms" of the house, and they give access to all the interior rooms as well as shading the house from the hot summer sun. The open porches, lined with windows, are the "front" side of the house, while the opposite, "back" side of the house, facing the neighbor's garden, is a solid wall. The solid back wall of the neighboring house provides privacy to the garden for each house, as it in turn provided privacy to its neighbor on the other side. In this way, every house has a private garden of the same size as the house, leading Clark to remark; "What an astoundingly elegant solution, merging urban pattern, response to climate and individuality."[9]

The narrow end of the house is set directly on the street, with a wall or fence often screening the garden from the sidewalk. At the opposite end of the lot, a separate kitchen structure, accessed by the porch-piazza, is set into the rear garden. The primary windows and doors of the house open towards the garden, as well as towards the street and rear garden, providing cross-ventilation, shading, and the smell of both garden and sea breezes. The house is raised several feet above the ground to facilitate cooling (cooler air being drawn in from beneath the house and hot air exhausted at the top of the central stair); to house the brick cistern that collects roof rainwater runoff for domestic use; as well as to protect its wood structure from the frequent flooding. The entry door opens to the porch-piazza, rather than to the interior rooms, so that the act of entry is through the porch-piazza, where one simultaneously inhabits both the garden and the house. The porch leads to the center of the house where the entry and stair hall is set between the two primary rooms. As Clark notes of the entry sequence; "This is an interesting architectural moment where the asymmetrical relationship to the street gives way to the symmetry of the house."[10]

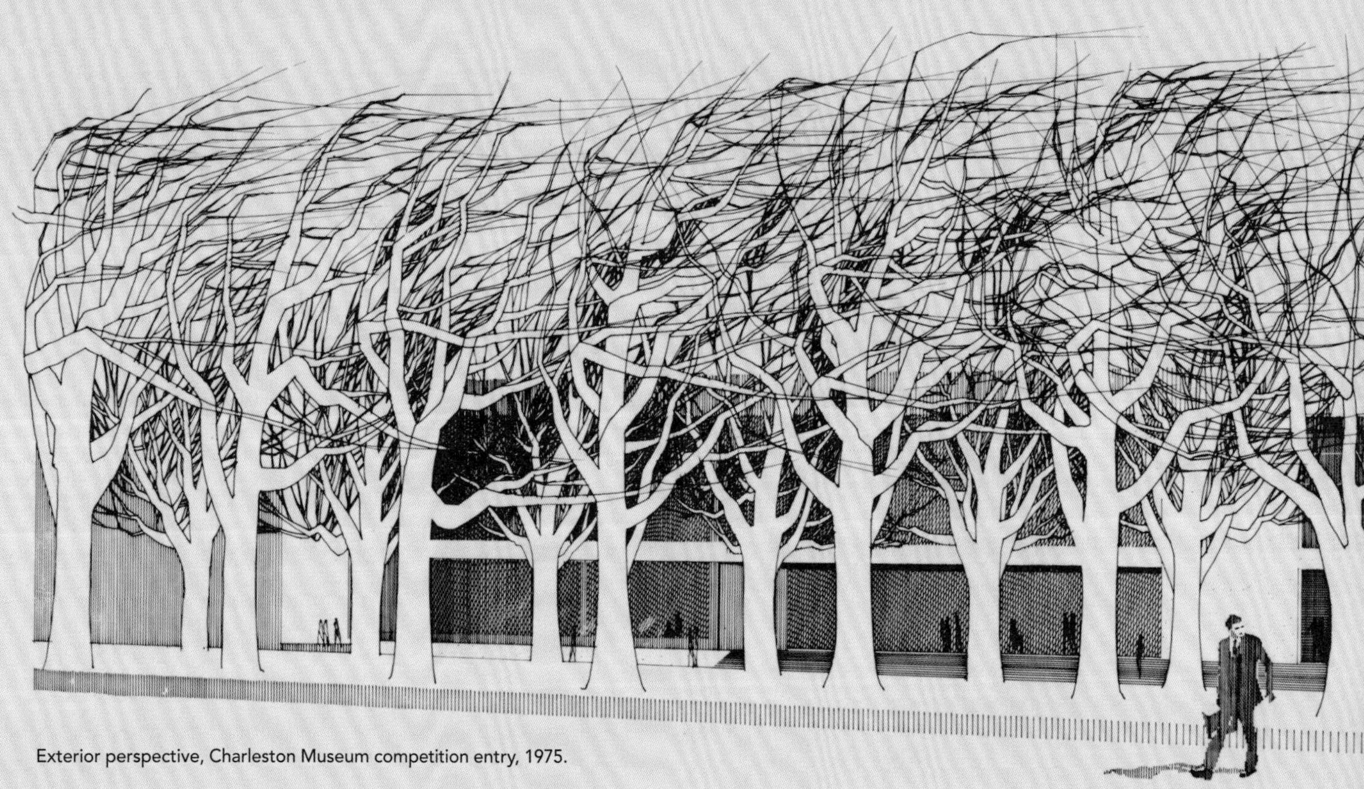

Exterior perspective, Charleston Museum competition entry, 1975.

From the beginning of Clark's career, the side-yard typology of the Charleston Single House has served as a particularly important inspiration for many of his designs. In noting the constructive qualities of the Single House, he said; "I find these houses so admirable because after all the sensible responses to climate and privacy, they emerge as elegantly proportioned forms contributing to the larger urban order. I admire the formal devices of the classical and the romantic joined. If you squint, you can see their influence at Middleton Inn."[11]

As Clark notes, contemporary Charleston is a place of "strong building traditions, formal typologies and a fierce determinism to preserve and extend 18th-century appearance" of its architecture. What Clark termed "a central question" of his practice in Charleston was: "How modern buildings may be made to strongly belong to, spring from, a place rich in historic tradition." From the beginning of his practice, Clark was committed to the critical evolution of modern architecture, and yet many of the citizens of Charleston "thought modern architecture was foreign; we wanted to prove that it is not, and [that it] could be intensely grounded in a local landscape as well as in a local culture."[12]

In learning from the way the city was built, and the lessons to be found in the work of previous generations of builders, Clark defined the modern architect's challenge regarding the constraint of local culture: "How to add to a beautiful place respectfully and critically. And how to prove that modern did not mean alien. This resulted in intense study regarding how to make new things fit, to belong. It meant that it was necessary to learn the history of the city to know its underlying principles of design: grain, texture, proportion, material, color, joints, responses to climate, and, of course, light … Only then could new work be infused with analogous traits, sympathetic character and sensibilities without simply aping old styles. Lesson one involved respecting a place."[13]

Charleston is also a challenging environment in which to build, and Clark notes that the second constraint the city imposes on architecture "was related not so much to formal design as it was to construction. Despite a calm, idyllic appearance, Charleston is a very difficult place in which to build. It has poor soil, earthquakes, hurricanes, flooding, ambient salt air, mildew and rot producing moisture, harsh sun, and Formosan termites [who attack buildings from above, entering through the attic, rather than from the ground below]. Almost nothing is built without careful soil analysis (foundation pilings can be a hundred feet long); windstorms destroy buildings; it is the second worst seismic zone in the country. Coastal salt air destroys normal hardware in weeks; the sun eats finishes; and the termites eat the wood."[14] As a result, Clark argues that Charleston "is not the place for amateur, negligent builders. Nor for normal modern Minimalist detailing."[15] But, if one is willing to engage the constraints, Charleston can be "a place for young architects to learn respect for nature, and for what it means to build. What valuable lessons: the constraints of both a stubborn Culture and a stubborn Nature, to be learned from in the effort to prove that a modern building could belong to its place."[16]

In 1941, the historian and cultural critic Lewis Mumford published *The South in Architecture*, a call for what would be given the name "critical regionalism" only 40 years later.[17] Mumford's book also raises many of the issues that Clark later engaged with while practicing in Charleston and Charlottesville. Mumford's definition of regionalism is one that does not result from simply imitating the forms of historic buildings in the region, or employing the local building materials, or engaging the regional climate. Rather, Mumford proposes a regionalism that results from an analysis of historical buildings and an engagement with contemporary social and cultural values, arguing that such an approach has—through the work of the architects Thomas Jefferson and Henry Hobson Richardson, both born in the South—"enabled the South, in particular, to leave an imprint on buildings far removed" from that region.[18]

Mumford begins his book with the observation; "Too much of our appreciation of historic buildings in America…has been confined to the surface" and to "a narrow antiquarian preoccupation with the past… [Yet] the great lesson of history—and this applies to all the arts—is that the past cannot be recaptured except in spirit."[19] Mumford argues for a deeper understanding of building, beginning with an understanding of "the gradual adaption of European modes of construction to American climatic and technical conditions," which recognized that "perhaps the most advanced technical adaption that has so far been made was the old-fashioned shutter, which controlled both the amount of heat and light that entered a room."[20] Mumford believes that a constructive contemporary architectural regionalism is the result of a local building tradition that is open to universal concepts coming from outside the region, which are in turn assimilated and adapted to local conditions.

Paralleling the "lessons" Clark later learned while practicing in Charleston, Mumford states, "Regionalism is not a matter of using the most available local material, or of copying some simple form of construction that our ancestors used, for want of anything better, a century or two ago. Regional forms are those which most closely meet the actual conditions of life and which most fully succeed in making a people feel at home in their environment: they do not merely utilize the soil but they reflect the current conditions of culture in the region." The evolution of an appropriate modern architecture in historic contexts, Mumford notes, involves the recognition of the inherent "tension between the regional and the universal … Every culture must both be itself and transcend itself; it must make the most of its limitations and must pass beyond them; it must be open to fresh experiences and yet it must maintain its integrity. In no other art is that process more sharply focused than in architecture."[21]

A modest house addition at 9 Price's Alley, built in 1975 in the heart of downtown Charleston, was the first building realized after Clark opened his office. Placed to the rear of an existing two-story brick veneer-wall garage with apartment above,

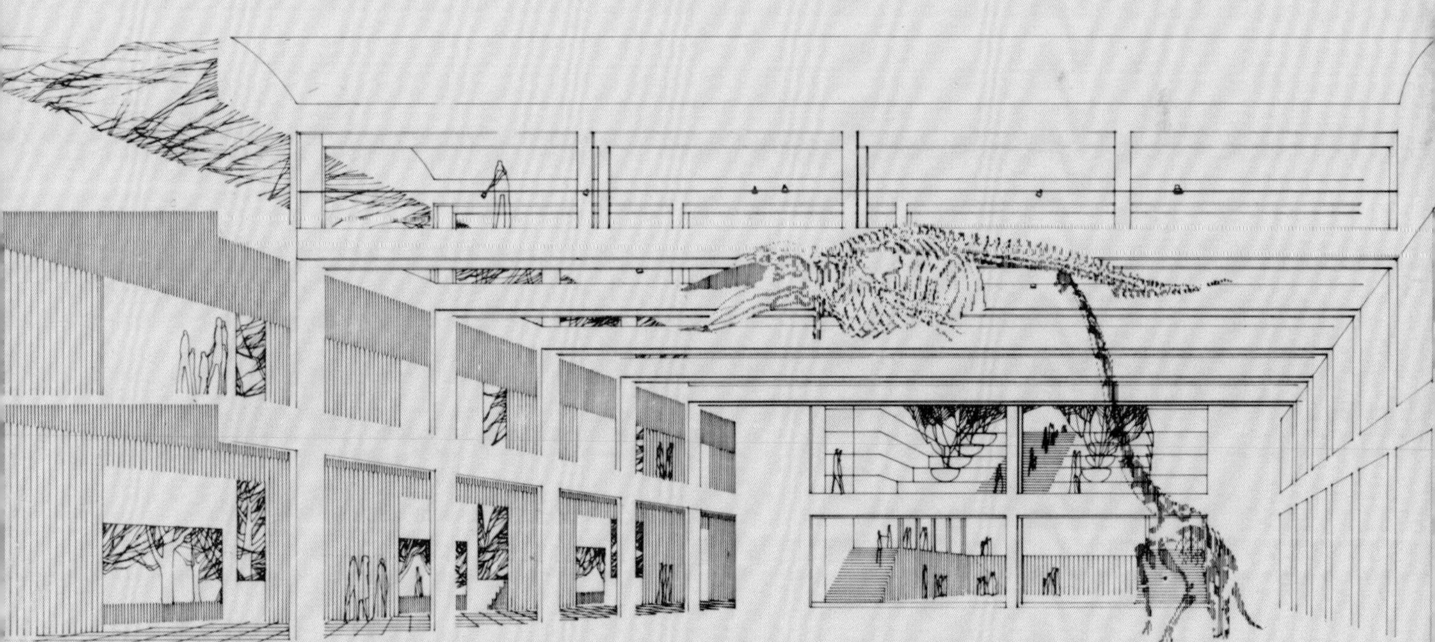

Section-perspective, Charleston Museum competition entry, 1975.

the addition has a solid, two-story wall set at the edge of the alley and following the curved property line to the west side. The recessed entry is set between the two-story wall and the one-story, fig vine-covered wall that extends along the alley, enclosing the private garden, onto which the rooms of the addition opened through double-height windows. Built of lightweight wood frame and stucco in response to the poor soil conditions, the addition contained the kitchen, dining room and utility on the ground floor, with a stair up to two bedrooms and a bath on the floor above. The renovated existing building housed the living room, with master bedroom above. Despite the addition taking the form of a Charleston Single House, Clark recalls; "Characteristic of Charleston's regard for things 'modern', the owner's own mother spoke publicly before the Board of Architectural Review to deny the project."[22]

In 1975, only one year after establishing his practice in Charleston, Clark received second prize in the national competition for the design of the Charleston Museum. The site for the large, 95,000-square-foot museum was on Meeting Street, with the oak allee, Wragg Mall, to the north, and to the south the Joseph Manigault House, a historic Huguenot building constructed in 1803 and important to both the city and the Museum, which owned it. Clark's intention was to link the three site boundaries of oak allee, street, and historic house with his design for the new museum. A garden, with a double row of trees, was placed along Meeting Street, aligning with the Manigault House, to which the garden opened to the south, with the museum entrance at the north end. In this way the mass of the museum was set to the east side of the site, framing the garden, the long axis of which was aligned with the Manigault House.

The gallery of the museum was designed as a single large room, framed by a promenade and with a gallery above, all of which recalled the old Charleston Museum, where, as Clark recalls, "all of its collection [was housed] in one large room, with the delightful result that things of many sizes and subjects were juxtaposed."[23] A series of stepped terraces above the museum spaces allowed visitors to climb up to a roof garden, where they could enjoy views of the city. In the exterior perspective, rather than being presented as an object, the museum is literally embedded in the historic city, with the allee of oak trees framing the monumental entry loggia on the

Schreck House, Street (left) and waterfront (right) view.

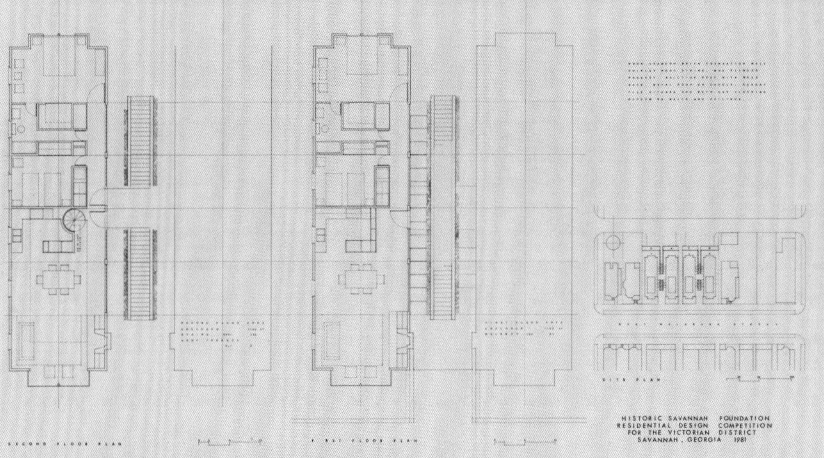

Plans, Historic Savannah Housing Competition, first prize, 1982.

north façade, while at the other end of the block the Manigault House can be seen, its façade aligned with the axis of the museum's walled garden. In both plan and perspective, the design subtly but unmistakably reveals Clark's careful study of the buildings of Louis Kahn.

One of the first complete buildings constructed to Clark's designs was the Schreck House, realized in 1981, which was constructed in Mt. Pleasant, on the east side of the Charleston harbor, facing the city. The cubic, two-story volume of the wood-framed house is clad in vertical cypress boards that were given a clear finish. Privacy from the street is provided by the absence of windows on the ground floor of the house, and by shielding the yard from view with a tall storage wall, which is also clad in vertical cypress boards. The living rooms on the lower level and the bedrooms on the upper level open to the harbor and city views through a large square window wall composed of four square fixed-glass panes. A double-height loggia runs along the south side of the house, framing a view of the harbor and city and facing onto the garden, with the entry below and a balcony suspended above, the whole a modern interpretation of the Charleston Single House. The geometric rigor, restrained detailing, and engagement of local building traditions and typological patterns of this early house would prove to be consistent characteristics of Clark's practice.

In 1982, Clark received first prize in a competition for new ideas in housing for Charleston's sister southern coastal city, Savannah, Georgia. Clark's design for the "Historic Savannah Foundation Residential Competition for the Victorian District," involved an ingenious pairing of two-story apartment buildings, with each floor-through apartment having windows on all four sides, with the living rooms on the street and the bedrooms on the alley. The pairs of apartment buildings were separated by narrow side yards so as to reinforce the rhythm of the lots of Savannah, while also being joined by a double stair, with landings at both the street and alley, which arrived to the covered entry porch at the center of the building – similar to the Charleston Single House. Clark's design was given national recognition through its publication in *Architectural Record*. That same year, Clark finalized the design and completed the construction documents for his first major project, the Middleton Inn.

The Middleton Inn was WG Clark's first major realized commission, and yet it resulted in a building of canonical significance. This is a building of such comprehensive spatial and constructive resolution, such formally restrained yet experientially enriching character, and such clarity of tectonic articulation that it remains hard to believe that the project was conceived in the first years of the architect's practice. The design for Middleton Inn, which many rightly consider to be Clark's masterwork, was finalized in 1982, when he was 40 years of age – still very early in the career of an architect. The design process was slow in unfolding, taking eight years from commission to completion of construction, and each step of the protracted process allowed Clark to become better acquainted with the landscape of the remarkable site.

Middleton Place is an early 18th-century plantation on the Ashley River in Dorchester County, 15 miles northwest of Charleston. In 1741 the main house was completed and the extensive gardens were begun by Henry Middleton, who later served as president of the First Continental Congress and became one of South Carolina's wealthiest men, owning 20 plantations totaling 50,000 acres and 800 slaves. Middleton's son Arthur, a signatory of the Declaration of Independence, was born at Middleton Place, and Arthur Middleton's son and grandson, Henry and Williams, oversaw the transition of Middleton Place from a country residence to an active rice plantation. In 1860 Williams Middleton signed the South Carolina Ordinance of Secession, marking the beginning of the US Civil War, and in 1865 during the last months of the war the plantation house at Middleton Place was destroyed by Union troops, and the remaining architecture consisted only of a few outbuildings at the edges of the gardens.

Middleton Place, a National Historic Landmark, is today most famous for its landscaped gardens, which are among the oldest in America. The gardens combine formal French and English garden design with landscape terraces and ponds related to the river topography and local rice farming practices. Slaves worked the plantation, and extensive slave labor was required to construct the formal gardens, landscape terraces, ponds, and rice fields. Middleton Place was also known for its variety of imported plants and animals, including the first water buffalo in the US, brought from Constantinople in the late 18th century for use as draft animals in the flooded rice fields. In the gardens are the first camellias imported to the US, and early samples of crepe myrtle and azalea.

The main house of Middleton Place, and the central axis of the associated gardens and terraces, was aligned by its builders with a long straight section of the Ashley River running from east to west. In this way, the river is constantly engaged in the experience of the inhabitants, forming the background for the views from the house and gardens. As the primary access to the plantation was by boats coming upriver from Charleston, the alignment of the house and its terraced gardens with the river also meant that the plantation was visible from a distance as visitors approached. This axial alignment of the plantation and its gardens with the river, and their location at a northward turn in the river, was important in Clark's designs for the site.

In designing for Middleton Place, Clark came to a realization that would prove pivotal for his practice – that engagement of the land and the place was the first and most important purpose of architectural design: "The most important quality of architecture is the way it relates to, signifies, and dignifies a place on earth. This is why most of the architecture we admire, be it the product of individuals or of civilizations, is that which has been built with a sense of allegiance to the land. Architecture is a disturbing art; it destroys places. Construction sites always have the scent of sacrifice, barely masked by the exciting and hopeful smell of building. It is our job to assuage the sacrifice and make building an act of respect for and adoration of the place."[1]

Middleton Inn, Dorchester County, South Carolina, 1977–1985

In association with Charleston Architectural Group, 1982–1985

View of terrace lawn and guestrooms of main building from the northeast.

During the time he worked on Middleton Place, Clark came to a second realization—that, as Louis Kahn said, rather than following the program of spaces as given to the architect by the client, as if filling a prescription, the architect often must act as "a philosopher" for the client by being critical of, modifying, and even rejecting the client's given program if it does not meet the architect's ethical, experiential, and economical responsibilities—which Kahn summed up as making what is appropriate; "I believe it is the duty of every architect … not to accept programs but to think in terms of spaces,"[2] and that "architecture … is not the filling of areas prescribed by the client. It is the creating of spaces that evoke a feeling of appropriate use."[3]

The first commission Clark received relating to Middleton Place in 1974, which was to design a new parking area, visitor orientation center, and administrative offices for the gardens, exemplifies both these realizations. For the orientation center, Clark was asked to provide a windowless, air-conditioned "black box theatre," in which one would view a movie before making the three hour walking tour of the gardens in the hot sun and humidity. Believing this was an inappropriate way for visitors to be introduced to the site, Clark proposed instead a shaded outdoor gallery as a part of the landscape, set along the edge of the gardens, so that visitors would never lose touch with the natural place they were visiting. In addition, he proposed that the video be replaced by a series of display panels mounted on a glass screen in front of the ivy-covered wall. The elongated, covered, open-air structure was sited along the southern edge of the rectangular pond, the largest element of the gardens. The two volumes of orientation center and administrative offices were set against a new ivy-covered berm and wall, which had the additional benefit of blocking the garden visitors' view of the parked cars. The existing pine grove planted in a grid allowed the new parking spaces to be inserted without removing trees, as well as shading the parked cars. The parking area was the only part of Clark's design to be realized.

The commission for a new Inn for guests visiting Middleton Place, to be called Middleton Inn, was given to Clark in 1977. Clark's three designs all located the Inn not in the historic gardens but along the heavily wooded bluff to the east of the gardens and south of the Ashley River. From the beginning, Clark envisioned the Inn as being composed of two primary components: linear thick masonry walls, often folded into L-shapes in plan, which housed the services, behind which the cubic, "cabinet"-like volumes of the wood and glass guestrooms were placed, with entry to the rooms through the wall, and a larger, semi-independent lodge at the end, anchoring the composition.

In response to the client's request that the Inn relate visually to the Middleton Place gardens, the first design positioned the Inn along the edge of the bluff above the Rice Mill Pond, with a longer linear building closest to the bluff, the guestrooms of which open to the gardens, and three smaller L-shaped buildings scattered to the east, the guestrooms of which open into the woods. The larger lodge is spaced away from the south end of the longer linear building and turned at a slight angle, establishing its independence even as it acts as a "head" for the long "body" of the linear building. The relationship of the lodge to the elongated guestroom bar is similar to the linear set of national buildings and larger, slightly rotated exhibition building that Louis Kahn designed for the "Interama" project, a widely publicized (though never realized) collection of buildings designed from 1965–69 for a Miami, Florida site by a group of leading US architects including I. M. Pei, José Lluis Sert, Marcel Breuer, and Kahn.

While the first design had the desired visual relationship to the gardens, Clark did not feel it had a strong connection to its wooded site. The second design placed the Inn deeper in the woods to the east, where it steps along the edge of a creek. In plan the walls and guestrooms are composed of L-shaped volumes, with the two

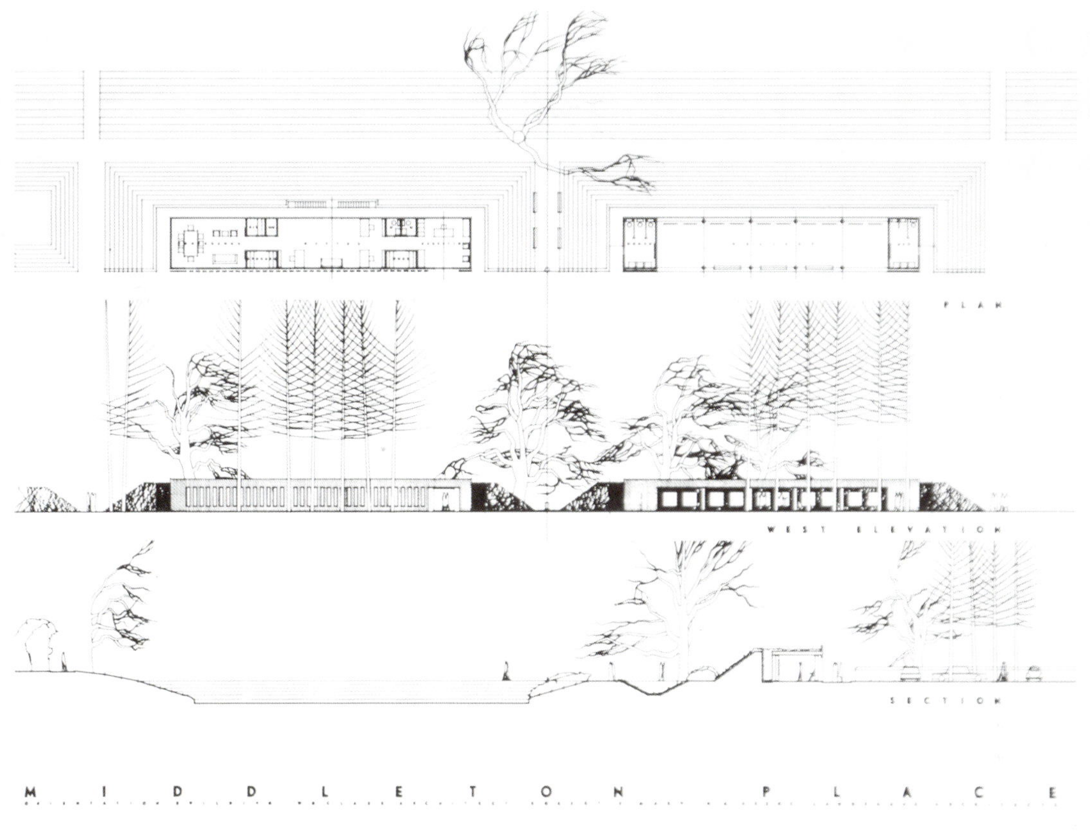

Plan, elevation and section of Visitor Orientation Center.

Aerial view looking towards northeast.

wings of each L-shaped volume being of the same length, and with the guestrooms facing east or north, away from the gardens. The L-shaped volumes are linked together to form a stepping figure in plan, shaping outdoor courts of contrasting character on each side, with clearings opening to the creek on the east side and woods crossed by paths on the west side. The larger lodge is again set at the south end of the plan, and it is rotated slightly off the rectangular grid organizing the stepped guestroom building.

The inspiration for the third and final location of the Inn came from Clark's "desire to make a building that truly belonged to its place, rather than just being sited on it."[4] This was paralleled by Clark's third realization—that being the importance of constraints on design, and the inspiration limitations may bring to design. In this case the constraint was what remained of an old riverside phosphate-mining operation, which had left two rectangular terraces, open except for a few pine trees, carved into the densely wooded hillside overlooking the river and its extensive marshlands. The terraces, the longer sides of which ran parallel to the river, were to be transformed during construction from raw, overgrown mining scars to grass-covered lawns, not dissimilar to the landscaped terraces of Middleton Place. Clark wrapped the main building along the L-shaped embankment of the uppermost terrace; "It is stretched the length of the terrace so as to become a boundary rather than an object," as Clark notes.[5] The main building is both boundary and space-shaper, separating and joining the dense forest to the south and the sunken lawn overlooking the river to the north. Clark said; "It became immediately clear that the Inn would not be a box, but a distended, occupied wall along the embankment, an inscribed mark of the long past occupation. It was satisfying to find a reason for shaping a building derived from the physical place and its history."[6]

It is this existing "constraint" that provides the convincing reason for the building and the landscape to be joined so as to make one entity. Yet it also meant that the third design, rather than being closely related to the gardens as the client had requested, was instead placed even farther away, along the edge of the bluff overlooking the Ashley River. Siting the main building of the Inn in the existing mining terraces meant it was set parallel to the straight east axis of this part of the river, which was used to organize the house and gardens of Middleton Place. But rather than engaging the axis of the river by aligning with it, as in Middleton Place, Clark placed the main building of the Inn parallel to and alongside the river—similar to the lateral opening of the porches to the garden in the Charleston Single House—so that the Inn establishes its own parallel relationship with the river, which is drawn up into the site of the Inn.

The tectonic order of the main L-shaped building, accommodating 24 guestrooms on three levels as well as the main lodge, which is placed nearest the river, is also deployed in three smaller L-shaped buildings, placed in the forest to the east and west of the main building, which accommodate 28 additional guestrooms on two levels. The L-shaped wall of the main building wraps around the guestrooms and encloses the lawn as an interior space, turning its "back" to the forest. In counterpoint, the L-shaped walls of the three smaller buildings wrap around and form entry courts as interior spaces on the forest side, with the guestrooms placed on the "back" side, opening to the river. Towards the dense surrounding forest, all four buildings present a massive two-story, gray stucco-clad, fig-vine-covered masonry wall, carved with large openings. Towards the lawn and river beyond, the buildings present pairs of airy, transparent two- or three-story, green-black-painted wood-framed towers, almost entirely opened with glazing. The complementary contrast of the tectonic character of the two sides of the buildings of the Inn could hardly be more emphatic or effective.

The thick masonry wall of the Inn, which is almost entirely covered by fig-vine, is opened between each pair of guestrooms to allow passage down the stairs to the lawn as well as views of the river beyond. The visitor approaching the Inn from the live oak forest is uncertain whether it is building or garden topiary, and whether it is occupied or abandoned, and in this quality it recalls the roofless ruins of the Sheldon Church, the most important "atmospheric" precedent for Clark's work. Built in Yemassee, South Carolina from 1745 to 1756, the church was burned in 1779 by the British army during the Revolutionary War, rebuilt in 1826, and then heavily damaged in 1865 by the Union troops at the end of the Civil War, and it has been a roofless ruin since that time. Today the ruins of the church stand in a clearing surrounded by the spreading limbs of large live oak trees. Its massive rectangular walls, opened on all four sides with large arched openings, and its freestanding Doric columns, are made of brick, and grass grows on the interior of the church. Clark notes that Sheldon Church, fifty miles to the southwest of Middleton Place, "is a ruin with missing roof, allowing it to be seen as both a building and a landscape."[7]

The tectonic rigor with which the materials and details are articulated throughout the Middleton Inn is remarkable, and raises this modest structure to the highest levels of architectural craft. In the main building, the thick, stuccoed masonry wall, placed against the dense forest at the upper edge of the terrace, functions as a retaining wall for the eight-foot difference between the lower and upper levels; frames the raised entry promenade along the forest edge; and houses the baths, dressing areas, and entries of the guest rooms. The cubic wooden-framed and extensively glazed bedrooms are stacked into towers and placed along the inner edge of the lawn, and each pair of bedrooms is separated by a masonry wall, which runs perpendicular to the thick outer masonry wall, and which accommodates the guestroom fireplaces.

At regular intervals along the entry promenade on the upper, forest side of the main building, tall narrow portals are opened in the thick masonry wall between the pairs of bedroom towers to accommodate the stairs descending to the lawn. Alternating with these narrow portals are wider portals into which the entries for each set of four guestrooms are recessed. A narrow, buttress-like concrete stair to the upper level, aligned with the masonry fireplace wall separating each pair of guestrooms, projects from the center of the large portal out onto the promenade, marking the entry to each set of guestrooms. The two upper guestrooms are entered from the narrow stair, the middle guestrooms are entered on the promenade level to either side of the stair, and the lower guestrooms, set at the ground level of the lawn, are entered from side doors at the bottom of the stairs connecting the promenade to the lawn.

A concrete lintel spans the large portal at the guestroom entries, and the lighter gray-colored stucco finish of the outer wall contrasts with the dark green-black paint of the wood-clad guestroom walls within. At the top of the large entry portal, an aperture allows a view of the terracotta chimney flues from the bottom of the stair; illuminates the upper floor guestroom entries immediately beneath it; and, by passing through the steel floor grates to either side of the concrete stair, the same light illuminates the guestroom entries on the middle, promenade level floor below. At night, lights shining up onto the curved ceiling beneath the narrow entry stair illuminate the promenade and guestroom entries.

The entry door to the guestroom opens into the dressing area, with a cedar closet on the outer wall and the large opening to the bedroom on the inner wall. The entry, dressing area, and bathroom are all within the thick masonry outer wall—a cool, shadowed, cave-like space, with a Carrara marble floor (less expensive than American slate at the time of construction), white ceramic tile partition walls and bathtub, cedar shelves, and light gray-colored stucco walls and low vaulted ceiling that rises towards the bedroom—its curve matching that of the curved ceiling beneath the concrete entry stair. The space is illuminated by natural light only through the outward-curving glass block window at the far end of the room, above the bathtub, and by a narrow beveled slot window next to the sink and mirror that is closed when the sliding bathroom door is opened, and which admits light but not views.

Complementing the cave-like spaces in the thickness of the masonry wall, the brightly lit, warm, transparent, lantern-like bedroom has an oak floor, cypress paneling behind the bed, a white plaster ceiling, and two sets of pine shutters, high and low, on the two wood-framed full-height glass outer walls. The gray-stuccoed masonry wall separating the two guestrooms houses the fireplace and its elevated slate hearth, which is set into a wood seat running the full depth of the bedroom. The ends of the glazed wooden frame of the L-shaped bedroom outer walls are separated from the thick outer masonry wall and the masonry fireplace wall by deep recessed slots, into which tall thin screened windows are opened, providing each bedroom with cross-ventilation even in the rain, and into which are set the rainwater downspouts. A similar thin window, with frosted glass for privacy, separates the entry door from masonry fireplace wall. With these three narrow windows, Clark employs slots of light to separate and articulate the primary building materials of wood and masonry for those inhabiting the interior (and slots of shadow to articulate the same relationship on the exterior) – a detail he shares with both Frank Lloyd Wright and Louis Kahn.

The lodge, the largest volume of the main building, is set at the end of the L-shaped plan nearest the river, and acts as a "head" for the "body" of the elongated building. The lodge is spaced away from the thick masonry wall and glazed cubes of the guestrooms wing by the widest of the stairs leading down to the lawn, indicating its more public program. On the outer, entry side, the façade of the lodge aligns with the outer face of the thick masonry wall, while on the inner, lawn side of the building, the glazed façade of the lodge is set well forward of the glazed facades of the private guestrooms, projecting out into the lawn and indicating its public, shared nature. The lodge serves as a lantern at night, when its extensive triple-height glazing is lit from within, and as a landmark in the day, anchoring and acting as a spatial pivot between the building and the landscape, the hinge point marked by the tall, monumentally-scaled masonry chimney rising from the massive fireplace, which is braced by a two-story variation on the buttress-like concrete stairs of the guestrooms.

The lodge comprises a single, large, double-height cubic room on the entry level, with wood floor, walls and ceiling, its interior opened on three sides by full height apertures, and the room is anchored at its southwest corner by the massive fireplace. The room is a layered, double-wall structure, with a second, outer, three-story wall on the north and east sides, opening to the river and lawn, respectively, through full-height glazing. The outer wall of the lodge is formed and structured by a large black-painted wood frame that rises to the full height of the building and wraps around the corner to join the north and east sides of the lodge. A second, shorter frame is set on the west side, and the lodge's main entry doors open in the space between the vertical piers of the two frames at the northwest corner. Between the inner and outer walls a stair slowly descends, its treads matching the slope of the landscape outside, to reach the lower level, where the breakfast room looks out to the lawn. The outer wall frames are infilled with glazing, similar to that in the guestrooms, up to the ceiling of the main room, above which they rise to form narrow roof bands, supported by cylindrical columns, running around the roof terrace that wraps the north and east sides, and onto which the penthouse guest suite opens.

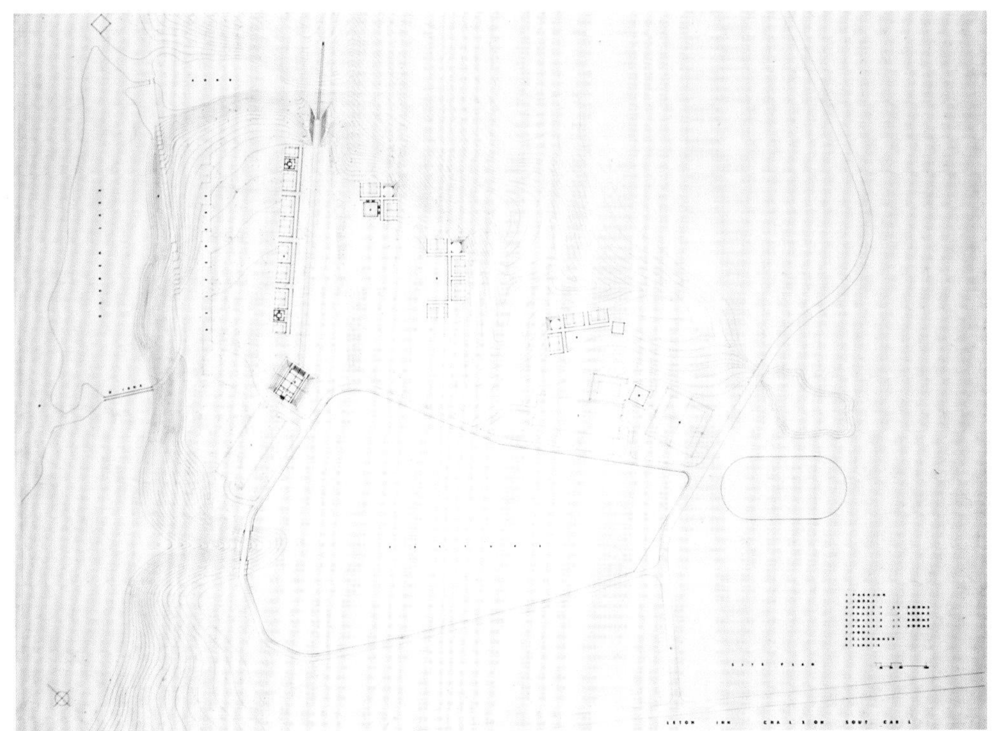

First site design, Middleton Inn.

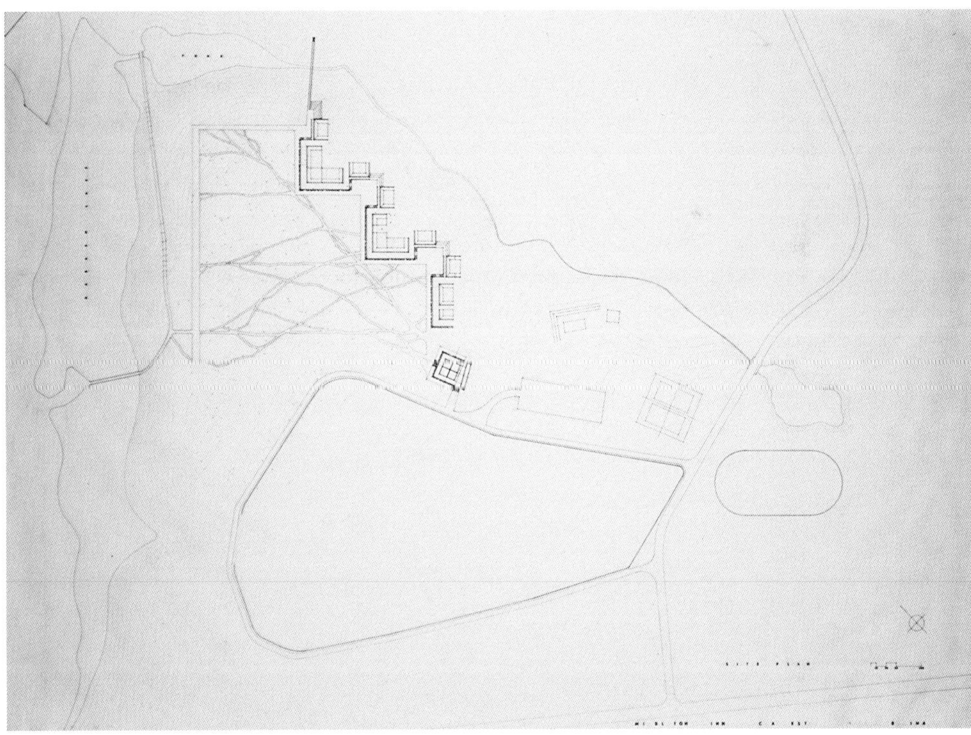

Second site design, Middleton Inn.

In terms of its general organization, it is intriguing to note that the design of the main building of Middleton Inn makes subtle references to both of Thomas Jefferson's buildings in Charlottesville, but here often inverted with respect to their original condition. The influence of the central Lawn at the University of Virginia is clear, but in Clark's building the promenades are placed against the forest on the outside, rather than along the edge of the lawn on the inside. On the other hand, Clark's and Jefferson's buildings share the regular rhythm of pedestrian passages from the inner lawn through the bounding inhabited wall. The influence of the embedded service spaces at the outer edge of the elevated lawn at Monticello is also evident, but in this case it is the primary served spaces of the guestrooms that are placed on the inner edge of the sunken lawn.

During the design and construction of Middleton Inn, Clark came to the realization that not one but three different places had been realized. The first is the physical place, having to do with the decision to site the building in the mining scar, around which the building's two components of thick masonry wall and glazed cubic volumes stacked into towers were wrapped, so that it belonged to its place. "This physical place resides in a cultural place. Habitation over centuries had resulted in local building traditions involving proportions, material use and details. These were in part due to climate and availability. Some of these were incorporated in the Inn."[8] Clark points out that these include the color and texture of the gray stucco on the exterior masonry walls, which matches that of St. Philip's Church, a prominent Charleston church; the wood is painted "Charleston green," a very dark green-black traditionally used to protect the wood and mask mildew; and wooden shutters and terracotta chimney caps that

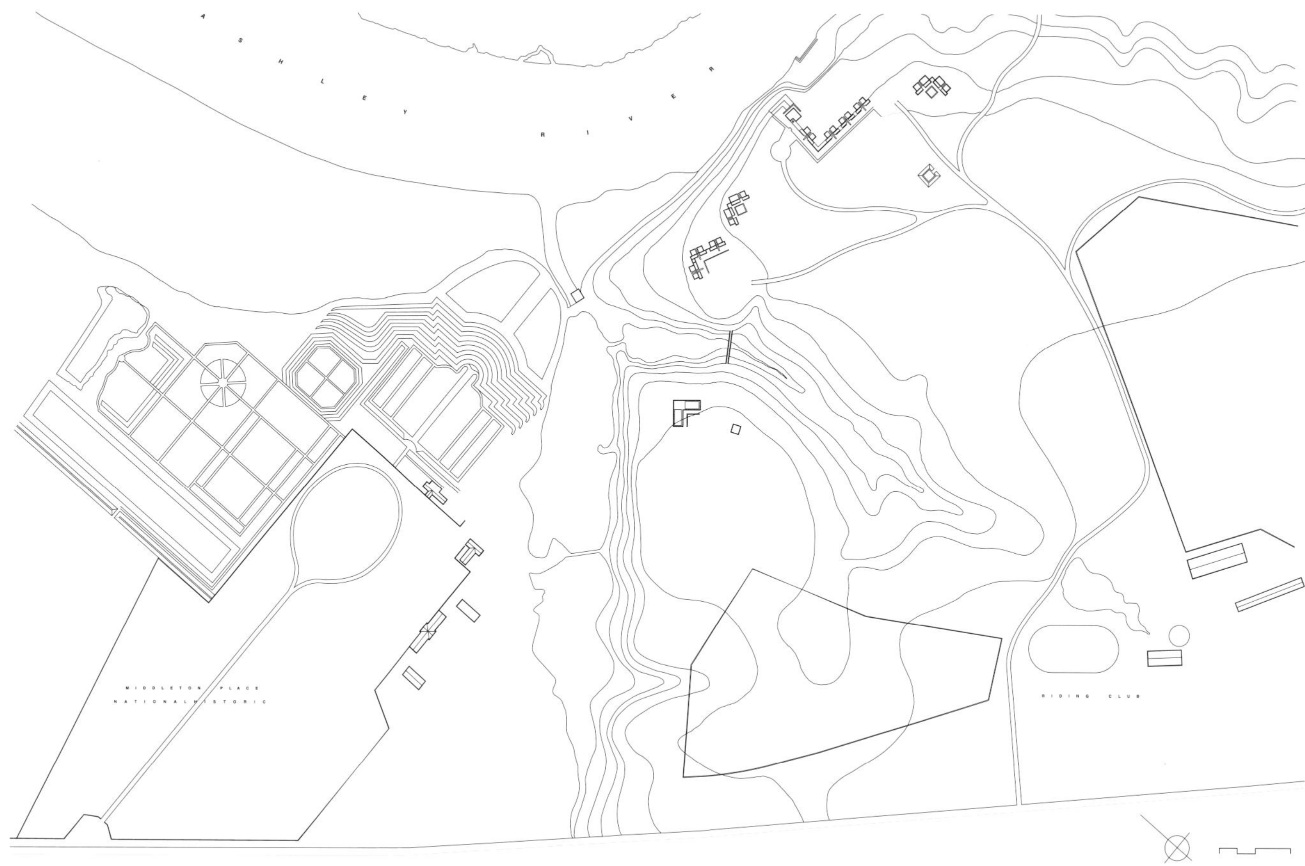

Overall site plan of Middleton Place (left) and Middleton Inn (right).

are part of the local building traditions. Finally, in the experience of inhabitation was realized a spiritual place, a place of evocation inspired by the image of the roofless masonry ruins of Sheldon Church; "The architectural strength of these ruins, and the quality we tried to evoke, is one of openness and transparency—the unsettling presence of grass and sunlight inside a burned church-become-cloister."[9]

The tectonic rigor, formal restraint, spatial integration, and experiential richness of Middleton Inn, Clark's first important building, is truly remarkable, and it bears comparison to some of the most accomplished domestic and institutional designs by Louis Kahn and Frank Lloyd Wright – both of whom it should be noted were significantly older when designing their best works than Clark's 43 years of age at the completion of Middleton Inn.

In a sad postscript to the story of the Middleton Inn, in 1989, only four years after the building was completed, Hurricane Hugo struck Charleston and its surroundings, doing extensive damage to the landscape and gardens along the Ashley River. While many of the enormous live oaks lining the entry drive to the nearby Drayton Hall were lost, the gardens of Middleton Place were largely unscathed. Yet, a short distance to the east, a staggering 85% of the trees in the live oak forest immediately surrounding the Middleton Inn were lost in the hurricane. As a result, until the live oak trees return, one approaches the masonry wall of the main building not from a dense, shadowed forest but across a sunlit field with widely scattered trees. As Clark notes; "One is prepared to lose one's building in such a natural disaster, but not to lose one's entire landscape."[10]

Site plan of Middleton Inn.

Aerial view looking across river towards southwest.

Model of main building.

   A PRACTICE OF MAKING PLACES

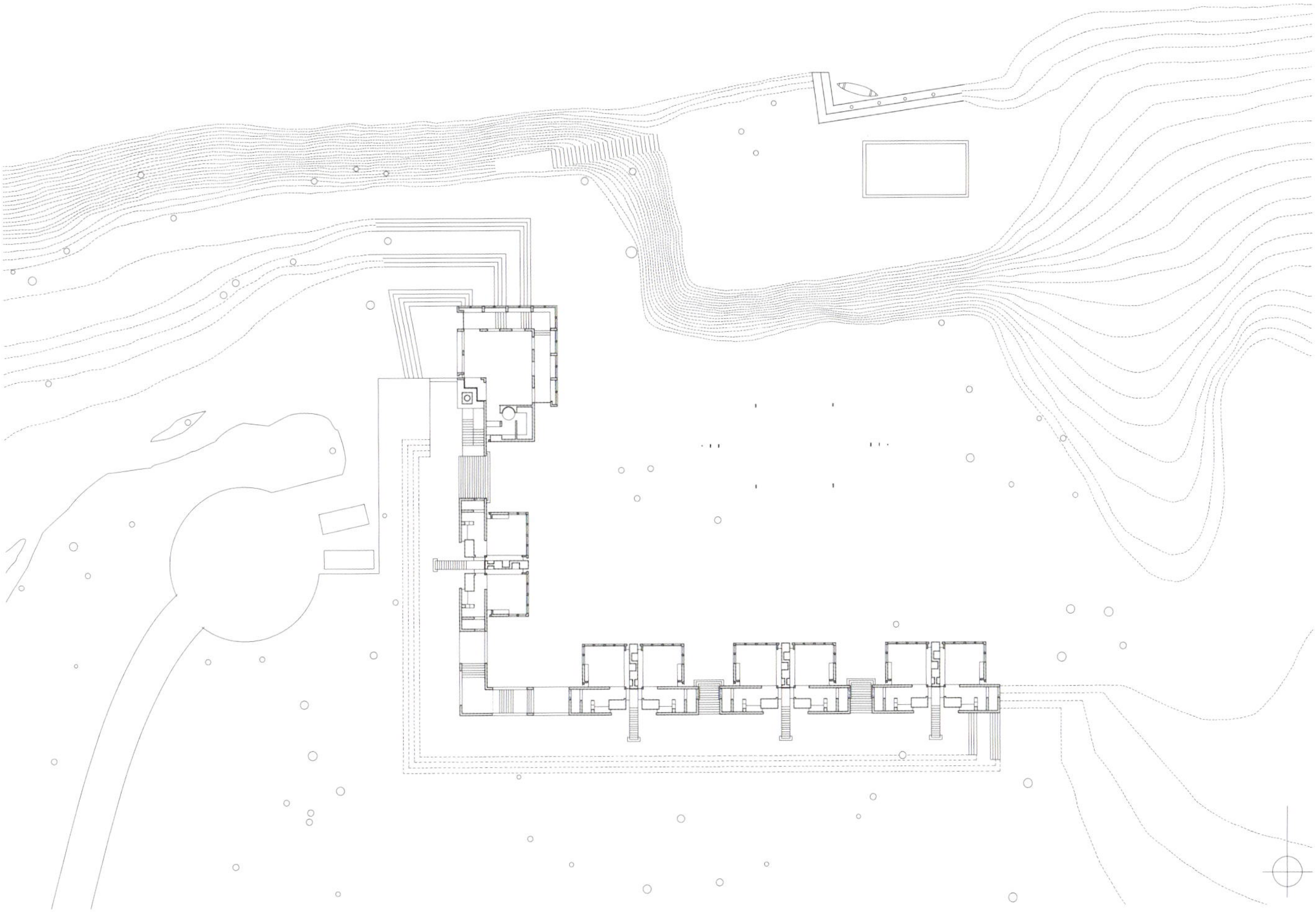

Plan of main building.

View of stairs to terrace lawn.

View of terrace lawn and guestrooms of main building from the east.

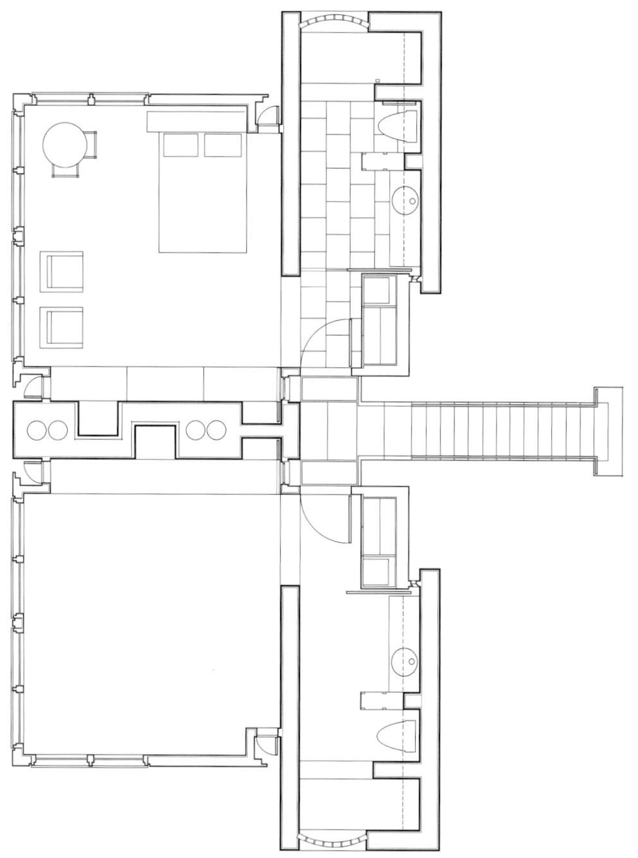

Plan of guestroom building.

Masonry wall seen from southeast.

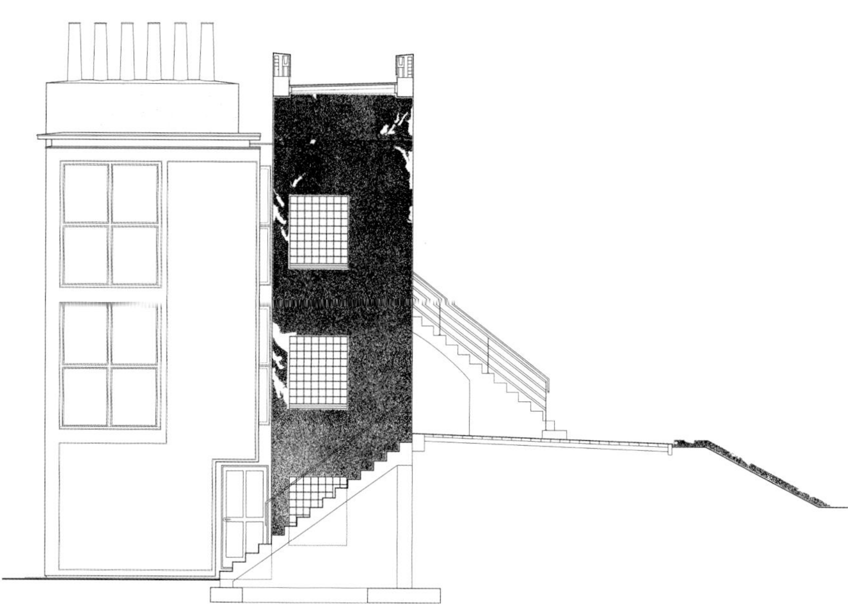

Section through wall, guest room elevation.

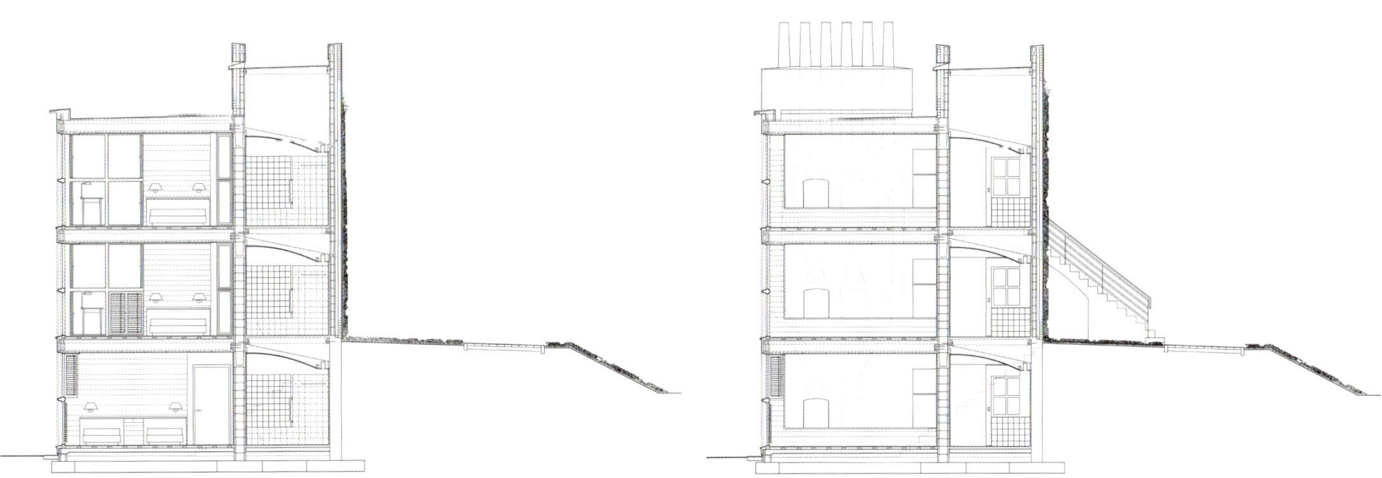

View of masonry wall and guestroom entry stair on smaller building.

Sections of guestrooms, looking toward bed (left) and fireplace (right).

Guest room bath.

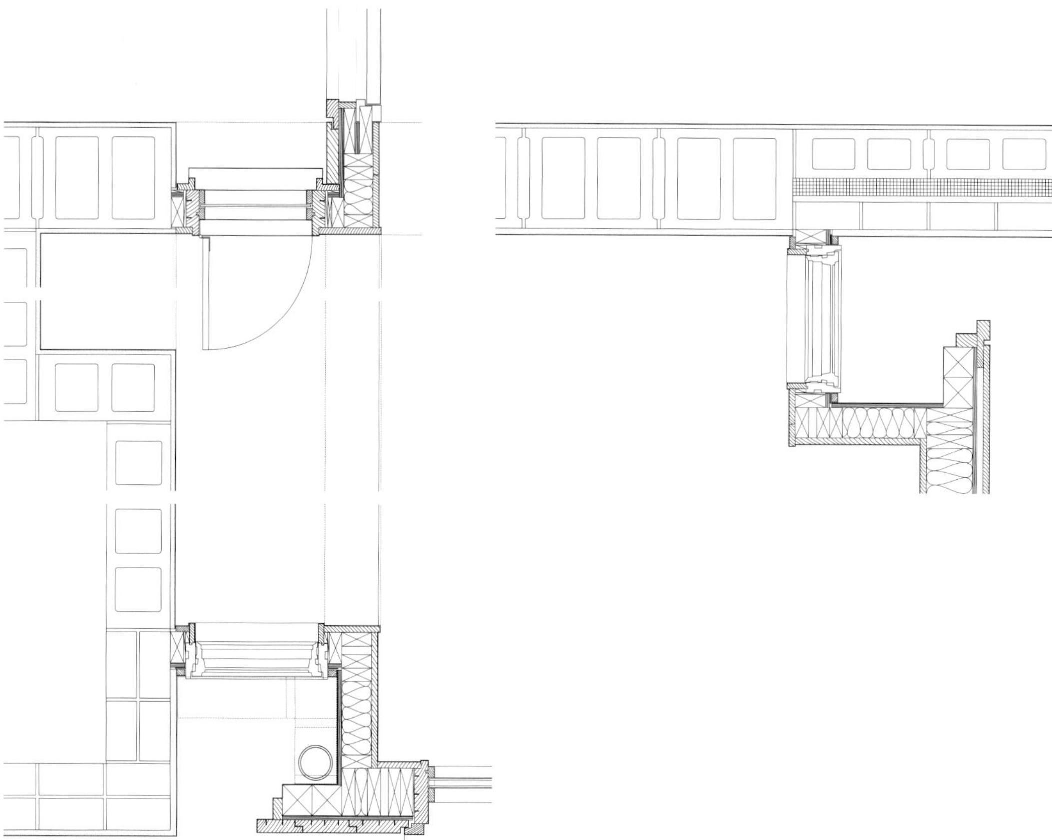

Plan details of recessed slot windows at corners of guestroom.

A PRACTICE OF MAKING PLACES

Guestroom interior.

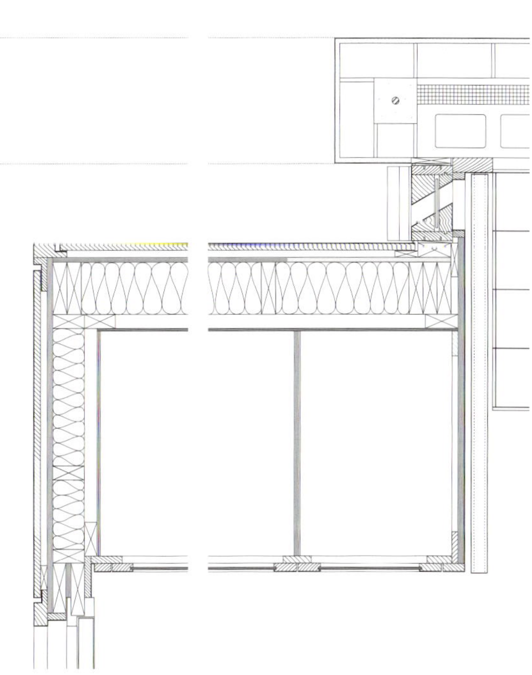

Lodge interior.

Plan detail of canted window at guestroom bath.

View of lodge seen from the northwest.

Perspective of lodge and entry seen from west.

     A PRACTICE OF MAKING PLACES

View of lodge and entry.

View of lodge seen through masonry wall.

View from lodge roof terrace.

The program for the national design competition called for an addition, housing galleries, workspace, storage, and a new auditorium, to the existing 1909 museum, a classical and axial symmetrical building designed by Samuel Marx, to the rear of which an earlier addition had been built. Clark realized that the existing museum and the City Park that surrounded it, while existing in close proximity, were nevertheless being used by different groups of New Orleans citizens, with many families regularly visiting the park but rarely if ever visiting the museum. Endeavoring to engage with both groups, Clark reinterpreted the program so that the new addition would, as he said, "strongly link" the existing museum to the natural landscape context of the surrounding City Park.

Rather than attaching the addition directly to the existing museum and aligning with its symmetrical north-south axis and east-west cross-axis, Clark placed the addition at a distance and diagonally, to the side and behind the museum. Instead of a self-centered symmetrical form, the addition was given an "incomplete" L-shape in plan, with the inner corner opening towards the existing museum. In this way the addition was sited more in the park than in the immediate museum precinct, thereby deferring to the existing building and framing a newly defined landscape formed between the two buildings.

The addition was also designed as an island, with the surrounding low land flooded to extend an existing lake, as Clark notes, "to form a lagoon upon which the addition was placed like a floating garden, an image which seemed appropriate for a city whose [ground] is largely below sea level."[1] The addition comprised a series of seven square galleries, each top-lit by a shallow circular dome lifted above the roof, with clerestory windows all around, and the diffused daylight entered the galleries through a large square aperture in the ceiling. On the levels below the galleries were the workspaces, storage, and car parking, and the new auditorium was placed at the southern end of the L-shaped plan.

An amphitheater, on the roof of the new auditorium, stepped down alongside the existing museum, while a terraced live oak tree grove, a colonnaded dining loggia and a paved sculpture court were set along the inside edge of the L-shaped gallery volume, opening to the existing museum while simultaneously serving as a connection to the City Park. The east-west sectional relationship between the new addition and the existing museum is particularly elegantly resolved, with the top-lit galleries opening to an arcade that overlooks the live oak terrace one level below, with the dining loggia set beneath the paved promenade at the edge of the live oak terrace – all three levels opening to the existing museum to the west. The dining loggia recessed beneath the outer edge of the live oak grove and terrace again recalls the hidden position of the service spaces at the edge of the grass terrace at Jefferson's Monticello, while the live oak grove and terrace elevated above the water level of the lake evokes what Clark called "the Venetian image" of the building in the lagoon[2] – where in order to have large trees, gardens are raised above the saline-saturated ground water.

The addition was linked to the existing museum by an elevated pedestrian bridge that connected the stair hall between the two sections of the existing museum to the tall, top-lit stair hall at the end of the addition's L-shaped plan, between the galleries to the north and the auditorium to the south, and the bridge continued out the other side of the addition to connect to the park lakefront on the east side. As Clark notes; "By introducing terraces, a grove of trees, a bridge and an amphitheater to the program, an attempt was made to make the building read as both building and landscape, a theme explored on subsequent projects as well."[3] In addition to the

New Orleans
Museum of Art,
Competition First Prize,
New Orleans, Louisiana,
1983 (unrealized)

In association with Charleston
Architectural Group.

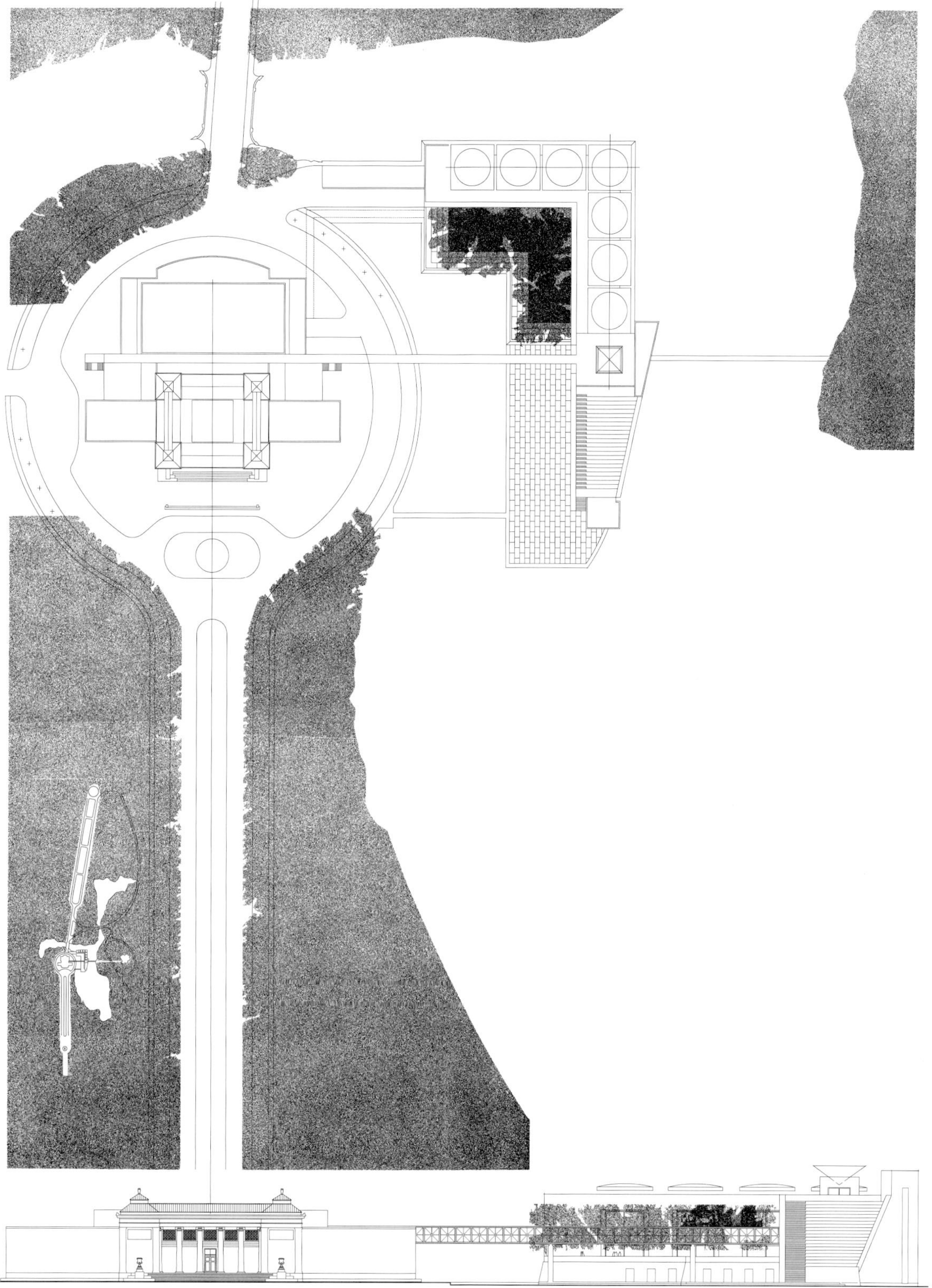

Site plan and elevation, NOMA Competition entry.

Venetian precedents, Clark also cites the Chateau de Chenonceau, a 16th-century building in France that spans across the River Cher, as a bridge-building precedent for the addition.[4]

In praising Clark's design, the competition jury noted that the design responded both to the museum's institutional program and its exceptional setting in City Park; "By accommodating the Museum expansion in a terraced building form actively engaging the landscape, Mr. Clark's design acknowledges the primacy of the Park as a public open space. At the same time, this project promises to create for the Museum a new and exciting public presence: a presence that will enhance enjoyment of the Park by defining new outdoor spaces accessible to the public while inviting public participation in a broad range of Museum-related cultural activities. Above all, the Jury finds this project worthy of the Park in that it reaffirms, freshly and passionately, the essential interdependency of human culture and the natural world."[5] This last echoed Clark's description of the larger intentions of his design; "At the juncture of the institution and the park, the design sought to intensify the meeting of the cultural and the natural, with an architecture that was allegiant to both."[6]

After awarding Clark's design the first prize, the museum staff and competition organizers made the highly embarrassing discovery that it would not be possible for the museum to build on City Park land. As a result, Clark was commissioned to design a much-reduced addition, which was directly attached to the museum so as to remain within the circular drive that circumscribes the museum property. Two new courtyards were formed between the original museum and an earlier addition to its rear, new stairs flanked the outer ends of the existing galleries, and new galleries were added to either side, stepping in plan so as to remain within the circular site. While this second and much reduced addition was built, in association with New Orleans architects Eskew Vogt Salvato & Filson, who made the construction documents, Clark's design was so modified by museum staff that he does not consider it to be among his realized works, and he has never visited the completed building.

Concurrently with completing Middleton Inn in 1985, Clark entered into partnership with Charles Menefee. Educated at Carnegie Mellon and receiving a Bachelor of Architecture degree in 1977, Menefee founded the Charleston Architectural Group in 1981, and he associated with Clark on the Middleton Inn from 1982 to 1985, during the final stages of construction documents and construction. The partnership of Clark and Menefee, which was located initially in Charleston, South Carolina and later in Charlottesville, Virginia, lasted for 15 years and resulted in eight built works, beginning with the Reid House.

Competition model seen from the south.

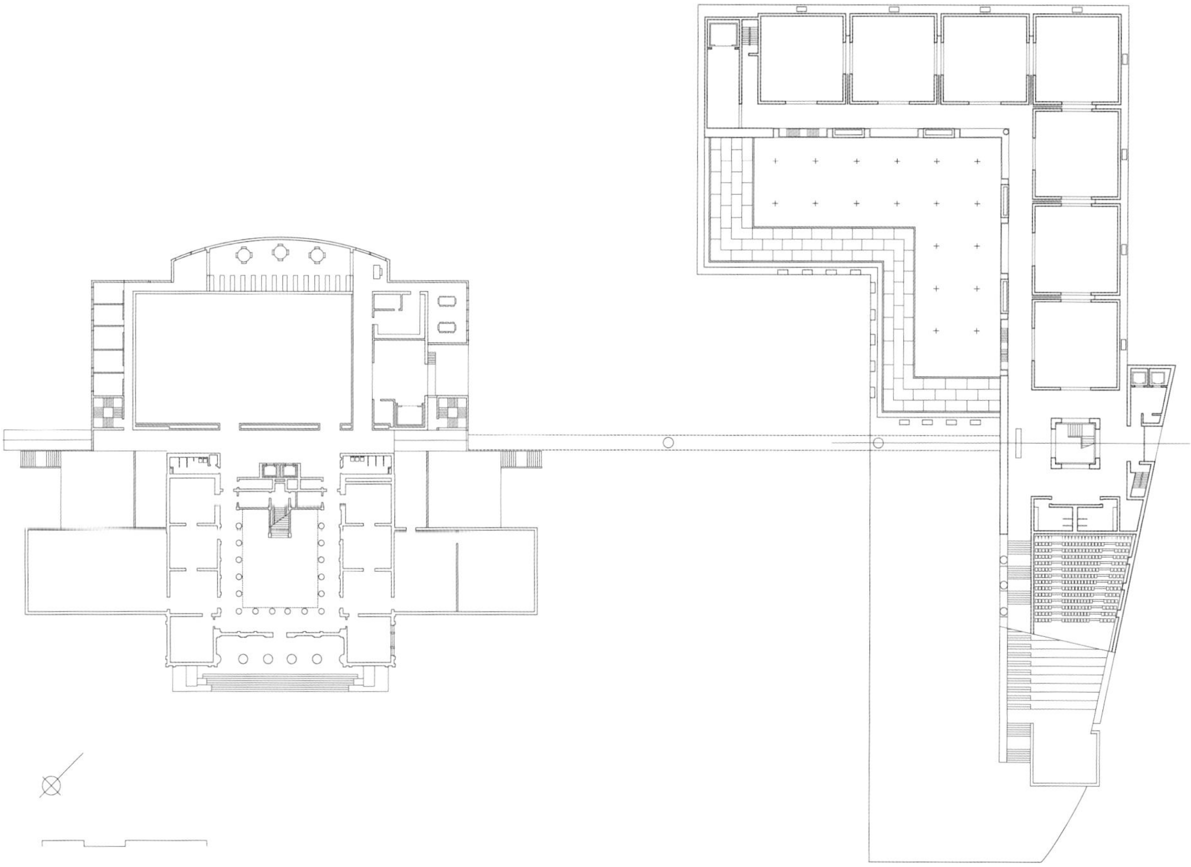

Plan of middle level with garden terrace.

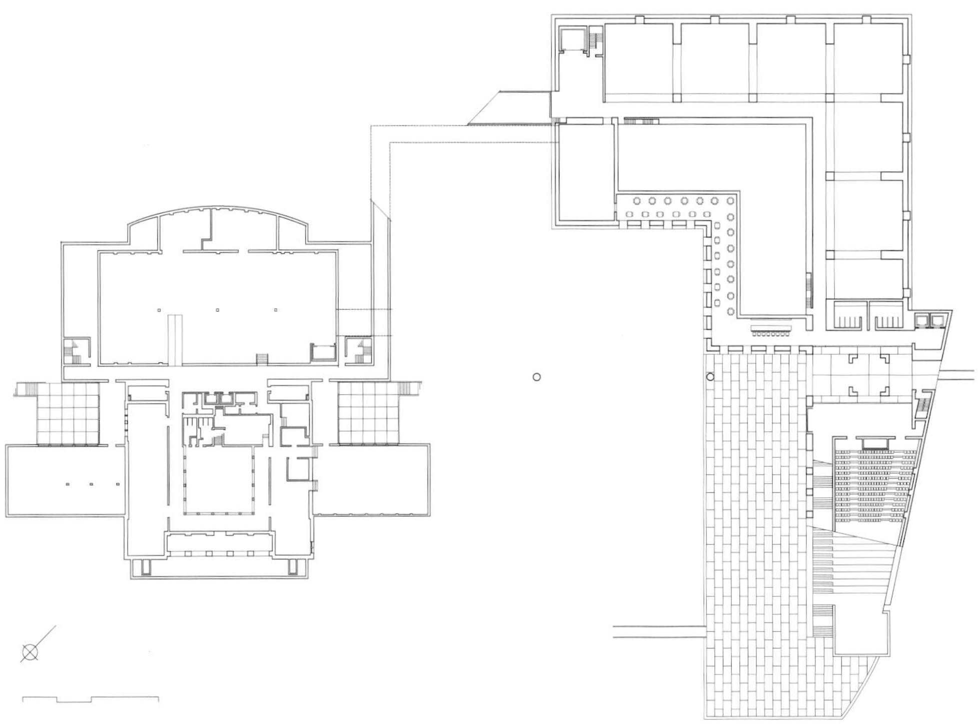

Plan of lower level, with café.

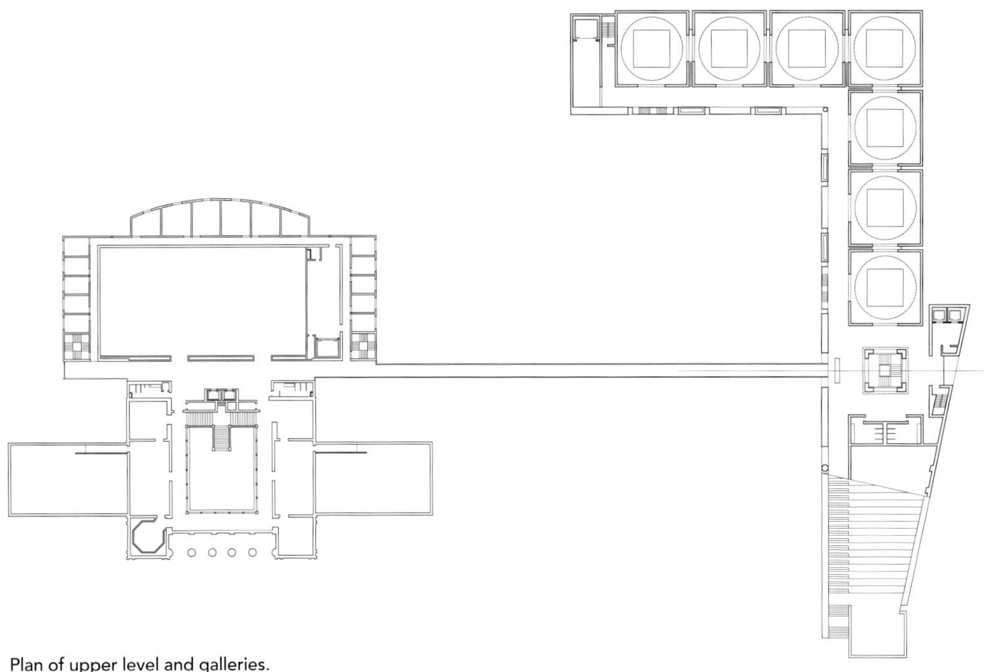

Plan of upper level and galleries.

A PRACTICE OF MAKING PLACES

Competition model seen from the east.

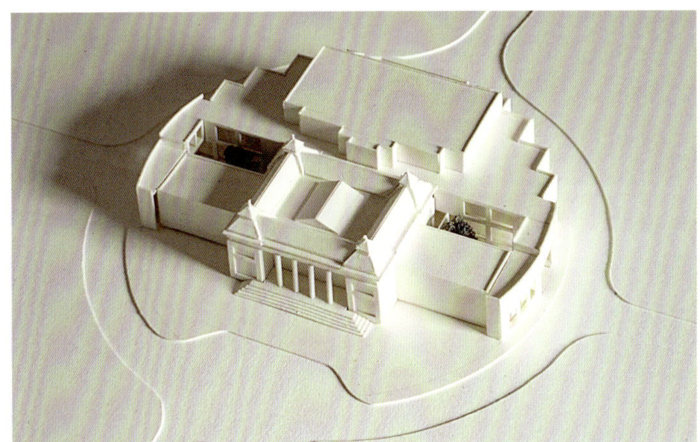

Model of second, realized design.

Long section through galleries, auditorium, and amphitheater.

The Reid House, located on John's Island, a rural community to the southwest of Charleston, is one of the lowest cost and most understated houses built by Clark, yet at the same time it engages its rural context in unexpected ways. The site is at the end of a dirt road lined with horse trailers, farm equipment, and cheaply built houses. With just a hint of irony, Clark notes that when he first met the client, an avid collector of agricultural, industrial and automotive detritus, he was living in two mobile home units joined to form an L-shape – the architect's preferred plan configuration. The design of the Reid House is at one and the same time appropriate to, and contrasting with, its rural agricultural context, in the way it makes references to both informal local vernacular farm buildings and the formal Palladian villas built on farming estates in the Veneto region of Italy.

Sited to precisely align with the cardinal directions, a 20-foot-square concrete block-walled three-story tower with a low pyramidal roof stands at the northern end of a large open grass field, with a fenced horse paddock to the west and the owner's two mobile homes to the east. The tower, which faces directly south, contains the entries and two bedrooms on the ground floor, and a double-height living room, with bedroom loft above, on the main floor – this is a *piano nobile*, or noble floor, as in an Italian villa, elevated to allow one to survey the landscape belonging to the villa, or, in this case, to give views above and beyond the owner's collection of vehicles and farm equipment scattered in the foreground. Behind the concrete block tower, a smaller 14-foot-square wood-framed, plywood and vertical batten-clad, shed-like volume with a sloping roof is placed to the north, containing the bathrooms on the ground and upper floors and the kitchen on the first floor. The two structures are joined on the interior by the masonry fireplace and chimney, around which the stair wraps on three sides, allowing the floor levels of the two parts to be slightly offset as needed.

In its vertical, tower-like proportions, the geometric rigor of its form, and its isolated position at the center of a large open field, the house makes no attempt to merge with the immediate landscape, and may instead be experienced as a local landmark, helping to organize and order the disparate collection of agricultural machinery and materials scattered around it. Yet the tower also evokes both local tobacco barns and grain silos, along with "their symbolic abundance," as Clark notes. In the frontal, formal symmetry of its south façade, facing the large field, the house evokes both the local examples of neo-Palladian houses as well as the originals to be found in the countryside around Venice.

On the other hand, the house belongs to its rustic rural place and cheaply built neighbors by way of the modesty of its materials and the straightforward way they are employed in the construction. The concrete block of the walls of the tower is exposed on the interior and given a coating of white waterproofing paint on the exterior, the rough bonding pattern clearly visible in raking light – thereby avoiding a too-"finished" appearance inappropriate on the working farms. In a similar way, the inclined asphalt shingle roof and plywood and battens walls of the shed-like rear section evokes lean-to construction, where in order to avoid the costs of a self-supporting structure, one part of the building leans on another. Clark notes; "The two parts of the house, the wood and the masonry, express the informal, accretive nature of the nearby buildings."[1]

Yet the house provides a setting of surprising experiential richness, the paradoxical result of the architect's formal restraint, geometrical rigor, humble materiality and revelatory detailing – the whole exemplifying Wright's aphorism regarding limitations being the best friends of architects. Seen from the open field to the south, the house presents a formal, symmetrical façade, precisely proportioned as a vertical golden section, with a large, double-height, vertical window above and two small windows below, and a slot-like horizontal clerestory window running beneath the cantilevered wood soffit of the low pyramidal roof, the ends of which are turned up to form pointed corners.

The formal "front" façade offers no means of entry, which can be found by walking around to either side, where twin entry doors are opened in the more informal and asymmetrical east and west facades – the impenetrable front façade flanked by side entries is also a characteristic of Wright's early buildings, in particular Unity Temple. Yet when the house is approached from the west side, one finds that the entry door aligns precisely with the road running along the edge of the horse paddock. On the west façade, the large double-height window and the single small square window beneath, are set towards the south, with the glazed entry door set towards the north. A horizontal clerestory window is opened at the top, and a tiny, enigmatic aperture holding two glass blocks is opened high up on the façade.

View from south-southeast.

The east façade is a mirror image of the west façade, except there is no large double-height window, and so the east façade is considerably more solid. Both entry doors open into the vestibule, with the doors to two bedrooms on one side, and with the stair leading upwards on the other side. At the top of the first stair, a full-height window is opened directly across the hall, giving a view to the paddock to the west. The kitchen, which is to the right at the top of the stairs, is opened with windows to both west and east.

The living room is entered from behind the fireplace, the masonry walls of which are painted white, so that it contrasts with the unpainted gray masonry outer walls of the tower portion of the house. The masonry core of the house, which contains the heating elements on the ground floor, the fireplace on the main floor and the chimney flue on the upper floor, is the spatial hinge joining the living room and bedrooms in the masonry tower to the kitchen and bathrooms in the wooden volume. In ascending and descending the stair that winds around the masonry fireplace core, the movement of the occupants going about their daily activities binds together the "servant" spaces in the wooden volume to the "served" spaces in the masonry volume – to employ Kahn's terms, which may be applied with equal appropriateness to all of Clark's designs.

The masonry walls of the double-height living room are opened on the west and south sides by large windows rising almost the full height of the space, with a larger, three-pane-wide window facing south and a two-pane-wide window facing west, towards the horse paddock. The exposed wood floor joists of the loft bedroom extend from the fireplace wall to the edge of the tall west window, where the low painted plywood-and-batten balcony rail is set. A black-painted steel beam, set precisely at the mid-point of the room, supports the loft bedroom floor joists, which cantilever three feet past the beam. The two ends of the steel beam are seated in small, glass block-glazed openings in the concrete block walls on east and west—the enigmatic apertures that were seen earlier on the exterior façades—so that throughout the day natural light reveals and literally "highlights" the structure in the shadows beneath the loft, while in the early morning and late afternoon sunlight plays along the steel beam.

The house has painted pine wood floors throughout, and the wood joists of the floor and roof structure are revealed in the ceilings below in every room in the house – with the notable exception of the double-height living room and bedroom loft. At the top of the masonry tower a flat, square, plywood-clad ceiling, painted a glossy white, conceals the wood frame structure of the low pyramidal roof. Clerestory window bands, extending most of the way across the room, are opened at the top of all four masonry walls. From both the living room and the bedroom loft, the smooth plywood ceiling can be seen to continue through the glass of the clerestory windows, from the interior ceiling to the exterior soffit, its glossy white surface reflecting the daylight coming in the clerestories. While the Reid House is simple and modest, it is detailed so as to reveal and articulate every aspect of its construction and materials, thereby enriching and dignifying the experience of the inhabitant. In this Clark is again close to Kahn, who said, "I believe that in architecture, as in all art, the artist instinctively keeps the marks which reveal how a thing was done."[2]

Site plan.

View from southwest.

View from west across horse paddock.

View from west.

Section perspective, looking west.

View from living room towards fireplace and stair.

Living room looking east.

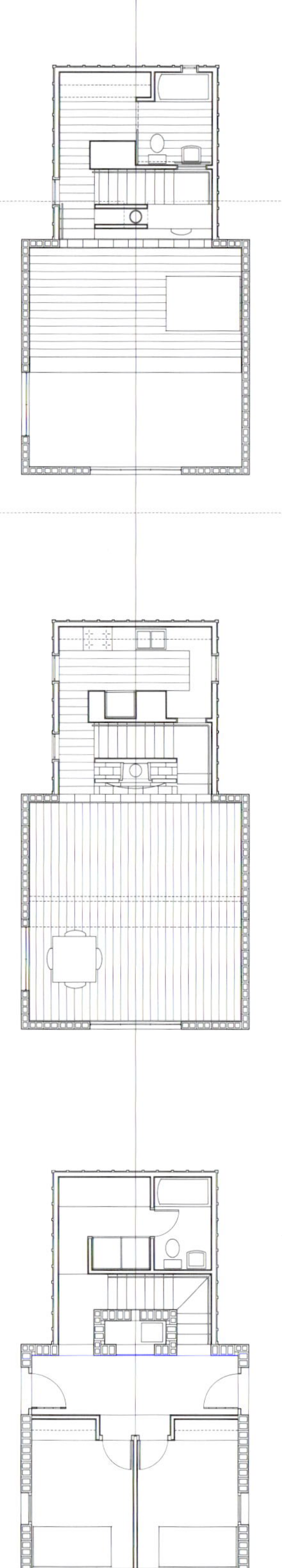

From top, plans of upper, middle, and lower levels.

A PRACTICE OF MAKING PLACES

Living room, looking west, view over paddock.

The competition was for a history museum for the State of Arizona, and the site was on a hillside at the southeastern edge of Papago Park, a large desert park north of Phoenix. Similar to the New Orleans Museum design, the museum design for Arizona was intended to relate to its desert place by fusing building and landscape, as well as by allowing the building to serve as a pedestrian pathway into the park – in this case a path parallel to the arroyo. The site is traversed at one corner by a desert arroyo, which carries floodwaters during the brief rainy season, and which is the only place in the desert that has green vegetation year round. The arroyo runs uphill into the park, and the museum is placed to the north, framing the dry desert landscape adjacent to the arroyo.

The largest spaces of the museum, the galleries, are organized into a single elongated rectangular volume, with a loggia and exit stairs along the south edge, which is embedded into the hillside. The single large space of the gallery is subtly articulated into four spaces, each a golden section in plan, by sets of columns that support the roofs, which form a series of four stepped terraces ascending with the slope of the hill. The flat-floored galleries, which are illuminated by continuous bands of clerestory windows opened beneath their stepping roofs, reach their greatest height at the building's west end, where they are most deeply buried in the hillside. Having the largest volume of the building buried the deepest into the ground, where the temperature remains cool year round, provides considerable benefits in terms of passive cooling. The series of stepped terraces of the gallery roof form a promenade ascending to the park, and as visitors climb the landscape stairs running alongside the stepped terraces, they are able to look down into the galleries through the clerestory windows to see what Clark described as the "treasures" of the collection.

The museum entrance, auditorium, and other non-gallery functions were placed at the downhill end of the building, nearest the entry from the road. The auditorium is housed in a low cylindrical volume with double outer walls, which projects from the south, front façade of the museum, forming the entrance both to the museum at ground level and, by way of a curving stair wrapping its exterior, to the roof terraces and stepped promenade to the park above. Also on the south side of the museum, and adjacent to the entry and auditorium, an amphitheater leads down to a large terrace that has been carved out of the ground, onto which the lower level galleries open. In order to merge the building and the landscape, the mass of the museum is partially hidden behind mounds formed from the earth excavated in the process of burying the galleries.

Indicating his understanding of the automobile-centered nature of the city of Phoenix, Clark notes, "From the highway, the building is seen as a path to the park, and from there the primary reason for burying the building can be understood: deference to the hillside, which is viewed unblocked over the museum."[1] As one of Clark's most comprehensive designs of a building as landscape, the Arizona Museum also relates to a series of regional precedents involving building with earth, such as Native American cave dwellings and kivas; excavating in the earth of the desert in order to escape the heat; and the way nature has evolved in the desert; "The burying of the building is remindful of the desert place, recalling mines, arroyos, fossils and animals seeking shelter beneath the sand. The shape of the auditorium, the carving of earth and the use of the roof for gathering recall ancient Indian dwellings."[2]

Arizona History Museum, Competition, Phoenix, Arizona, 1986 (unrealized)

Clark and Menefee

A PRACTICE OF MAKING PLACES

Site plan.

Aerial view of model in site.

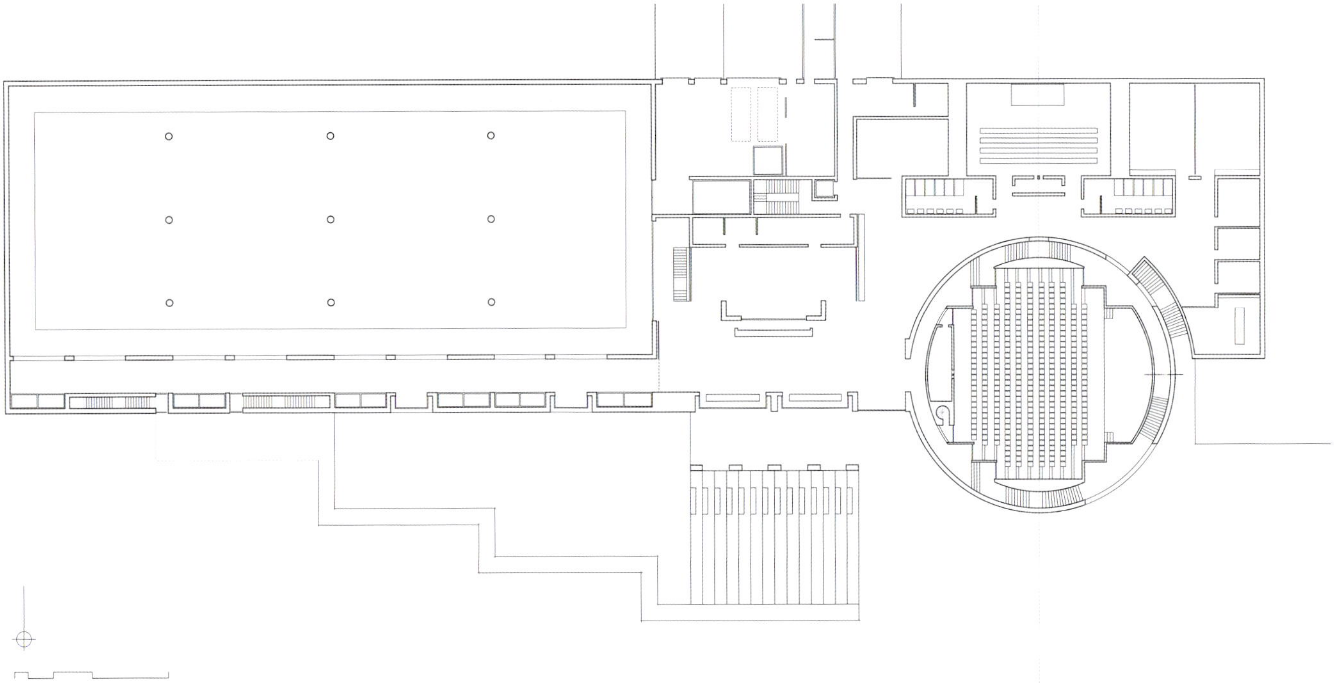

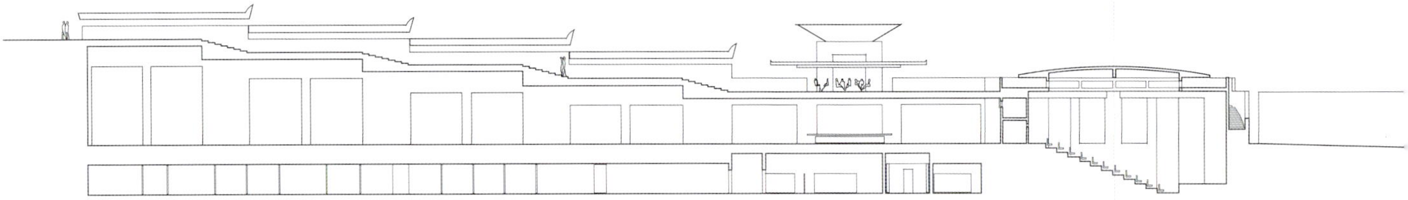

First floor plan (above) and east-west section through promenade (below).

Model in site, showing stepping section.

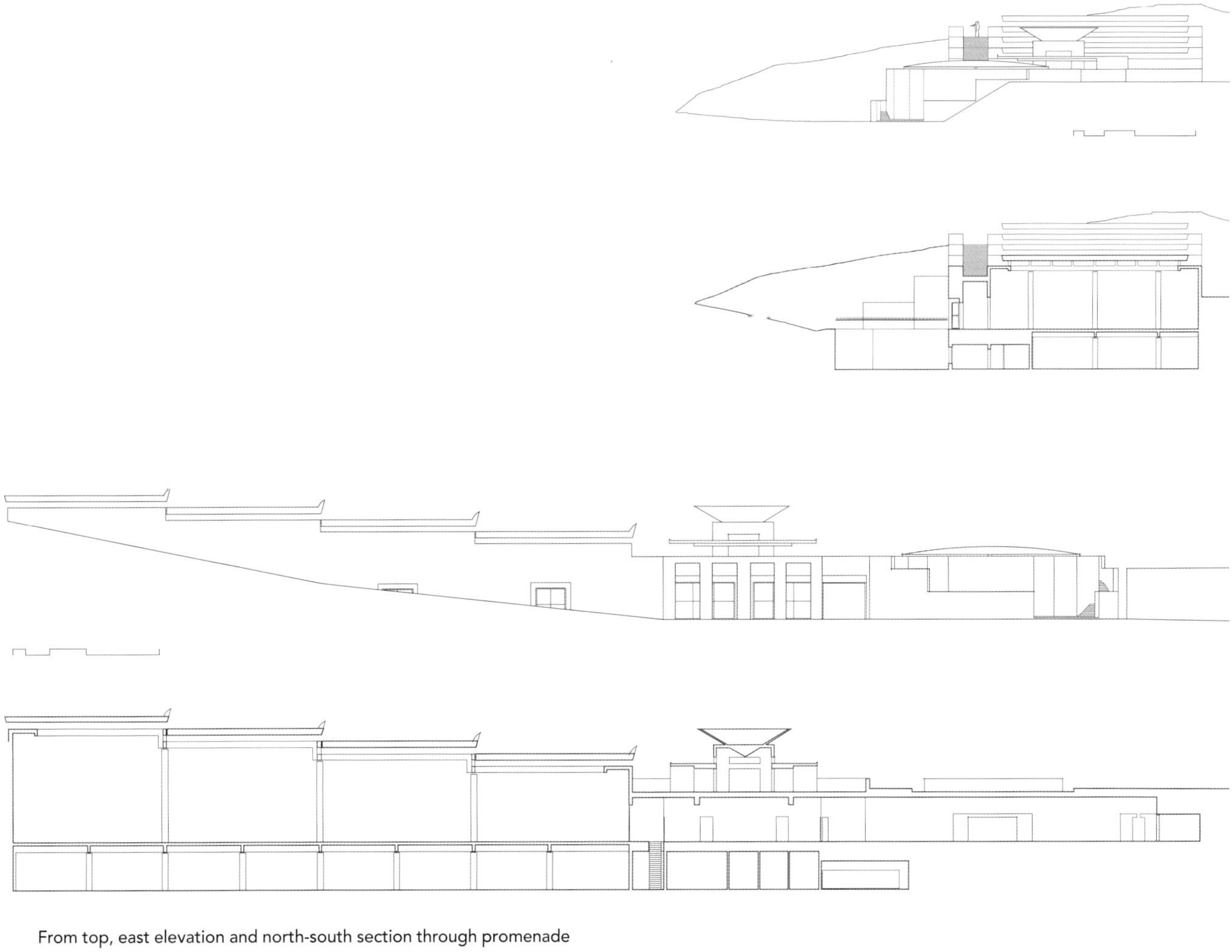

From top, east elevation and north-south section through promenade
and galleries; south elevation and east-west section through galleries.

The set of prototypes for bus shelters, commissioned by the City of Charleston, are assembled from a standardized set of components that can nevertheless be configured in a variety of ways so as to serve a wide range of locations. The sites for the bus stops are in the greater Charleston metropolitan area, and vary from narrow streets and sidewalks in the Old City to more open suburban and rural areas surrounding the city. As the architects note, "The Charleston Bus Stop was designed to extend the tradition of eighteenth- and nineteenth-century Charleston ironwork, with the consciousness of the modern city. Like other elements of the Old City, these shelters are designed to become a Charleston artifact,"[1] part of the quotidian life of the citizens of the city.

The bus shelters may therefore be understood as a modest but important exercise in extending the local and regional "tectonic culture,"[2] intended as an addition to the material culture and constructive history of Charleston as it is embodied in existing works of architecture and urban infrastructure. The bus stops consist of two fundamentally different types of elements: the standardized steel components, which are pre-fabricated off-site, and which can be deployed anywhere in the city; and the site specific element of the cast concrete floor slab that also serves as the foundation, which takes on a different configuration in response to the particular characteristics of the ground on each site.

The shelter consists of a steel structure, with central columns composed of pairs of L-section steel pieces (double pairs are employed at points where two sections are joined); which support a central spine-like beam composed of pairs of deeper L-section steel pieces; which supports tapering T-section steel outrigger struts that are cantilevered out to either side of the central beam; which in turn carry the sheet steel canopy or roof. The double canopy, which is slightly sloped to the center to collect rainwater, takes the form of a "butterfly" roof, an image that is accentuated in this case by the tapering of the cantilevered struts.

The pairs of steel L-sections that comprise the columns and the spine-beams are spaced away from each other, forming a slot of light in the center of the columns and a slot of shadow in the center of the spine-beams. The steel T-section cantilevered struts are notched on their inner edge so as to accommodate the rainwater channel recessed into the center of the canopy. A circular hole has been cut in each of the cantilevered struts at its deepest point, close to the central spine beam, which allows a play of light and reflection.

The shelters can be assembled in bays to any length necessary and can be either full-width (cantilevered to both sides of the central columns and spin-beam) or half-width (cantilevered to one side only), as needed to accommodate site limitations. The shelter can also carry cantilevered wind-screens, steel mesh panels, and signs, all detailed in steel similarly to the primary structural components. The load-bearing steel columns are anchored to the cast concrete slab-on-grade, which defines the perimeter or edge of the shelter in a similar way as the stone curbs and sidewalks define the pedestrian territory in the Old City. The concrete floor slabs can also accommodate up-lights that illuminate the underside of the steel canopy. The steel components are all painted the dark "Charleston green," and the design was scaled and detailed so as to be able to accommodate the traditional Charleston "Battery" benches.

Charleston Bus Stop, Charleston, South Carolina, 1987–1992

Clark and Menefee

Detail of canopy structure.

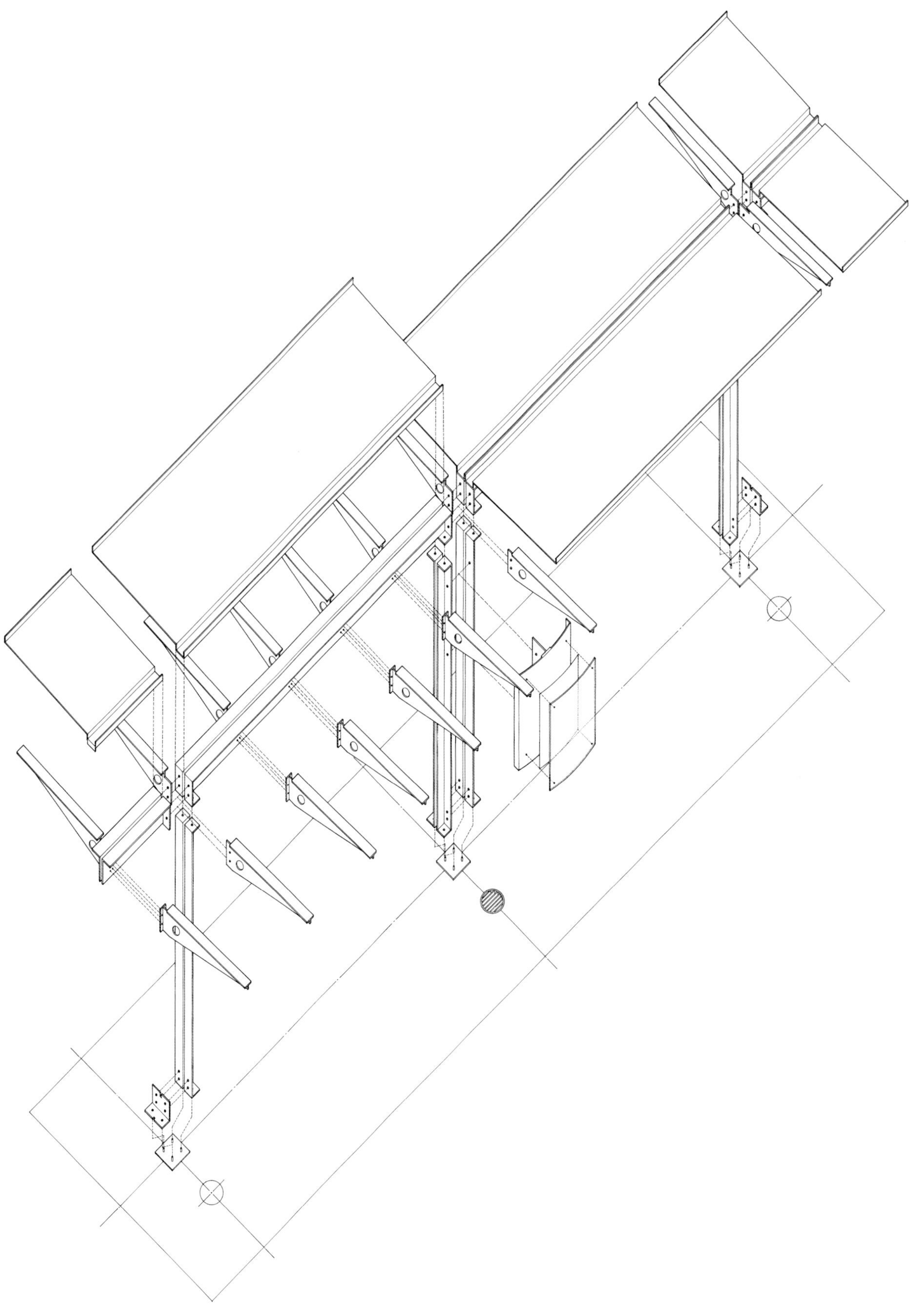

Axonometric showing assembly.

     A PRACTICE OF MAKING PLACES

Bus shelter as installed on site.

Detail of column and spine structure (left) and canopy (right).

n 1986 Clark and Menefee, in association with Eskew, Vogt, Salvato & Filson, Architects, received first prize in the South Carolina Marine Science Museum competition, a three-day invited competition with four other architects: Antoine Predock; Emilio Ambasz; Michael Graves; and Esherick, Homsey, Dodge and Davis. In developing the design for the aquarium, Clark engaged in intensive research into the history of the proposed site on the Cooper River, in both its natural and inhabited aspects – an initiatory method that had become a consistent starting point for his design process. The waterfront site was formerly occupied by a creek, which had been filled in over time, and Clark's landscape plan referenced this history by carving a canal that marked the original waterline and connected Calhoun Street, an important city street that terminates at the site, to the River. The stepped sidewalls of the canal, which provided seating as well as allowing access to the water, were proposed to turn and run along the river edge, allowing people to sit on the waterfront. The aquarium was an urbanized island set into the river and connected to the land by a pedestrian bridge.

The competition design proposed three parallel volumes housing the exhibit spaces and stepping down in height towards the south, with a service block appended to the tallest, north side of the building. Each exhibit space extended out onto the roof of the adjacent volume to form three stepping terraces facing south to the views of the Charleston waterfront and the natural areas of the Cooper and Ashley Rivers and their wetlands. The lowest terrace, beyond the open-air entry loggia, was proposed to be an oak tree grove, and the upper terraces were extensions of the aquarium floors housing screened aviaries. In this way the building turned its back on, and blocked the visitors' view of the commercial docklands to the north, with its gigantic cranes, docked cargo ships, and acres of parked cars and shipping containers. The three entry halls were roofed with inverted copper domes that reflect light down into the public spaces, the last and highest of which housed the large cylindrical glass ocean tank. The copper domes also captured rainwater, which spilled from the highest to the lowest and then into the river, and were intended to symbolize "the passage of water from the mountains to the sea in South Carolina."[1]

Clark and Menefee were given the commission as design architects (with Eskew, Vogt, Salvato & Filson as executive architects) for what was now to be called the South Carolina Aquarium, and the design evolved into a building that is both more compact and more monumental than the competition design. The primary design intentions were to house the aquarium in a structure capable of "holding its own" and standing up to the large-scale commercial port directly to the north; to house the thousands of aquatic animals so as to allow the visitors to focus on a sequence of exhibits without distraction; to address the issues resulting from the introduction of natural light into the aquarium (such as glare, reflection, and algae growth); and to avoid housing the exhibits in a "black box" by opening and directly connecting the interior exhibits to the aquatic environments immediately around the site, as well as to those visible in the distance, at the confluence of the two rivers that defined the peninsula of the city.

The Aquarium comprises a long volume set perpendicular to the shoreline and extending some 200 feet into the Cooper River, which is framed on both long sides by large-scale parallel pairs of structural walls supporting the exhibit floors spanning between them. The two ends of the building, in the river and on the shore, house two different aquatic habitats in elevated screened enclosures. The deep ocean tank, which rises through the three Aquarium floors, contains 385,000 US gallons (almost 1,500,000 liters) of salt water and over 700 aquatic animals, and is set at the

Clark and Menefee, in association
with Eskew, Vogt, Salvato & Filson as
executive architects

center of the north wall, where it forms the central figure around which the other exhibits are arranged on all three floors. The solid back wall of the deep ocean tank is exposed on the north elevation of the building, with a crane mounted above for lifting large aquatic animals. The sections of the north pair of parallel walls to either side of the deep ocean tank house service, mechanical, and circulation spaces, allowing the central exhibit spaces to be reconfigured as needed. The pair of parallel walls on the south are opened by repetitive bays, forming an arcade (similar to a Charleston Single House side-yard "piazza") that houses the entry hall and ramp, and allows views from within the Aquarium to the harbor. The primary structure of the building is reinforced concrete, so as to be able to support the enormous weight of the water tanks inside, "as well as being a tough material that can tolerate the marine environments that the building contains and that it sits within."[2]

The Aquarium is approached from the end of Calhoun Street, across a pedestrian plaza. On the building's west façade, the solid ends of the two pairs of massive concrete parallel walls are set to either side of the cubic aviary habitat, which is screened and framed in black steel, and which projects forward at the center of the building. A steel-framed glass butterfly roof hovers over the aviary's screen enclosure, the central rainwater drainpipe of which descends in the slot between the pair of steel

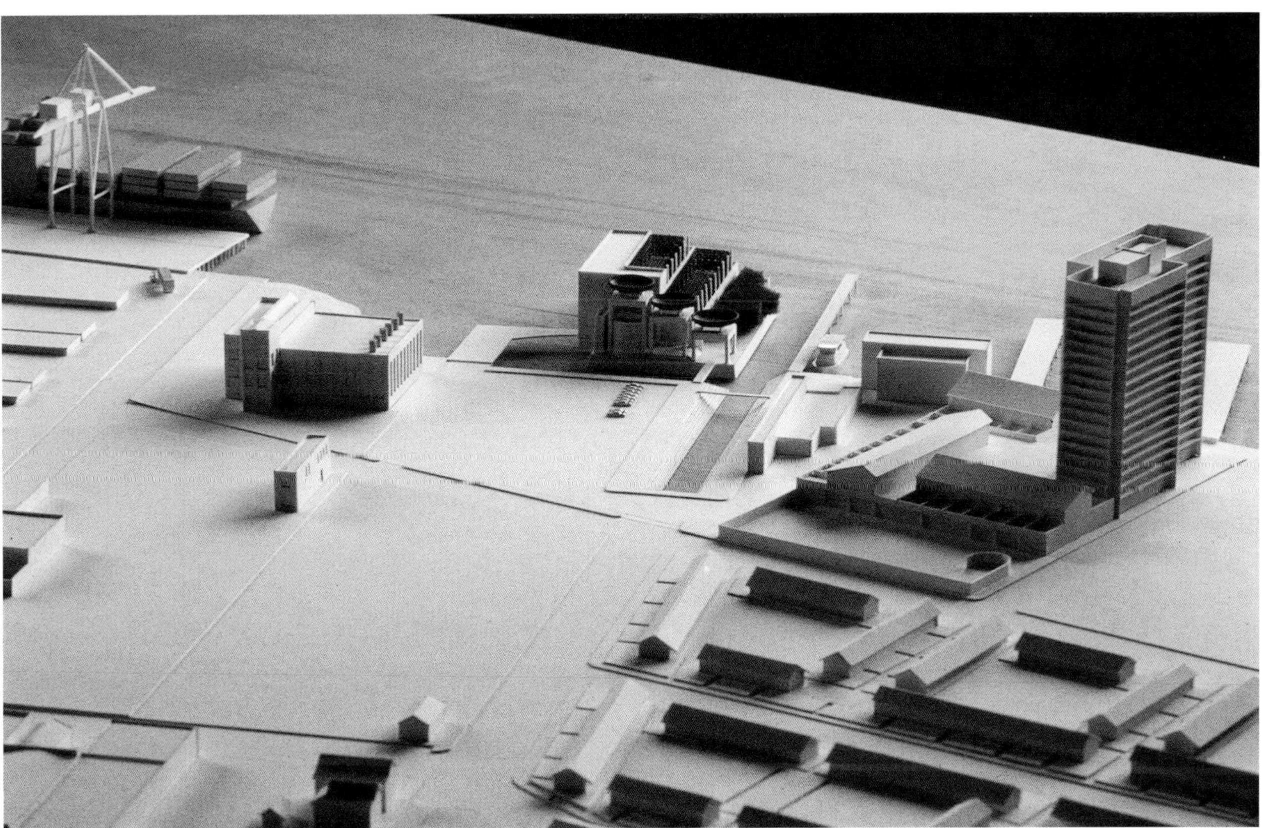

Site model of competition design.

columns at the center of the aviary. The volume of the aviary, solid at the bottom and open at the top, is spaced away from the south parallel wall by the horizontally framed windows of the main hall of the Aquarium, elevated one floor above the ground and over the building entry.

A steel-framed glass butterfly roof projects out over the entry doors, beneath the main hall windows above, and from the outer vestibule, one can enter the lower level of the Aquarium directly. However, the glazed volume of the main hall staircase above projects out of the building to the south, inviting one into the loggia and subtly suggesting that the more compelling and honorifically important entry sequence lies that way. After passing beneath the lower ceiling, one enters the concrete colonnaded loggia, structured by widely spaced piers, that runs along the south side of the building.

As one ascends the broad, slowly rising ramp suspended within the colonnaded loggia, the passage is marked by the regular rhythm of the concrete piers along the inside wall, and the space becomes progressively taller and more monumentally scaled the farther one walks from the shoreline, rising from one story and one bay wide at the shoreline; to two stories and one bay wide in the middle; to four stories and two bays wide at the river end, where suspension cables support the ramp and terraces above at the mid-points of the two-bay wide openings. The entry ramp and loggia culminates in a broad terrace overlooking the river and harbor at the east end of the building, and anchored by a second steel-framed aviary. At the eastern edge of the concrete floor of the terrace, stepped seating descends towards the water, inviting views away from the building and towards the aquatic environments across the harbor.

From the harbor-front terrace, one enters the main hall of the Aquarium, a double-height space that runs along the south side of the building, which is opened with full-height, horizontally-framed glass walls, giving views of the harbor through the piers of the loggia. The north side of the main hall opens to the nine galleries which today house more than 3,000 plants and 7,000 aquatic animals, all arranged around the massive Great Ocean Tank that rises through the three exhibition floors. As a way of providing orientation for the visitors coming and going from the dark and labyrinthine exhibit spaces, each of the three exhibition levels opens to the views to the south, so that the visitor is always aware of where they are in the building. On the middle level of the Aquarium, one level above the main hall, are the entries to the two aquatic habitats and aviaries at the east and west ends of the building, and a wood-floored terrace runs the length of the south loggia, above the entry ramp. On the upper, third level, a café is set on the roof terrace above the eastern end of the main hall, offering views across the harbor.

The Aquarium building that was completed and opened in 2000, described above, closely conforms to Clark's final design in general configuration and construction. However, changes made during construction, including the entirely unnecessary painting of the exposed concrete, as well as the project managers failing to heed Clark's advice, led to Clark resigning from the Aquarium project, which he does not count among his realized works, and which he has never visited. Yet the Aquarium as it stands today is almost entirely of Clark's design, and, even when the aspects that failed to conform to his design are taken into consideration, the building nevertheless merits inclusion in any comprehensive assessment of his works.

Arguably the most troubling aspect of the final, realized design for the Aquarium is the failure of the client, the City of Charleston, to perceive the importance of implementing Clark's brilliant and historically articulate competition landscape plan.

As built, the Aquarium is connected directly to the shoreline, so that it is analogous to a pier or peninsula, rather than to an island, as Clark had proposed. Also lost was Clark's inspired idea to reveal the history of the site by reconfiguring the shoreline and recalling the original watercourse, so that visitors to the Aquarium would discover something of the history of their city as they walked to the building. Instead, the Aquarium stands as yet another example of contemporary society's failure to value landscape and architecture equally, resulting in the ever-increasing difficulty of realizing the merging of architecture and landscape – one of Clark's core ideals.

Plans of two historical (left) and proposed (right) configurations of Charleston waterfront.

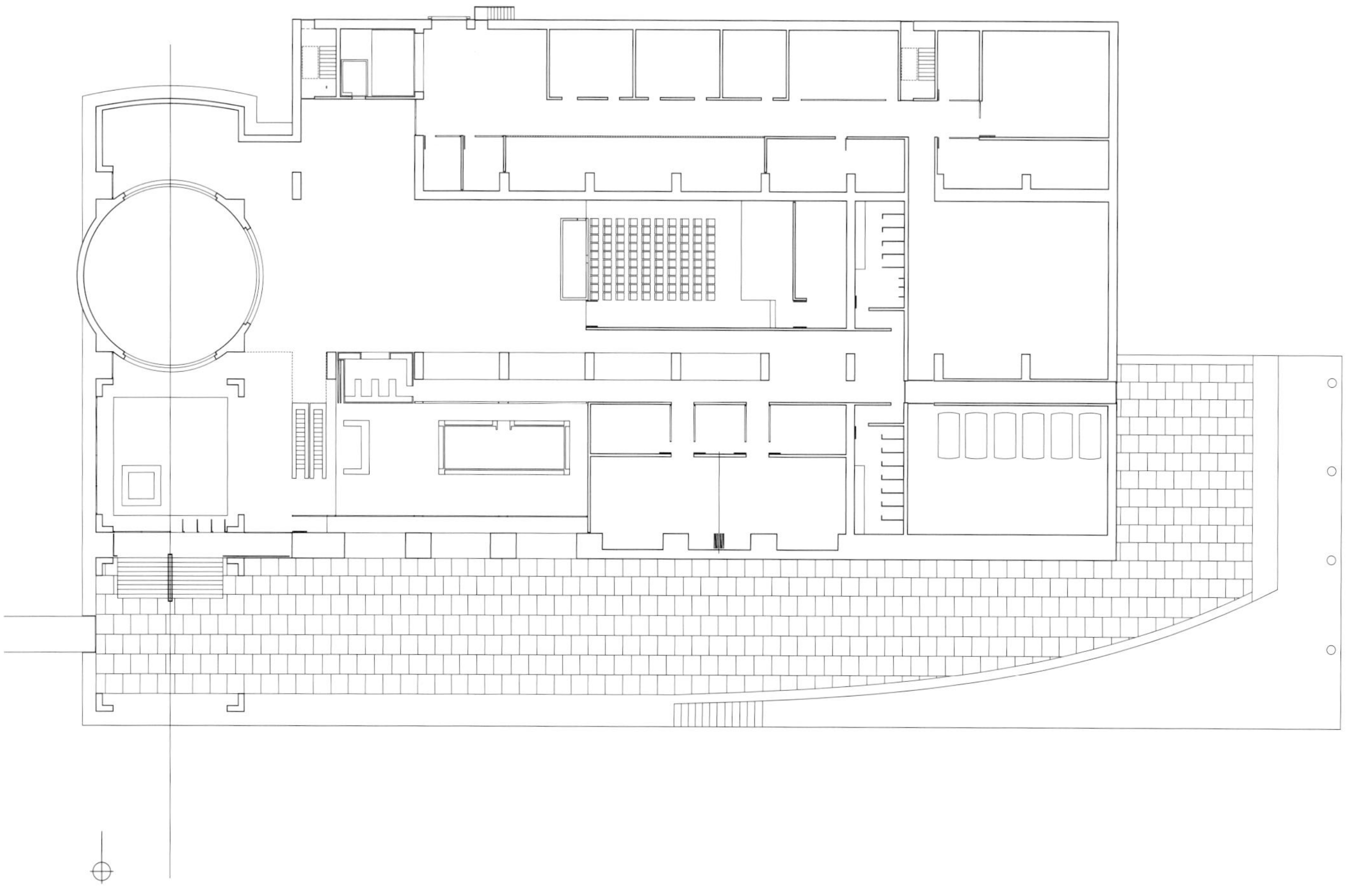

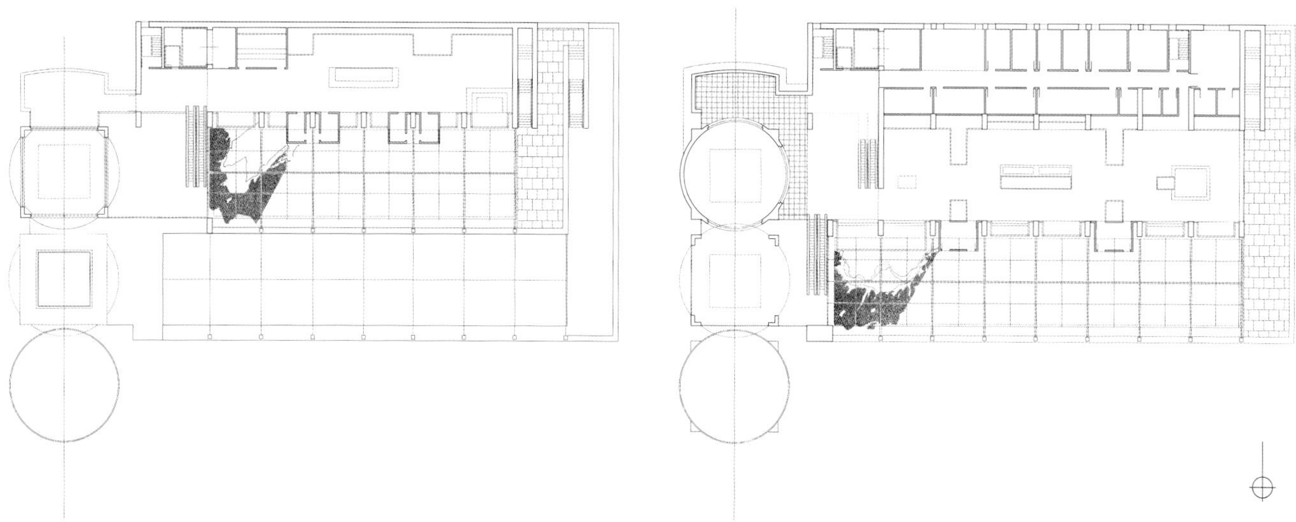

Plan of lower, entry level.

Plan of upper (left) and intermediate (right) levels.

 A PRACTICE OF MAKING PLACES

Aerial view of site model of competition design.

Perspective of approach, with view across new canal.

From top, models of realized design; aerial view, view of entry from southwest, view of terrace from southeast.

View from south with entry arcade and cranes of port to north.

View of entry from southwest.

Terrace suspended in entry arcade on south side.

Main hall of aquarium, with windows opening to south and east.

L ocated south of Charleston and across the Ashley River, the Croffead House is on a remarkable corner site at the confluence of two rivers, to the north and west, with dramatic and extended views to both rivers and their shorelines. The site is at the end of a suburban street lined with houses that share consistent spacing between and setbacks from the street. A line of large, mature live oaks, roughly parallel to the street, runs through the center of the lots, in front of the existing houses, and extends along the entire block. After analyzing the site, the architects positioned the new house to match the setback and spacing of the existing houses, extending the existing neighborhood pattern and terminating it in the riverfront. The house is organized into a compact plan, three floors tall, so its front façade and massing align with the adjacent houses, and it stands behind the row of trees. This resulted in the house being positioned in the southwestern quadrant of the site, close to the shorelines of the confluent rivers.

The main part of the house is contained in a concrete block cube, 32 feet on each side, precisely aligned with the cardinal directions, which contains the living spaces.[1] A detached loggia, with cast concrete frame and glass block infill, containing the entry porch and internal stairs, is set on the east side of the house, facing the street. The loggia is slightly angled to align with the row of live oaks, giving a view of the trees for those using the stair. The square plan of the house may be related to the "four-square" plans of Wright's similarly cubic Prairie houses (including his own Oak Park house of 1889) in the way a central masonry column structures and divides the interior of the cubic volume into four squares, and the bathrooms and kitchen are located in the southeast corner of the plan, thereby forming a large, L-shaped primary volume at all three levels that opens towards the two rivers and accentuates the house's position at their confluence.

In an echo of the reciprocal, two-part, solid-void characteristic of the Charleston Single House, the central column also divides the house into two halves, with the lower, more closed spaces on the south side, towards the neighbors, and the taller, more open spaces on the north side, toward the rivers. On the main, middle level of the house (the *piano nobile* – the noble floor), the double-height living room is to the north, while the kitchen and dining room are to the south (the living and dining rooms forming an L-shaped space), with the master bedroom, dressing and bath on the upper, balcony level, overlooking the living room. On the ground floor is a painting studio beneath the living room, a bedroom (which can be opened to the studio to form an L-shaped space) beneath the dining room, and a bath and utility room beneath the kitchen.

Seen from the street, the house is nestled among the massive trunks and unfurling limbs of the live oaks, with the open space of the river behind. The front façade of the house is formed and framed by the loggia's outer surface, and, as if to emphasize this fact, a thin, projecting concrete edge band, like the frame of a painting, demarcates the outer edge of the loggia at the roof, ground, and both sides. Reflecting the interior organization of the house, the façade of the loggia is divided in half by a central concrete pier. The left half of the concrete frame of the loggia, which stands behind a cluster of trees, is entirely infilled with glass block, and the right half of the loggia is opened to reveal an elevated entry porch set against the concrete block and glass façade of the living room. The recession of the entry porch within the shadows of the loggia is complemented by the extension of the concrete entry stair out of the loggia, and the entry stair axially aligns with the projecting fireplace and rotated chimney above – the whole quite similar to the guestroom entries at Middleton Inn. The spatial sequence of entry, seen from the street, embodies a transformation

Croffead House, James Island, South Carolina, 1986–1989

Clark and Menefee

View from street of entry stair and chimney.

from horizontal (walkway), to diagonal (stair), to vertical (chimney rising from firebox, passing through loggia roof, and silhouetted against the sky).

The house is approached from the east on a stone walkway leading to the entry stair, on which one ascends to reach the thin concrete floor of the entry porch, with the rectangular concrete block fireplace directly ahead, framed by narrow windows on either side. The fireplace and its tall chimney, which is rotated to a 45-degree angle, stand outside of the living room, in the entry porch. The chimney passes through an opening in the loggia roof, above, and a large window is opened behind the chimney, giving views through the top of the double-height living room. The glass entry door opens from the porch to the stair, where, directly ahead, one is given the view back along the line of live oaks. A large opening in the concrete block wall to the right leads from the loggia to the living areas on this, the elevated *piano nobile* of the house, and one enters by moving along beneath the lower ceiling of the kitchen and dining room, with the double-height living room opening to the other side. The entry sequence is experienced as a series of overlapping thresholds from entry walk to stair to porch to loggia to low-ceiling, shadowed interior to high-ceiling, bright interior.

The double-height living room, its walls and ceiling finished in white painted stucco, is opened on all four sides. On the east side, glass surrounds the freestanding fireplace, which projects out onto the entry porch, the masonry walls continuing down to the ground below, while the rotated concrete block chimney, seen through the large upper window—as in Kahn's Esherick House—rises above the concrete lintel that runs the full width of the room, and penetrates through the porch roof above. Opposite the fireplace, a double-height bay window with glass corners projects outward towards the river to the west, framing a view of live oak tree limbs. Similar to the fireplace and chimney on the east wall, the bay window on the west wall is celebrated by way of its articulate detailing: the three glass surfaces terminate in a cantilevered cast concrete sill at the floor and header at the ceiling, and the outward projection of the bay window is counterpointed by the narrow recess in the wall that runs around its four sides, and from which the window projects, floating out over the landscape. The vertical east and west walls, each opened by a single, large aperture, together establish a spatial dialogue across the living room: the fireplace shields the living room from the street, while the projecting bay window orients the views to the river and trees.

On the north wall of the living room, two double-height windows open towards the river and the oak trees at the end of the allee, and the windows are divided at their center by a pier aligning with the central column. The south wall has four large openings, the two on the lower level giving onto the wood cabinet-walled kitchen on the left and onto the dining room on the right, and both rooms have glass block windows to the south, for privacy from the neighbors. The two openings above, into which a continuous low wood balcony wall is set, give onto the master bedroom and its dressing area and bath, and allow views across the top of the living room to the rivers and trees. The horizontal south and north walls, each opened by pairs of apertures centered on the central pier, establish a spatial dialogue across the living room: the two pairs of horizontal openings interconnect the interior spaces of the house, while the pair of vertical windows provides a wide panorama of the confluence of the two rivers.

The cast concrete-framed loggia and staircase, set outside the cubic, concrete block-walled volume of the interior rooms, is essentially an in-between space – reminding us of the porch-piazza of the Charleston Single House, part of both house and garden. The loggia and staircase are at one and the same time an interior space and an exterior space: enclosed with glass and glass block, and opening to the white stucco-walled rooms within the concrete block volume, with which it is intertwining by our circulation; and outside the thick-walled cubic enclosure of the main house, where one is held against the exposed concrete block exterior wall of the house, suspended in the air and surrounded by light, standing on thin floor slabs and beneath a wood-framed roof (the only time horizontal structure is exposed in the house), with distant views of the line of live oaks on one side and the far shore of the river on the other.

The experience of the Croffead House is heightened by the complementary contrast of a geometrically pure cubic volume housing the quotidian needs of daily life. As Wilfried Wang notes, the house "becomes a distilled manifesto of the differentiation to which a perfect cube can be thrust so that a tension exists between the varied reality of everyday occupation and the abstract ideal of a simple marking in the landscape."[2]

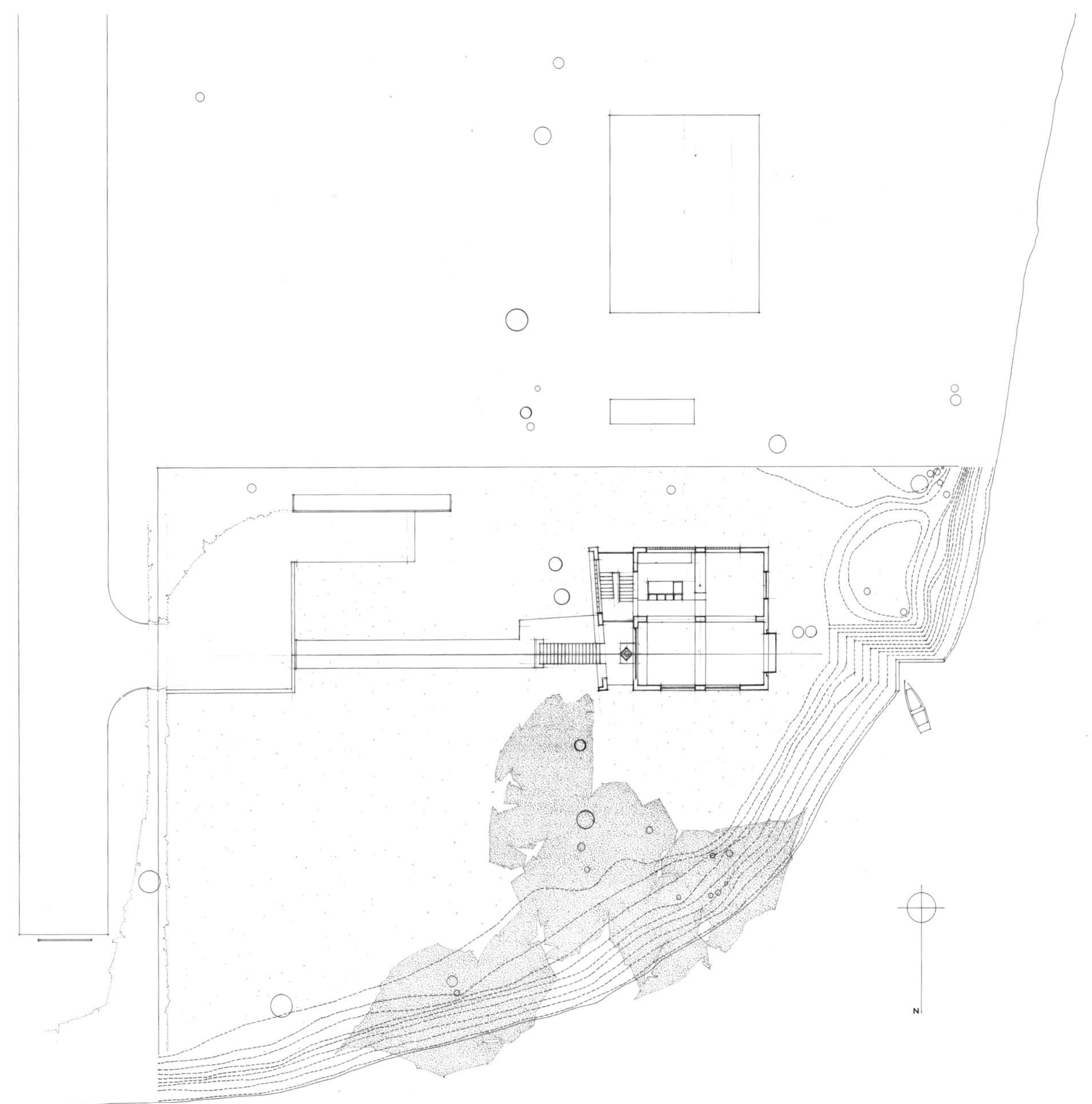

Site plan.

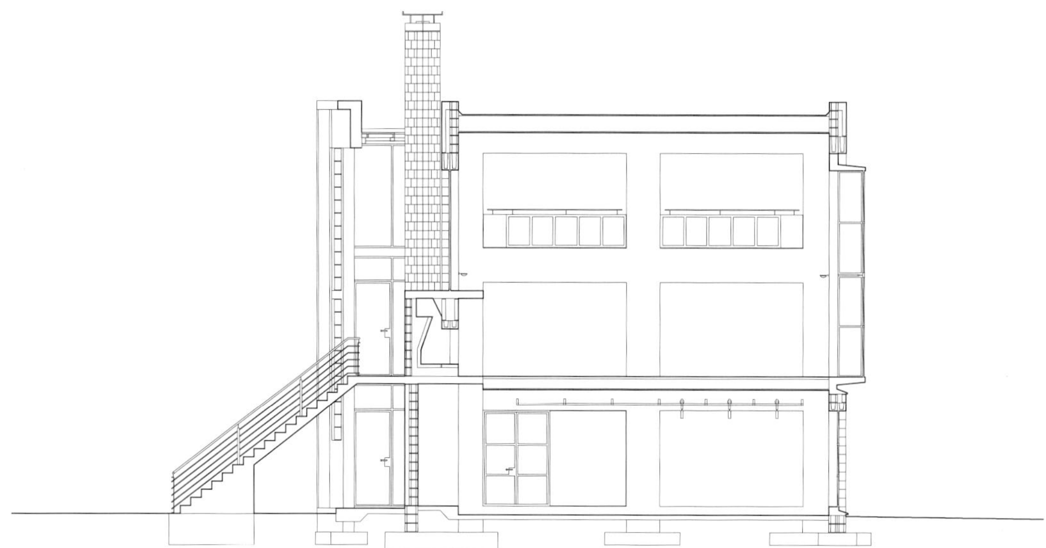

East-west section through entry stair and living room.

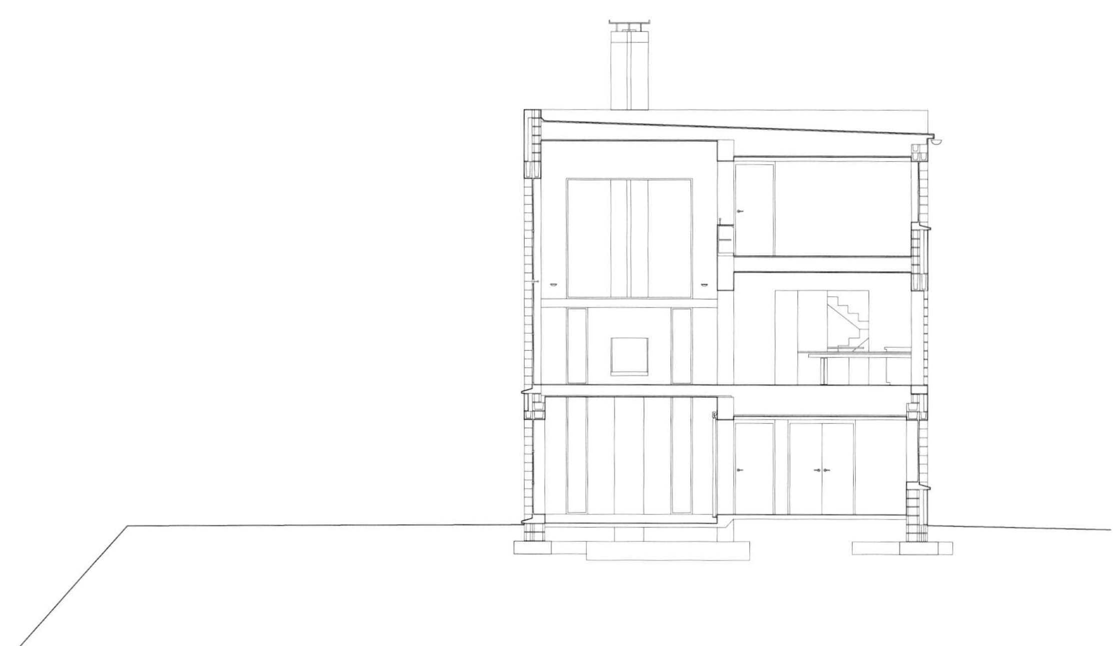

North-south section.

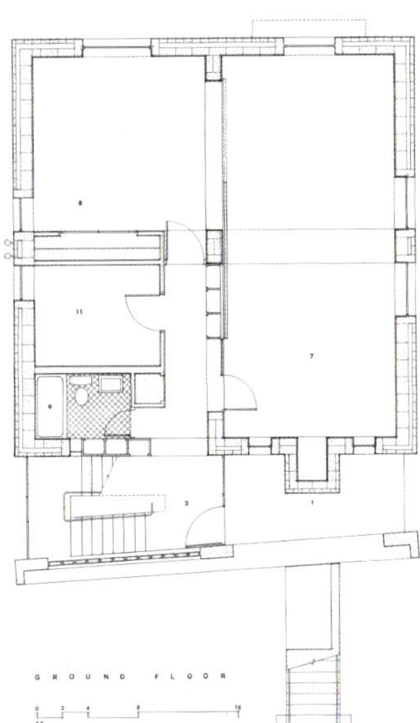

View from southwest.

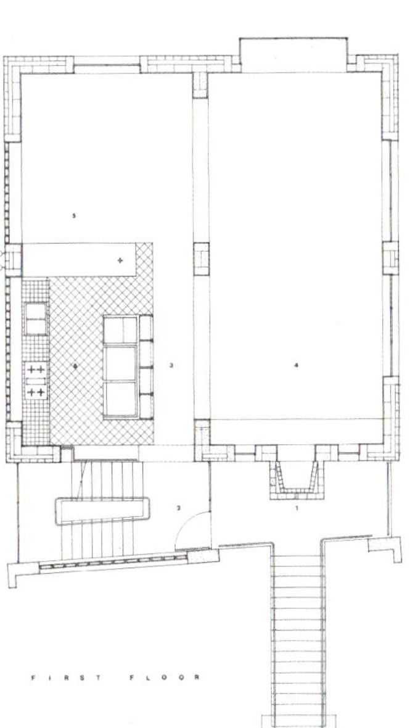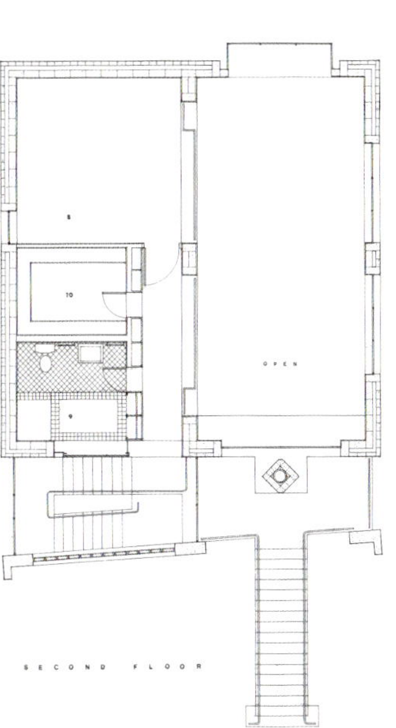

From left, plans of lower, middle (main), and upper levels.

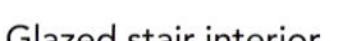

Glazed stair interior.

Entry stair and door from outside.

Living room, looking east.

Living room, looking northwest.

View across living room towards river, seen from upper level balcony.

Glazed stair interior.

Interior detail of projecting bay window.

East façade with bay window projecting towards river.

The building is located on a wooded hillside site just south of Lake Crabtree and in the outskirts of Cary, a suburb of Raleigh. Though the area immediately surrounding the foundation and preschool has a number of corporate office buildings distributed along a busy four-lane divided parkway, the large site, which is generously scaled for the relatively small program area, the dense stand of trees, and the northern slope of the hillside together shield the occupants of the building from views of its much larger neighbors. A gently curving access drive leads uphill from the parkway to the north and arcs around the east side of the building, with parking along its curve for the foundation and a drop-off and parking area for the preschool to the south of the building.

Two separate yet related programs are accommodated in a single building: a preschool that also offers developmental therapy for children and counseling for their parents, and which by regulation and program needed to be on one floor level; and a foundation that promotes local programs related to psychoanalysis and research. Similar to the Middleton Inn, the building is an L-shape in plan, and the building's two wings accommodate three components. The largest of these is the preschool, which is housed in the longer wing of the L-shaped plan, running east to west. The six, single-story classrooms make up three-quarters of the wing, and the offices, therapy rooms, play therapy rooms, waiting room, and entrance foyer are housed in a smaller volume set at the east end. The foundation is housed in a two-story L-shaped volume placed at the north end of the building's shorter wing, running north to south, and comprises a library, research room, interview room, and offices. The preschool and foundation are spatially and programmatically linked by the third component, a lecture and meeting room shared by both programs, which is positioned at the northern juncture of the two wings of the L-shaped plan. A playground is placed in the sheltered space formed by the two wings of the L-shaped plan, on the same level as the preschool classrooms, which open to it.

Due to the program's focus on child development, the architects designed the building to respond to both their and the client's desire for transparency between the spaces within the building, as well as from interior to exterior. In addition, the architects felt it important that the children be able to perceive how the building is constructed, how its parts fit together, and how it worked, and to that end they clearly articulated the building's construction, materials, details, and hybrid structure of concrete and steel—cast concrete beams and frames, concrete block piers and walls, and steel beams and columns—which is exposed wherever possible. In this intention, Clark again parallels Louis Kahn, who said, "Architecture is the thoughtful making of spaces. But these spaces must be clearly defined in their making."[1] For Kahn, it is an ethical imperative that construction materials and building structure are always to be left exposed, becoming the only ornament appropriate to modern building. In Clark's designs, there is a similar intention to construct rooms that, when inhabited, allow us to see how they are made and how they are structured.

The preschool is entered from the south side of the building, where a paved entry court is sunken a few steps below the level of the adjacent ground, and well below the parking, which is at the uphill end of the site. A low concrete bench runs along the south edge of the court, facing the entry, providing a place for parents and children to wait in good weather. A wing-shaped frosted glass canopy, supported on a single freestanding steel column, cantilevers out from the concrete masonry walls and provides cover for the area in front of the entry doors. Upon entry, the reception desk, waiting room, therapists' offices, and play therapy rooms are ahead, and, to the right is the principal's office, which has a window overlooking the entry court, and which

Lucy Daniels Foundation
and Preschool, Cary,
North Carolina,
1990–1992

Clark and Menefee

Aerial view of building from northeast.

opens to and aligns with the wide, concrete-floored hallway leading to the classrooms.

The south-facing classroom hallway is opened to the wooded hillside by large steel-framed windows that run from the concrete bench raised two feet above the hallway floor, matching the ground level outside, to the exposed concrete beam at the ceiling. As is typical throughout the building, the glazing takes the form of a large bay window, with the central glass wall set towards the outer face of the concrete masonry piers, with returns forming recesses at both ends (within which the tall narrow operable windows can open even in the rain), and each concrete bench is wrapped in glass on three sides. The concrete bench, warmed by the south sun in winter and shaded in the summer, is a natural gathering place for the children. Across the hallway, the classrooms are paired into three sets, with shared entry foyers recessed within the depth of the wood-paneled walls containing the bathrooms and storage. The thick, solid-walled service zone protects the classrooms from the noises of the hallway, yet the wood walls do not reach the ceiling, allowing the classrooms to also receive bounced south light through the band of clerestory windows above.

Inside the glass entry doors, each pair of concrete-floored classrooms is joined by a shared storage wall adjacent to the entry on the south side, which houses wood cabinets above and children's individual cubbies below. Towards the back of the room, the storage wall expands to house the wood-walled children's washrooms, on the outer face of which are a long counter and sink. The shared central storage wall stops well short of the ceiling, and a continuous frameless, butt-glazed clerestory window, the same depth as that over the hallway service blocks, runs the length of the classrooms, which share a continuous ceiling. Each pair of classrooms is also joined by the skylight opened in their shared ceiling, which extends from the entry door to the children's washroom, illuminating the cabinet and cubby wall. Each classroom is opened to the playground to the north through large steel-framed bay window, detailed similarly to those in the hallway, and beneath which a concrete bench is set. In the niche behind the washrooms, shelves line the wall next to the glass door, recessed so it can be opened in the rain, which gives onto the playground.

The cast concrete beams and concrete masonry of the outer south and north walls are complemented by the steel I-beam that runs across the center of the ceiling of each classroom from east to west, parallel to and equidistant from the two outer walls. At the shared storage wall and skylight of each classroom pair, the steel beam is joined to and supported by a steel column, which stands in a slot opened in the wood cabinets. The steel columns in each pair of classrooms do not meet, and the gap between them is directly beneath the skylight, which literally highlights the independence of the steel structural frames of the two classrooms. On the exterior of the preschool, tall inverted V-shaped skylights rise above the roof and the concrete masonry parapets at the outer walls are lowered, aligning with the entry vestibules, skylights and washroom blocks, together marking the location of the paired classrooms. On both north and south façades, the rainwater downspouts located between each pair of classrooms are celebrated by being recessed into slots in U-shaped concrete masonry piers.

The foundation is entered from the east side of the building, where a paved entry court is set into the inner corner of the L-shaped plan, one floor below the preschool level. Approaching the entry court, the wall directly ahead is static and symmetrical, with a cast concrete frame wrapping all four edges, which is spaced away by glazed recesses from the building volume behind. Inset within the concrete frame—though seemingly independent of it—is a steel-framed bay window, with clear glazing above and glass-block below, which returns to form deep recesses at both sides and

   A PRACTICE OF MAKING PLACES

the top, and within which can be seen the piers and beams of the concrete structural frame. In contrast, the wall on the left is asymmetrical, being comprised of roughly equal L-shaped areas of solid concrete masonry wall and recessed steel-framed glass, the whole forming a dynamic, rotating composition. The entrance doors are set into a deeply recessed porch-like space in the inner corner of the entry court.

On the lower level of the foundation are the reception area, an interview room, and the research room, which the glass-block outer wall both illuminates and protects from views of those in the entry court. A cast concrete staircase, with a semi-cylindrical wall at the mid-point landing, rises to the main floor. At the top of the single flight of stairs, one arrives to one of the two glass-walled vestibules or thresholds that connect the three program components in the north-south wing of the building. These narrow glazed vestibule spaces are set between the solid concrete masonry walls of the adjacent building masses, opening to the forest to the east and to the playground to the west. They also open to north and south, giving views along the hallway from the foundation to the lecture room and beyond to the preschool offices and entry. To allow the three program spaces to be acoustically isolated from each other as needed, each glass vestibule is divided at its center point by a glass wall and door running east-west, which when closed still allows views through the building.

On the main, upper level of the foundation, the rooms of which are wood-floored, a wide hallway and waiting area is illuminated and opened to views of the forest and the entry court below through the inward-folding glass wall. The offices are set on either side, behind wood walls with clerestory windows above, and the director's office overlooks the entry court through a large square window with recessed operable returns at both sides. Above the research room is the foundation library, one of the most beautiful rooms in the building, with an L-shaped wall of bookshelves on its north and west wall. On the east side of the room, the cast concrete structural frame wraps the floor, walls, and ceiling, and the steel-framed glass wall projects beyond and runs outside of the structural frame, returning behind the piers at both sides, descending past the floor beam below and rising past the ceiling beam above. The glass door opening from the waiting area to the library, and the glazed opening directly across from it, constitutes one end of the visual axis that runs continuously through all three components of the program at this level.

The north-south movement axis of the hallway is complemented by the exposed double channel steel beam at the ceiling, which, in a way similar to the steel beams in the preschool classroom ceilings, runs down the central axis of the foundation, lecture room, and preschool offices, terminating at its north end in the concrete structural pier of the library window, and terminating at its south end in the steel column supporting the glass canopy at the preschool entry. This steel ceiling beam runs across the center of the lecture and meeting room, which is shared by the foundation and school programs. The identical sides of the wood-floored lecture room, each flanked on its north and south sides by wood cabinets, open through large steel-framed bay windows onto the forested hillside to the east and onto the preschool playground on the west, and the room receives sunlight both morning and afternoon. In the everyday activities of the preschool and foundation, the transparency desired by both the clients and the architects permeates the experience of the place, providing every room with generous natural light from several directions and varying throughout the day; engendering social connection and interaction among the inhabitants of the building; and allowing all activities that take place within to be characterized and accompanied by the numerous beautiful views to the surrounding forest hillside.

Foundation, seen from east.

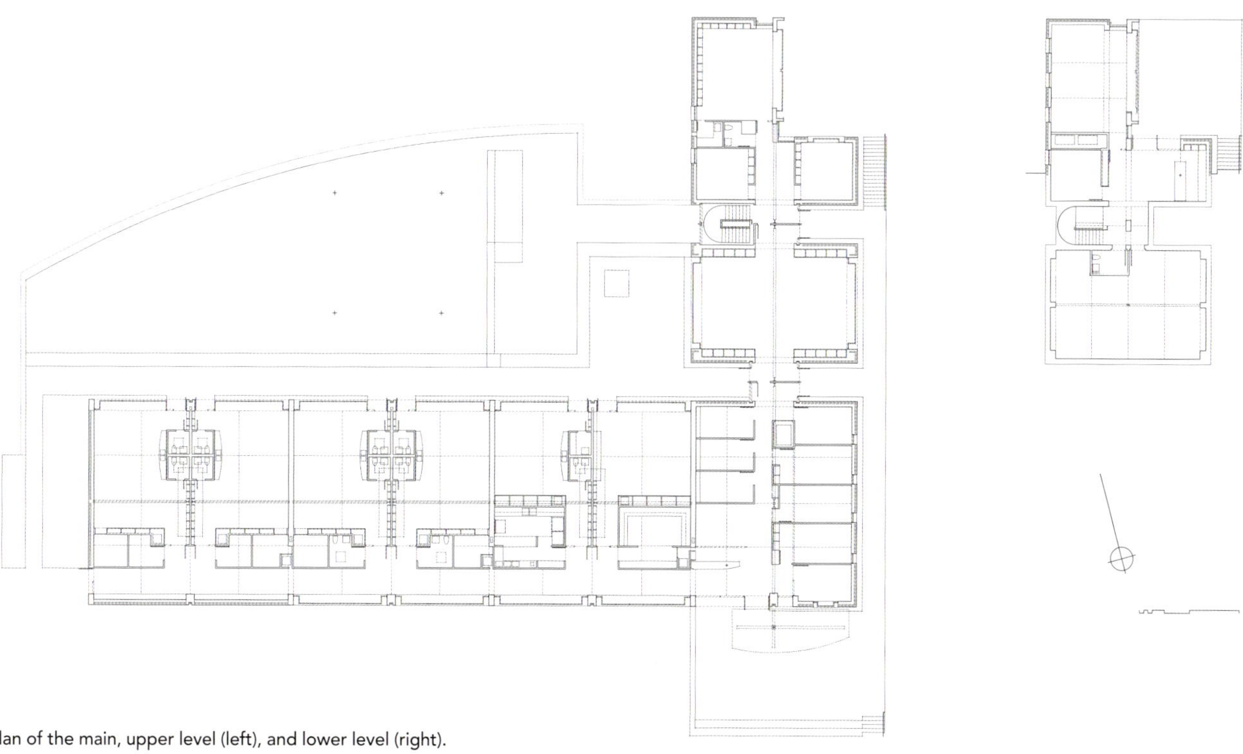

School entry court, hallway, and skylights, seen from southeast.

Plan of the main, upper level (left), and lower level (right).

School entry court, canopy, and door.

View from above of classrooms and playground.

Classroom, with skylight and clerestory glass to neighboring classroom.

Glazed south hallway with classroom entries.

Playground and classroom façades.

Detail of classrooms (left) and foundation entry façade (right).

View to foundation library.

Entry to paired classrooms.

Classroom, with windows onto playground.

Foundation library.

Lecture room, overlooking playground.

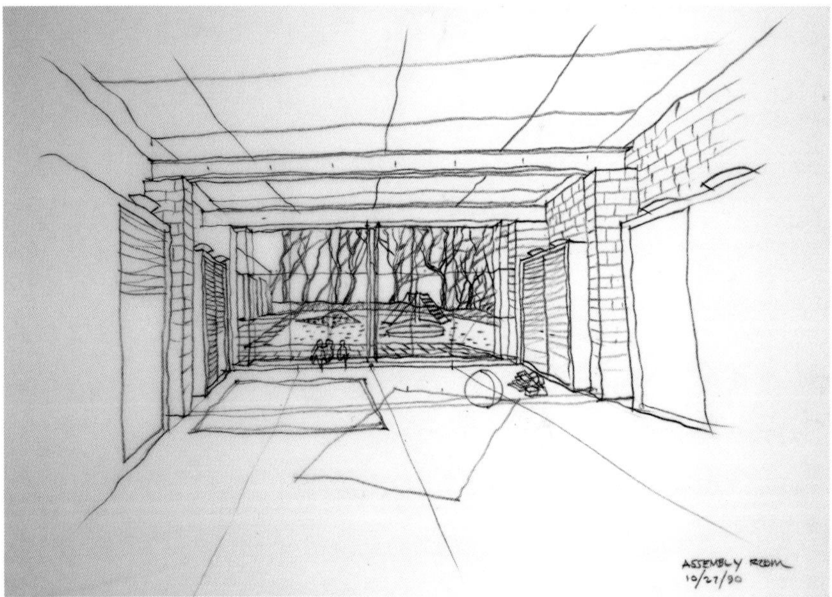

Design sketch study of lecture room.

   A PRACTICE OF MAKING PLACES

Lower entry court and façade of foundation.

T he house was designed for Menefee's parents, who requested a dwelling "from which they could explore and study the mountains, a new landscape for them."[1] The house is placed high up on a heavily wooded, south-facing slope overlooking the Green River in the mountains of southwestern North Carolina, south of Asheville and close to the South Carolina border. In siting the house just below the top of the hill, the architects paralleled Frank Lloyd Wright's principle of building on the "brow" of the hill, so as to frame the hilltop, rather than building directly on it, and thereby erasing the hilltop from our experience.

The small house is a double square in plan (which, along with the square, was Wright's preferred plan proportion), 16 feet wide and 32 feet long, and it is oriented precisely to the cardinal directions. The wider façades are to the east and west, facing along the slope, with its shortest narrow façade to the north, and its tallest narrow façade to the south. The concrete masonry walls, exposed outside and inside, form a solid-cornered, tower-like volume, and the west and south façades are opened with large, three-story-tall windows, to allow the warm sun to enter in the winter, while the east and north façades are mostly closed and solid, having only small windows to protect the interior from the cold winter winds. The roof appears to float above the concrete lintel at the top of the concrete masonry walls, from which its white-painted wood soffit is separated by a thin line of clerestory windows. The roof cantilevers beyond the concrete masonry walls all around, rises in a low curved arc from east to west, and is sheathed in stainless steel.

The house is approached along the slope from the west, where the concrete masonry fireplace and chimney mass is set in front, and at the exact center, of the façade. The thin edge of the roof cantilevers out over the west wall of the house, shading the clerestory window band just beneath it, and an opening at the center of the roof allows the chimney to pass through. A concrete masonry retaining wall emerges from the fireplace mass and extends along the slope, anchoring the house to the landscape, forming a brick-paved terrace and entry porch on the uphill side and a gently descending path on the downhill side, which leads to the entry to the lower level bedroom. There the glass entry door opens onto a raised concrete landing that wraps the west and north sides of the concrete-floored lower bedroom, and into which steps are cut and onto which the fireplace opens. The private lower bedroom, only accessible from the outdoor path, is experienced as opening to the forest to the south and west, and at the same time as withdrawing into the excavated concrete foundations.

On the western, entrance side of the house, the concrete masonry walls form solid outer corners and frame the full-height steel-framed glazing that renders the wide middle section of the façade largely transparent. The fireplace and chimney standing at the center of the glass wall anchor the sectional transitions that take place within the house as it steps down to the south in parallel with the sloped site. A thin concrete slab emerges from the glass wall to the right of the fireplace mass, paralleling the middle floor level of the double-height living room within, while to the left, at the transition between the fireplace and the chimney, a curved concrete floor slab emerges from the glass wall, paralleling the upper floor level of the bedroom loft within, while also providing a sheltering roof over the glass entry doors.

The entry door opens onto the pine wood floor of the dining area, ahead, and the concrete-floored kitchen to the left, both of which are illuminated by the window opened in the east wall directly across from the entrance door. The entry foyer, dining area, and kitchen are all set beneath the low ceiling formed by the wood floor framing of the bedroom loft above. Similarly to the Reid House, the loft floor framing is

Menefee Mountain House, Zirconia, North Carolina, 1990–1993

Clark and Menefee

View from the southwest.

supported by a black-painted steel beam, set at the mid-point of the double-square space, which spans from wall to wall and bears above the center of the fireplace, where a concrete lintel extends over the entry door and marks the transition in section from fireplace to chimney.

Moving from beneath the low, wood-beamed ceiling at the entry to the high, white-painted plywood and batten ceiling of the double-height living room culminates the act of entry. The wood flooring extends across the living room to terminate in a steel beam that spans across the south wall, allowing the large, three-story steel-framed window to run continuously from the lower bedroom level beneath the floor to the ceiling above. At the center point of the west, entry wall the fireplace opens onto a raised concrete hearth that gently curves out to form the landing of the steel stair that ascends to the loft bedroom above.

The pine-wood floored bedroom loft is framed on its south side by low white-painted cabinets that screen the views from the living room below, and on its north side by continuous white-painted wood doors that stop short of the ceiling, behind which are the bathroom and closet. Small windows are opened in the shower on the north wall and adjacent to the wood doors on the east wall. The large steel-framed windows rising from the living room open to expansive views to the south and west, where the chimney stands just outside the glass.[2] At the top of the double-height space, the steel-framed windows and concrete masonry walls terminate at the continuous concrete lintel that runs all the way around the room, and the flat, plywood-and-batten ceiling is lifted above the lintel and cantilevers out beyond the walls all around, its glossy white surface reflecting the light coming in the continuous band of clerestory windows.

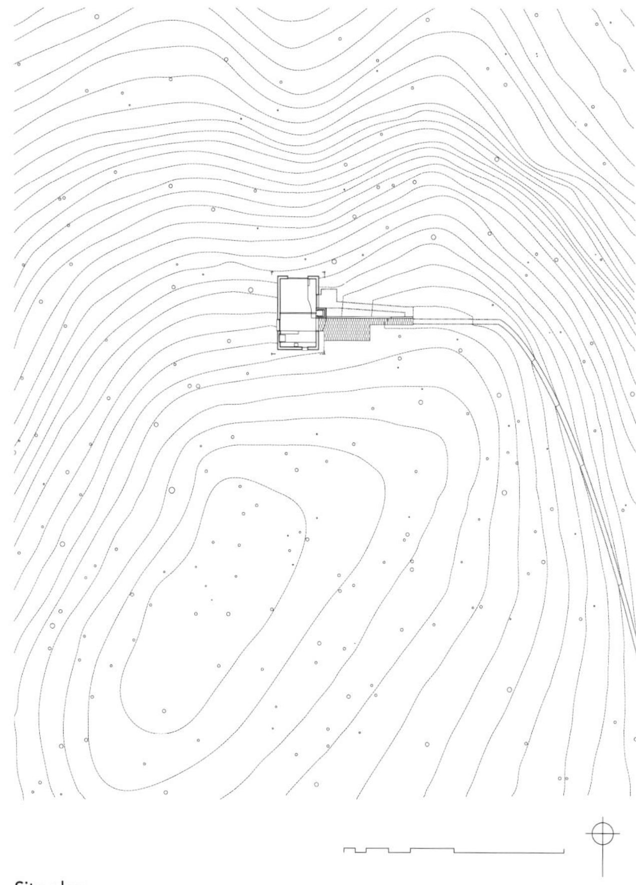

Site plan.

A PRACTICE OF MAKING PLACES

View from northwest (left) and west (right).

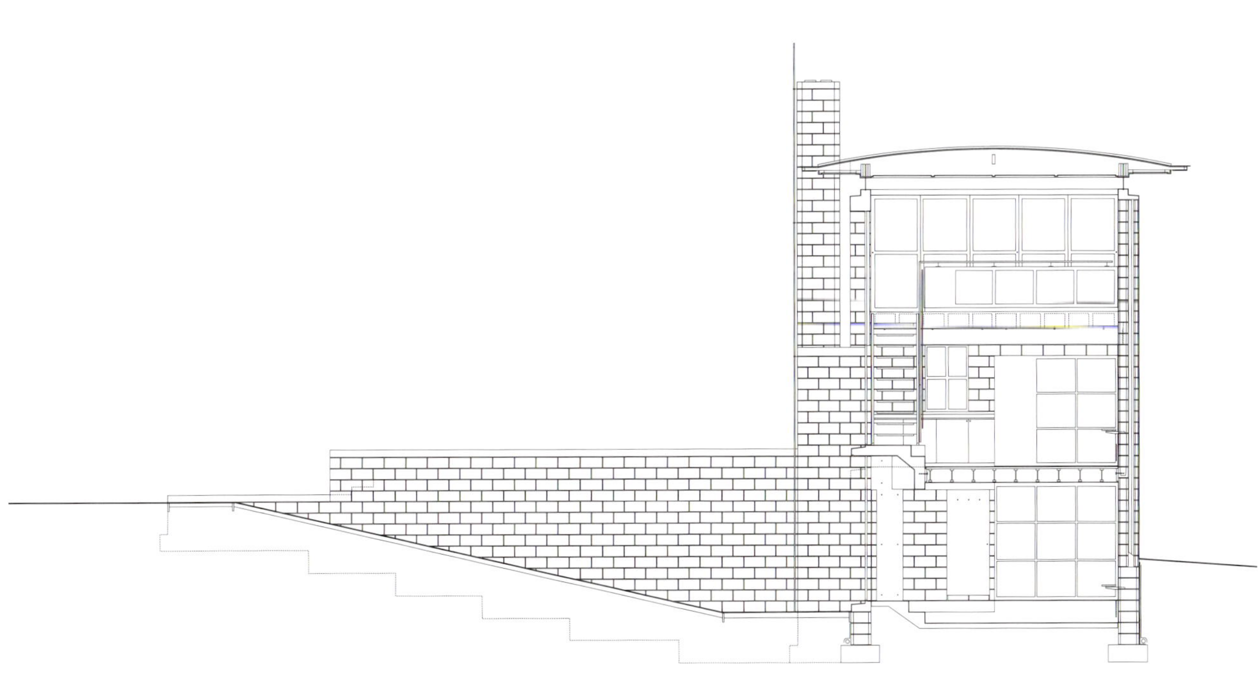

East-west section.

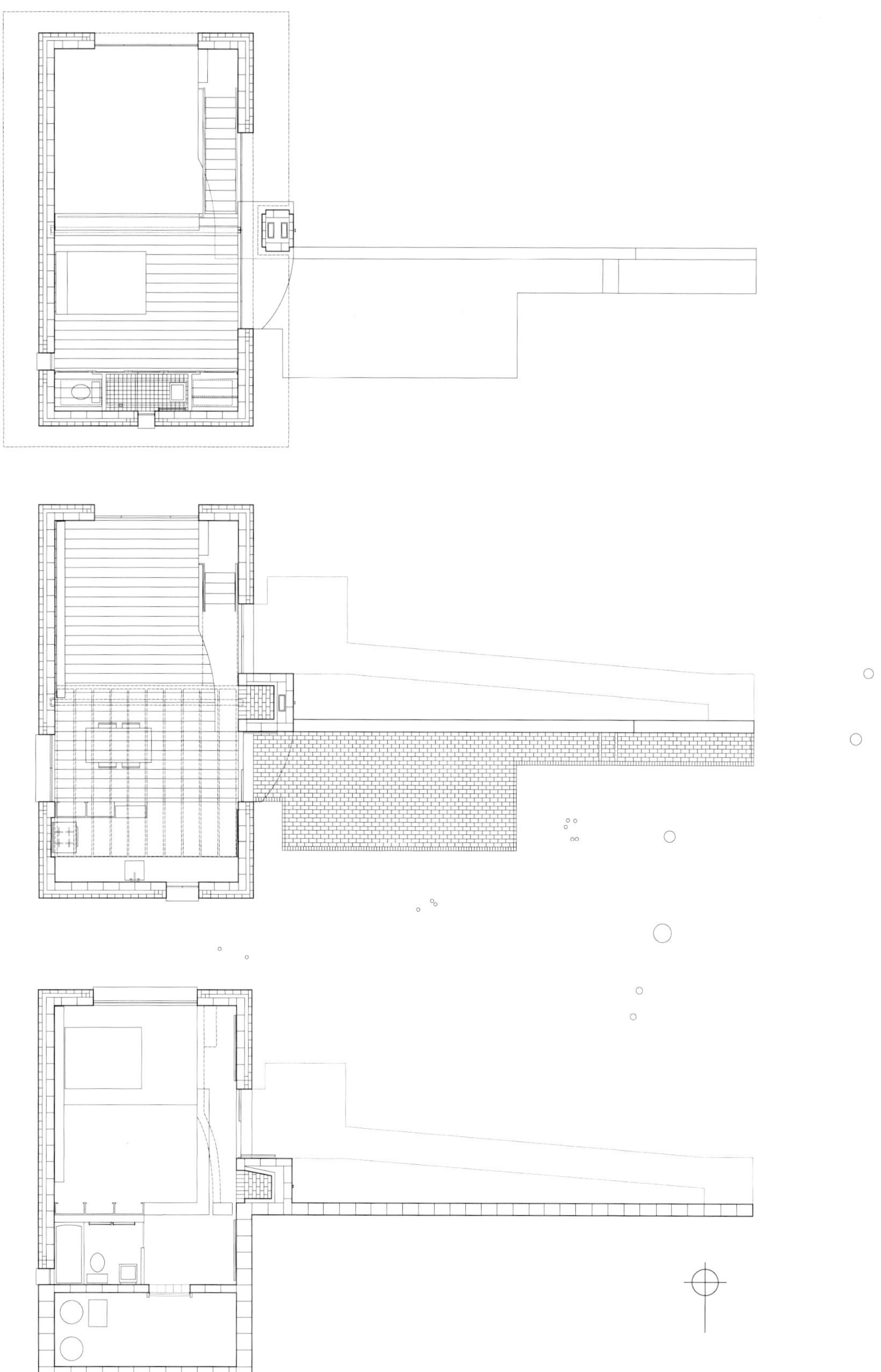

From top, plans of the upper, middle (main), and lower levels.

Lower-level bedroom (upper left); main-level living room, fireplace, and stair (upper right); main-level living room with south-facing window (lower left); upper-level bedroom and storage wall (lower right).

Upper-level loft bedroom, with clerestory window band at ceiling and exterior chimney.

     A PRACTICE OF MAKING PLACES

Main level living room, stair, fireplace, entry, and kitchen.

T he architect's own house is sited on the edge of a steep, wooded bluff, overlooking commercial buildings at the bottom of the hill and a highway in the
distance to the north, with extended views of the hillside forest to the east
and west, and entry from a suburban cul-de-sac to the south. The design precisely
responds to the conditions of the site by having translucent, glass block-glazed win-
dow-walls to the north and south, giving both privacy and abundant light but also
diffusing the views both in and out, and by having large transparent windows to the
east and west, opening to views that, as the architect says, "go on forever" along
the slope of the wooded hillside. The design also engages with the topography of
the site by embedding the three-story house into the hillside parallel to the slope,
so that the south, entry side of the house is two stories tall, while the north, downhill
side of the house is three stories tall.

In designing plan and section of the house, Clark again employed Frank Lloyd
Wright's favored geometric figures and proportions of the square and double-square.
The floor plans are each a double-square, 16 x 32 feet, and the double-height living
room is a square in section, 16 feet wide x 16 feet tall. The fireplace and chimney
mass are set at the third-point of the plan, dividing each floor into a larger, primary
or "served" space and a smaller, secondary or "servant" space. Yet, as is typical in
Clark's architecture, these "ideal" geometric figures and proportions, when used to
determine the interior dimensions of the spaces, are also grounded in the mundane
and circumstantial dimensions of the materials of their making: the 4 x 8-foot sheets
of plywood that clads the ceilings (which another architect has called "the tatami mat
of America"[1]) and the 8 x 8-inch and 8 x 16-inch concrete blocks used to make the
walls and fireplace.

Unlike the typical suburban houses that surround it, which have driveways
extending from the street to the front door, the approach to Clark's house from the
street is a purely pedestrian experience. Cars are parked at a small paved area at
the edge of the cul-de-sac, and one approaches the house on a slowly descending
walkway that runs straight towards, and is aligned with, the two-story, recessed, glass-
block-walled entry porch, which is the only opening in the solid concrete masonry
front façade. The entry walk also aligns with the sidewall of the fireplace, seen just
inside the glass block wall, and the unusually tall chimney, which rises above the front
façade. The front façade matches the double-square proportion of the floor plan, and
the recessed entry porch is opened one-third of the way in from the left side. The
façade is given a vertical emphasis by the square concrete blocks of the wall, set in a
running bond (with the vertical joints staggered), and the square glass blocks of the
recessed entry porch, set in a stack bond (with the vertical joints aligned).

The entry porch has a stone-paved floor, elevated one step above the path,
and the glass-block back wall is bracketed by a solid black wall, with high window
above, to the left, and the glass entry door to the right. The threshold of the entry door aligns with edge of the glass-block wall and the front edge of the concrete
hearth of the fireplace, and from there one steps onto the wood floor of the double-height living room. This, the primary space and largest volume of the house, is
placed on the main, middle floor along with the entry porch and the kitchen, which is
placed behind the fireplace, at the west end of the floor. A guest bedroom and bath
are in the loft or mezzanine above the kitchen, overlooking the living room, and the
bedroom and bath is on the lower floor. There are no partitions in the house, and the
fireplace is the only element that divides the spaces of the house, with storage always
built into an outside wall. As a result, the entire three-story volume of the house is
spatially interconnected.

Clark House, Charlottesville, Virginia, 1994–1996

Clark and Menefee

Living room and east window, seen from kitchen.

The house is experienced as a carefully crafted exercise in spatial and material point and counterpoint. The inward projection of the two-story recessed entry vestibule, glazed on three sides, into the volume of the house is counterpointed and complemented by the outward projection of the three-story window or "vitrine" out of the volume of the house, extending beyond the concrete block walls to form the primary element of the north façade of the house. The north face of the "vitrine" is entirely glazed with glass block to provide both daylight and privacy, while its tall and narrow east and west ends are steel-framed clear glass windows, and its floor and ceiling are cantilevered concrete slabs. The two sets of cast concrete stairs—one above the other—centered on the fireplace mass and accessed from the main, middle level of the house, are cantilevered out into the western half of the projecting window, giving both access and acoustical connection to the loft studio above and the bedroom below. When ascending or descending on the stairs, one is outside the masonry walls of the house, and one is given extended views through the clear-glass end-walls to the hillside outside, making each use of the stairs a kind of "walk in the woods," as the architect-occupant describes it.

The small house was inspired by the one-room cabin of Clark's grandfather, and while measuring only 1,400 square feet (600 sq. ft. on two floors and 200 sq. ft. on the mezzanine), the space is nevertheless experienced as a "large-scaled" house, filled with elegant material details and intertwining spatial joints. This expansive character is the result of the spaces of the house interpenetrating, interlocking, and forming a continuity with one another, which is complemented and contrasted by the material components of the house being made elemental, distinct, and independent of each other, never touching.

Yet, in our experience of the house, we find that each material element and spatial volume engages both point and counterpoint. The large, three-story steel-framed window opened in the east wall continues past the wood floor of the "public" living room above and down into the "private" bedroom below, providing both rooms with an expansive view of the wooded hillside. In a similar way, the cantilevered concrete stairs only occupy one-half of the three-story "vitrine" window projecting out past the north wall, the other half of the space constituting a vertical void connecting the "public" living room to the "private" bedroom below, allowing the two rooms to share the daylight and lateral views. This spatial "joint" between the living room above and bedroom below is demarcated and celebrated by the long low bench-seat-table at the edge of the void in the living room of deep red-brown mahogany wood, which contrasts with the pale birch plywood ceiling and oak floor.

The rough, gray concrete masonry walls are made of 8 x 16-inch blocks on the interior, giving a subtle horizontal grain to the vertical walls, which is complemented by the smooth, polished horizontal surfaces of the wood floors and plywood ceilings, as well as the plywood cabinets, which fold to form inhabitable niches in the masonry mass. In the complementary qualities of the bedroom below, half buried in the ground yet opened to the east and north, and the guest loft above, open on all four sides and yet shielded from views, the continuous wood planes hover overhead and underfoot, providing a calming counterpoint to the dynamic space of the living room.

The house is experienced as a single great room projecting out over the hillside whose characteristics it articulates and restates. The cubic, wood-floored living room is anchored by the pinwheel composition of the masonry fireplace, illuminated by the south sun coming in the entry vestibule, and it opens to the forest to the east and to the luminous grid to the north, and expands overhead to encompass the entire volume of the house, capped by the 16 x 32-foot birch plywood ceiling. As the architect indicates, the house is a variation on a larger theme; "This house, with the Croffead House and the Mountain House, represent a series of houses of similar spatial, material and constructional patterns. They represent permutations of a type. Each of the houses is three stories and each has a mezzanine overlooking the living space. Each is built of concrete block integrated with poured concrete and utilizing a wood floor frame. The repetition of a type allows for the continued refinement of details."[2]

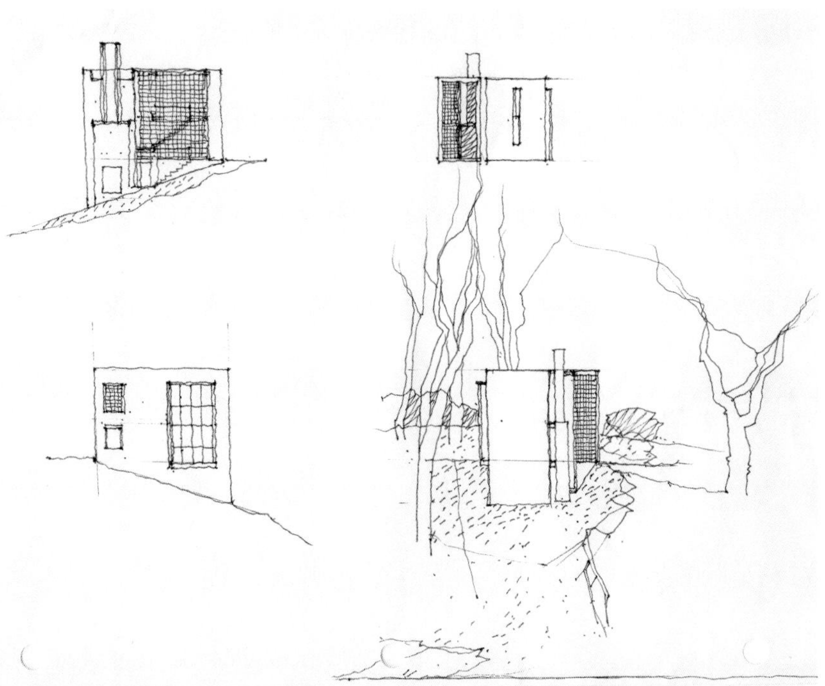

Design sketch studies of elevations.

Design sketch studies of living room interior.

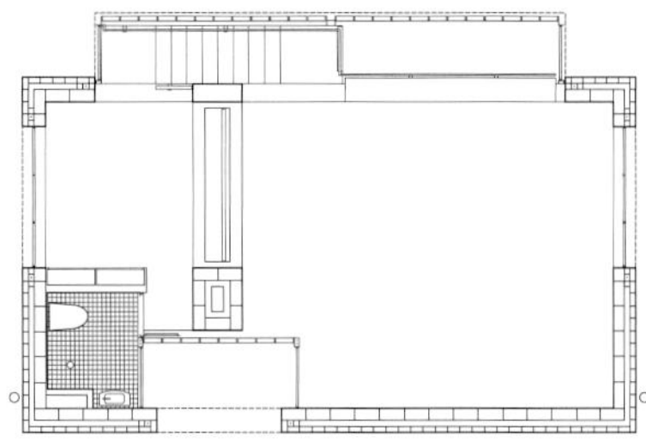

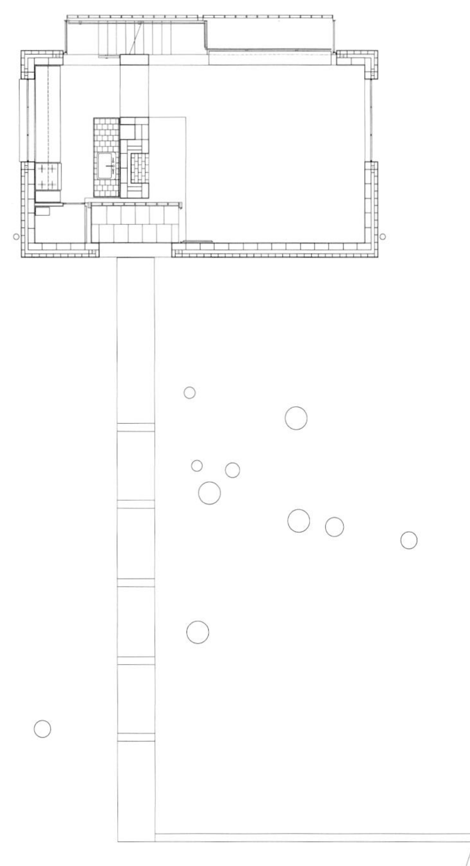

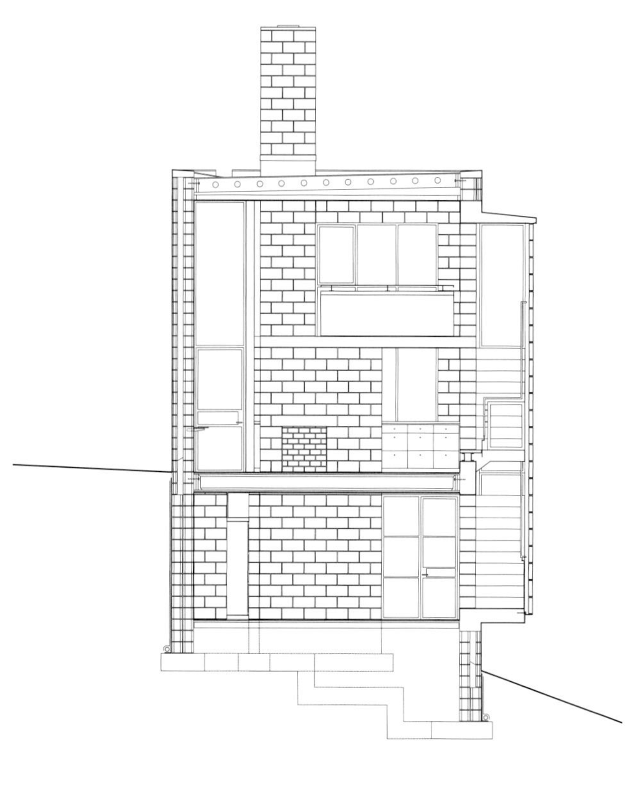

North-south section.

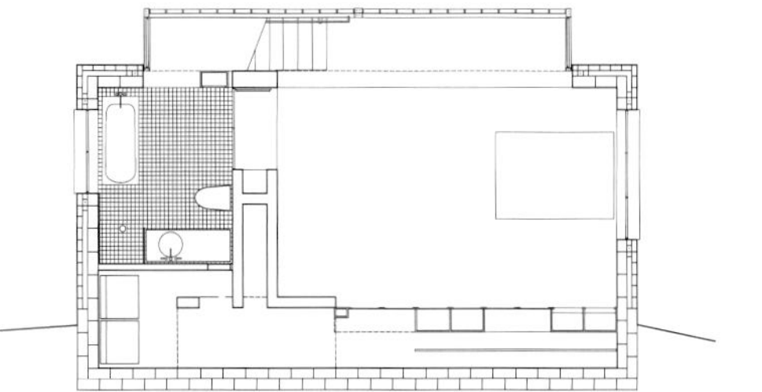

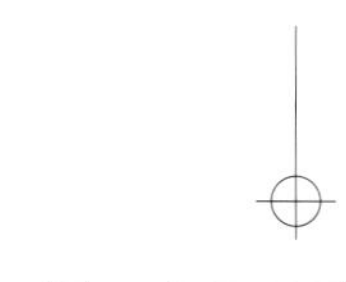

From top, plans of upper, middle (main), and lower levels.

View from southeast (above) and of approach from south (below).

Living room looking towards entry, fireplace, kitchen below, and loft above.

Detail at entry.

Living room view to glass block vitrine window to north.

Detail at kitchen (left) and loft (right).

Living room looking towards kitchen and stair to loft.

View from stair into living room (left) and view of lower, bedroom level (right).

View from loft down into living room.

Details of lower-level bath and stair (above) and bedroom and storage wall (below).

View of house from northeast.

The residence at 8 Bedon's Alley is located in the oldest section of Charleston, a short distance to the west of the harbor, in an area originally dedicated to the commercial shipping industry, and which is today one of the epicenters of preservation activities in the city. The commission involved the renovation of and addition to a shipping warehouse built in 1738, a rectangular brick-walled building running east to west, with two open floors without partitions, a largely solid wall to the north and windows opening to a brick-walled courtyard to the south. The building had been extensively altered in the 1930s to make it a residence, resulting in additions built into the courtyard, a central stair inserted, and the open floors partitioned into smaller rooms.

The new design began with the demolition of the 1930s additions in the courtyard as well as on the interior, replacing the floor beams and the entire roof structure of the warehouse, thereby effectively returning the building to its original spatial order of two, loft-like floors within a brick-walled shell, which open on its south side into a brick-walled courtyard of equal dimension. The new house employs the open loft-like interior spaces of the warehouse as living and dining room on the ground floor, and bedroom and study above, both of which open to the courtyard to the south through the original jack-arched window and door openings. The architects placed a new addition behind the original warehouse volume, to the east and northeast, which houses the kitchen and utility room on the ground floor, adjacent to the living and dining room; a dressing room and bathroom on the upper level, adjacent to the bedroom; and a small study on the third floor, located in the roof rafters.

The front façade of the residence on Bedon's Alley, to the west, retains the original appearance of the warehouse, its brick wall opened by four windows, two on each floor, and a small ventilation aperture in the pediment above. Entry is through a square-grid woven steel gate immediately to the right, between the brick wall of the house and the lower brick wall of the courtyard. The courtyard is experienced as both a variation on the side yard garden of a typical Charleston Single House, and as a forecourt, which one traverses to reach the new entry door, placed towards the back of the courtyard. The courtyard is paved in traditional Charleston bluestone, and a planting area containing a number of existing trees, runs the length of the courtyard on its south side, adjacent to the existing brick wall. Between the paving and the planting area, a narrow, slot-like rivulet of water flows from the street wall to a black-bottomed reflecting pool set beneath an existing flowering peach tree.

At the point where the line of water flows into it, the reflecting pool widens and the bluestone paving narrows, its edge aligning with the transition from the original brick wall of the warehouse to the concrete and stucco wall of the addition, as well as demarcating the location of the new front door of the residence. The addition is structured by a deep cast concrete frame, aligned with the wall of the original building, which is entirely opened on the ground floor, with a recessed steel-framed glass entry door, set adjacent to the original brick wall to the left, and a projecting steel-framed glass "vitrine" breakfast room on the right. The more solid wall of the upper floor, into which a large steel-framed window is opened above the entry door, complements the recession and projection of the fully glazed ground floor. A steel-framed glass canopy cantilevers out from the wall, its gently curved edge covering both the entry door and the glass ceiling of the projecting breakfast room.

The entry vestibule just inside the door opens on the left to the living and dining room on the ground floor of the existing building; on the right to the new kitchen and breakfast room; and directly ahead to the new mahogany staircase, set outside the face of the original building's back wall. On the other side of the mahoga-

A PRACTICE OF MAKING PLACES

Spiral stair to third-floor study; photographed during construction.

ny staircase, a steel and sandblasted glass scrim wall rises the full two-story height of the addition, separating the mahogany stair from the kitchen below and the dressing room above. The material dialogue of the stair and scrim wall is typical throughout the addition, where mahogany shelves, cabinets, doors, and tables are supported by black-painted steel structural elements. As an example, the steel-framed glazing of the breakfast room "vitrine" is complemented by the mahogany bench, running the full width of the breakfast room, and shorter table, both of which are supported by black steel posts and frames. The kitchen opens at both its ends to the dining and living room in the existing building, and is opened through steel-framed glass walls on all sides to the courtyard, patio, and garden, which wraps around the back of the house to terminate in the existing garage on the north side of the house.

On the upper level, a large steel-framed window illuminates the landing of the mahogany staircase, which opens on the left into the bedroom in the existing building, and on the right to the dressing and baths. The two baths, each with a large steel-framed window, mahogany walls and cabinets, are placed at the east end of the addition. Between the baths and the steel-framed frosted glass scrim wall is the elongated dressing room, with frosted glass and steel walls, mahogany-walled closets, and a mahogany shelf. The dressing room provides access to both baths and is terminated at its southern end by a steel spiral stair leading up to the new study above. The sculptural form of the spiral stair can be seen from the bedroom through an opening in the existing wall, as well as while ascending or descending the mahogany stairs.

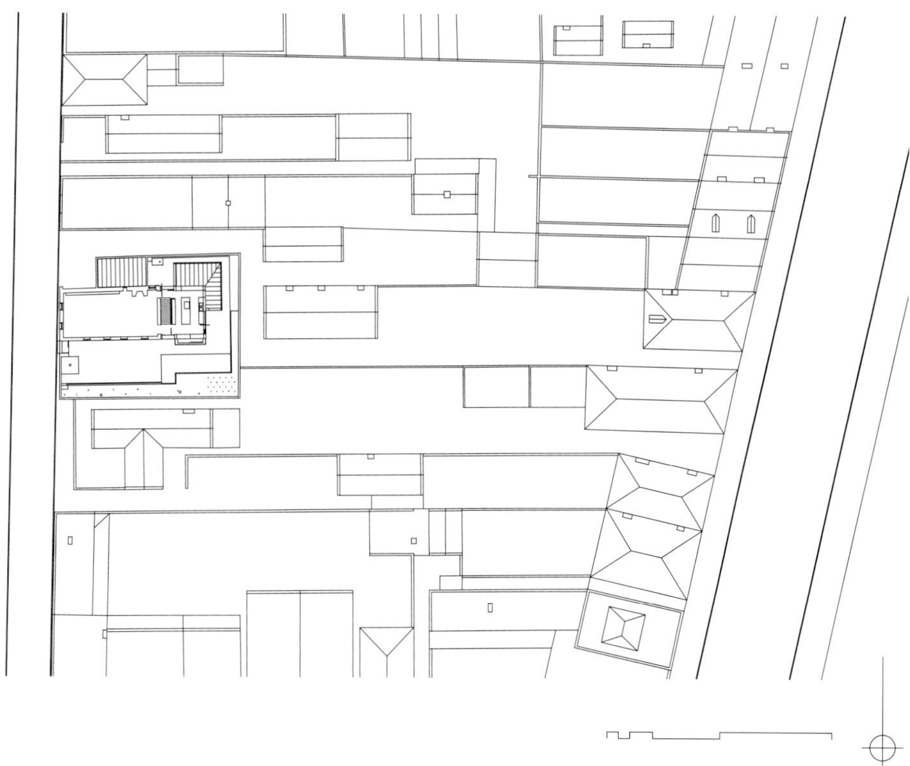

Site plan.

A PRACTICE OF MAKING PLACES

In the manner in which the addition and renovation is detailed, as well as the way the inhabitants are offered views that layer new and old, and are invited to move through the new and old spaces, the architects have intertwined the pre-existing and the contemporary in the daily lives of those who live here. This is accomplished by engaging the concept of complementary contrast on at least two levels in this design: the first being the complementary contrast between the massive brick-walled old building, with its small apertures opened in thick walls, and the thin, light, steel-framed elements of the new addition, with its interior and exterior walls largely made of glass; and the second being the complementary contrast within the new addition between the "cool" steel and glass exterior walls, interior scrim wall and structural elements, and the "warm" mahogany wood staircase and built-in cabinetry and furniture. In this design, the architects achieve a transformation of place that merits comparison to the equally convincing renovations and additions carried out in Venice by Carlo Scarpa, where, in a similar way, the contemporary and the existing built fabrics are laminated, intertwined and joined to make a new place that is at one and the same time ancient and modern.

In 1999, coinciding with the publication of *Clark and Menefee*, a monograph authored by Richard Jensen (Princeton Architectural Press, 2000), WG Clark and Charles Menefee decided to terminate their partnership. They opened separate practices based in Charlottesville, Virginia, where they both are professors at the University of Virginia School of Architecture.

Existing street façade (left) and new entry court and pool (right).

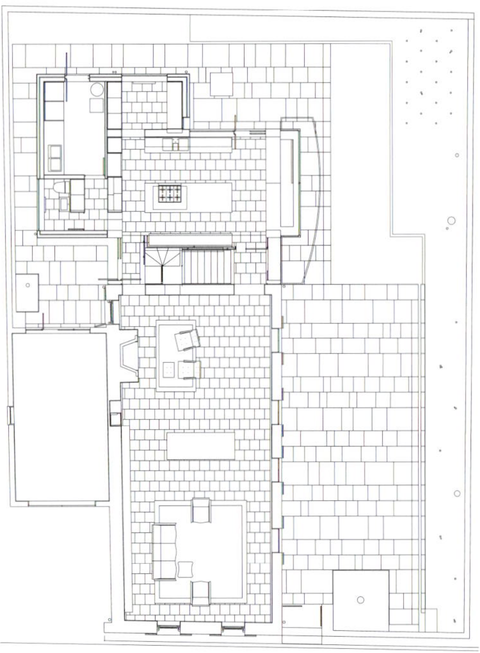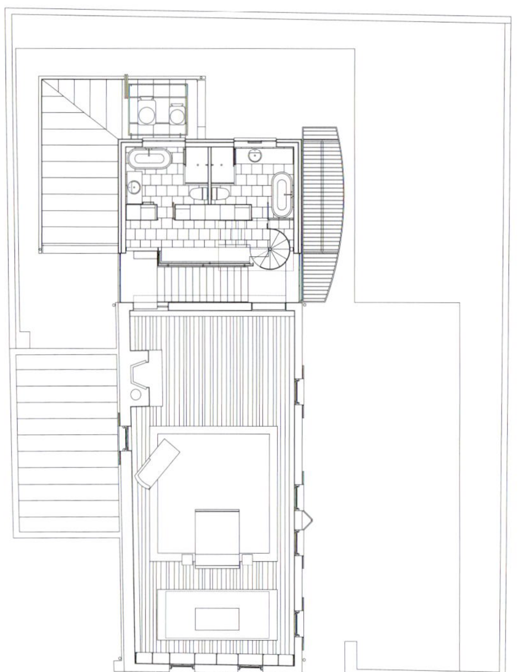

Plans of ground floor (left) and upper level (right).

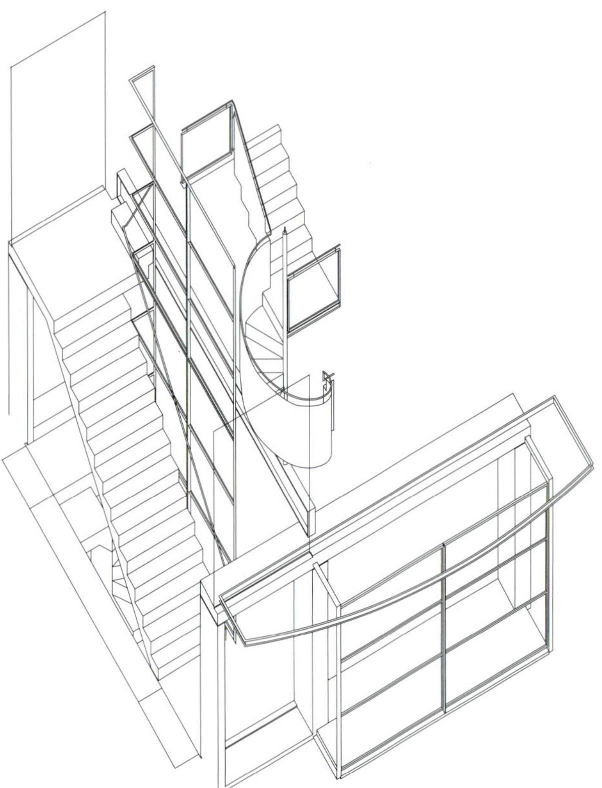

Axonometric (left) and dressing area and spiral stair (right).

Glass vitrine window at breakfast room projecting out into court.

Entry and breakfast room vitrine window at night.

View to living room from kitchen (left) and view to court through glass vitrine (right).

Glass vitrine, with breakfast room.

Designed for a family that for several generations has commissioned works from leading American architects, including Frank Lloyd Wright, Bruce Goff and Steven Holl, the house was to be located on a spectacularly scenic site in the Rocky Mountains outside Telluride, Colorado. The site was a meadow with expansive views to the south to the dramatic vertical spire of Lizard Head Peak, and north to an extensive aspen grove with mountain peaks behind. The two different views, to the south towards the distinctive profile of the peak and into the sun, and to the north to the aspen wood and mountains illuminated by the sunlight, became the primary inspirations and constraints of Clark's design.

The house takes the form of two volumes of unequal floor area and equal sectional dimension that are placed at either end of an elongated composition running from east to west. A large rectangular volume, framed by parallel walls on the north and south, occupies the eastern half of the composition and contains the main rooms of the house, with one level partly embedded in the earth and three levels above. A smaller cubic volume, also framed by parallel walls on the north and south, occupies the western end of the composition and contains the garage below and the rooms of the guesthouse above. An exterior entry terrace is opened between the two equal-width volumes of the main house and the guesthouse. The approach to the house was from the north, through the aspen grove, and the terrace acts as a threshold to the landscape, with the walls of the main house and guesthouse framing the spectacular view of the mountain peak to the south. The slightly elevated terrace is paved with stone except at the top of the entry stairs at the northwest corner, where it is paved with glass over the sunken water reservoir, which is used to battle wildfires.

Parallel exterior walls to the north and south frame the three-story volumes of the main house and guesthouse. The thick, massive walls are made of an outer and inner layer of cast concrete with insulation in between. In counterpoint to the thick massive walls to the north and south, at the eastern and western ends of the main house and guesthouse, steel-framed walls infilled with glass and metal panels open to the landscape and entry terrace, and are expanded to accommodate support spaces and built-in furnishings such as the low-ceilinged entry foyer, powder room, shelves, and cabinets.

The main house comprises a single triple-height great room framed by the thick, massive, parallel outer walls and scaled to the seemingly infinite heights and distances of the surrounding mountain landscape. In contrast, an intimately-scaled vertical tower stands within the great room, in-between but not touching the massive horizontal walls, dividing the entry, living, and dining rooms to the west from the bedroom to the east, and rising from the basement and projecting through the roof. The stairs occupy the space between the tower and outer walls, so that in use one is simultaneously in close proximity to the massive concrete walls and the delicate frame and infill panels of the tower. The steel-framed and glass and metal panel-clad tower contains the kitchen and bath on the main floor, two baths and closets on the bedroom level above, a sauna on the third floor, and a spiral stair ascends up to a glazed cupola on the roof. The lantern-like cupola provides access to the roof terrace as well as ventilation for the great room in the form of a thermal chimney, allowing hot air to naturally rise and be exhausted, while simultaneously drawing in cool air from windows below to replace it.

The thick, massive parallel outer walls on the north and south of the main house are both scaled to the surrounding mountain landscape, yet, in response to their opposite orientations with respect to the sun, they are articulated and detailed in complementary ways. Due to the high altitude and intense solar radiation, the thick wall

Telluride House,
Telluride, Colorado,
2000–2001
(unrealized)

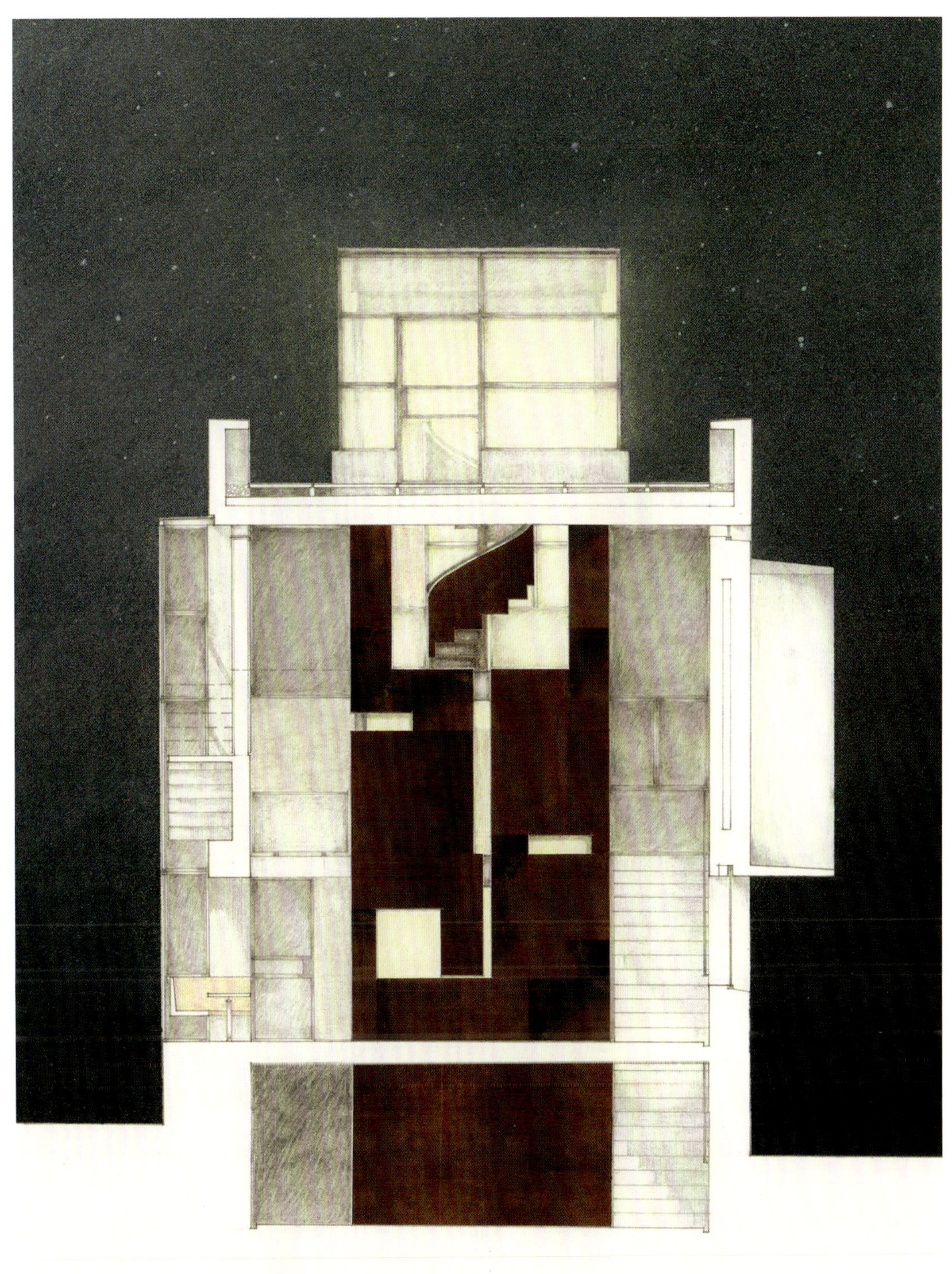

Section, showing masonry outer shell and steel inner tower.

facing south, towards Lizard Head mountain peak, is carved open with narrow vertical and horizontal slots, the larger of which are shielded with projecting cast concrete "sun shelves" that shade the windows and the interior. When struck by the strong southern sunlight, these projecting planes combine with the dark window apertures to form what might best be called a calligraphy of shadows on the south façade.

In contrast, the thick wall facing north, away from the sun and towards the brilliantly illuminated aspen grove and distant mountain slopes, is carved open with three much larger rectangular apertures at the bedroom, the tower, and the living room. The large vertical window adjacent to the tower projects out as a bay window, containing the breakfast room on the main floor and the stair up to the sauna above. In the living room, the fireplace box also projects out through the north wall, with the chimney rising outside the wide window above.

The dimension of the cantilever of the bay windows on the north wall equals that of the cantilever of the "sun shelves" on the south wall. The complementary contrast between the two monumental, three-story tall, thick walls on north and south engage the occupants in a syncopation of light and view, with the smaller framed views to the south being counterpointed by the large expanses of glass on the north, where the cool blue light from the sky illuminates the family's extensive contemporary art collection on the south wall. This expansive landscape-scaled dialogue between the north and south walls is complemented by the delicately layered and interwoven patterns of the intimate, human-scaled, interior surfaces of the tower and the east and west end walls, reflecting and representing the quotidian rituals of domestic life.

South view to Lizard Head (left) and view to aspen grove to north (right).

Site plan, north down.

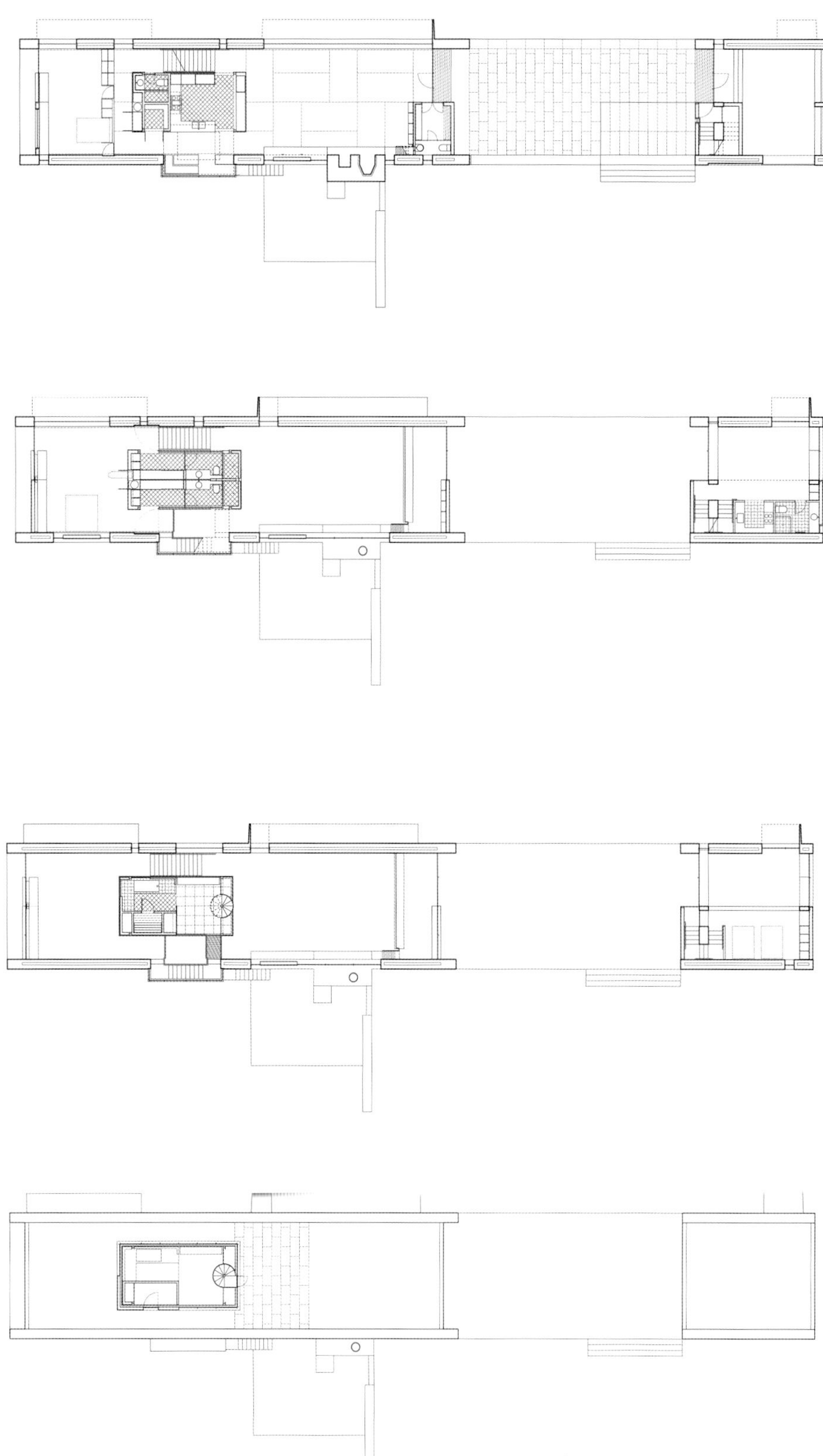

From top, plans of main, entry level; second level; third level; and roof and tower level.

     A PRACTICE OF MAKING PLACES

View looking down into model with roof removed.

Model of main house with north wall and roof removed.

Model seen from northwest, with north wall and roof removed.

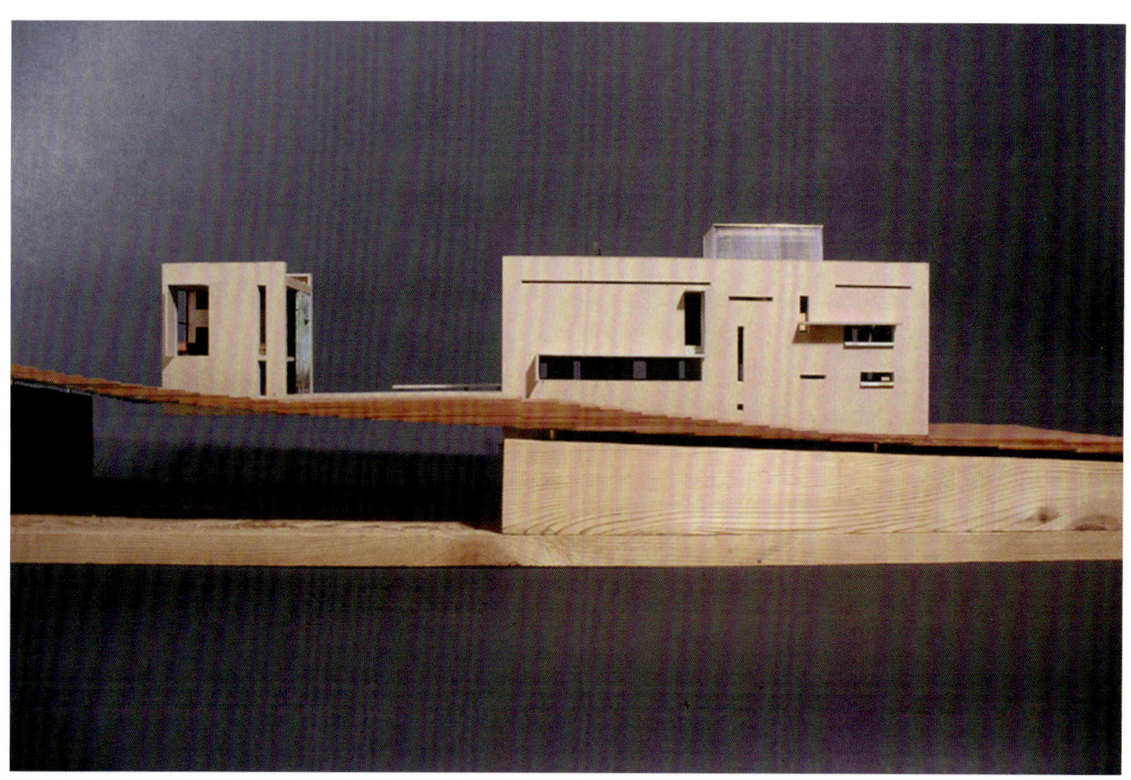

Model seen from south (above) and north (below).

The house is on a site overlooking the Chickahominy River, near Williamsburg, Virginia. The river is to the northeast, and the approach to the house is from the southwest. The house is composed of two rectangular, two-story volumes of equal length, width, and height, one containing the double-height entry foyer, living room, dining room, and kitchen with loft study above, and the other containing the bedrooms, utility room, and office on two levels. The two volumes are set adjacent to but offset from each other, with the double-height volume projecting to the northwest giving the living room light, views from three directions, and an expansive view of the river, and the two-level volume projecting to the southeast. The two volumes are separated by a double-height slot of space, which contains the staircase.

In its plan composition, the house is similar to the Frederick Robie House of Frank Lloyd Wright, where the living and dining rooms are opened to each other within the primary volume, overlooking the Midway Park, while the partitioned private and service spaces are set in a separate, secondary volume, placed behind the primary volume, and the two volumes are offset from each other to allow the living room to have light and views in three directions.

The house may be understood as a development of the Croffead House, in its composition as a "diptych," with two distinct but equal volumes, and in its construction type, being built of concrete masonry walls exposed on the exterior and plastered on the interior, wood floor and roof framing, steel-framed windows and doors, and interior cabinetry and fittings of plywood, black steel, and frosted glass. In addition, the Beckerdite/Scholly house is designed around an extensive collection of African artifacts, which is displayed throughout the house in niches and ledges made of plywood, steel, and cast concrete.

The house is approached on the gravel walkway leading from the parking area to the southwest to the entry porch, which is raised two steps above the ground. The privacy of the rooms within the house is protected by the long concrete masonry wall of the nearer, bedroom volume, which is only opened by three small vertical and horizontal apertures cut into the otherwise solid wall. In contrast, the projecting end of the farther, living room volume is almost entirely open, with the steel-framed glass entry door set beneath a glass block wall giving views through the house to the landscape beyond. The freestanding double-height cast concrete frame that stands in front of the recessed volume forms the spatial threshold of the entry porch. A double-height window is opened in the end wall of the nearer, bedroom volume on the near right, with glass block below to shield the office within, and clear glazing above at the master bedroom. Beyond the concrete frame of the entry porch, the masonry fireplace and freestanding chimney project out of the end wall of the living room.

The entry door gives onto the foyer, which is set at the end of the slot of space between the two volumes at the bottom of the stairs, and is given views into the living room through a full-height opening in the inner wall. Ascending four steps, one turns, passing beneath a cast concrete lintel, and enters the double-height living and dining room. Across from the entry, a wide bay window, with clear glazing below and glass block above, projects towards the river. A column is set at the third-point of the bay window, subtly demarcating the larger living room from the smaller dining room. On the end wall next to the entry foyer, the concrete masonry fireplace anchors the living room, and a large double-height window gives views along the hillside. Across the room from the fireplace wall, a folded, freestanding plywood wall shields the kitchen below and the loft study above from view, while allowing acoustic connection. The wall also houses display niches and projecting stands of black steel for artifacts.

Beckerdite/
Scholley House,
James City County,
Virginia,
2001–2005

    A PRACTICE OF MAKING PLACES

View down into living room from loft study.

Living room looking to kitchen, stair, and loft study.

In a similar way, the long, thick, white-plastered wall across from the large bay window, behind which is the staircase, entry foyer, office, and bedrooms in the volume beyond, has recessed plywood cabinets and cantilevered cast concrete ledges and recessed niches for the artifacts.

The four walls of the living and dining room are each different in character, and the two pairs of facing walls are of contrasting openness and material: a densely layered enfolding interior wall carrying artifacts and enclosing spaces within, across from an expansive, exfoliating glazed exterior wall opening to views and light. These four walls, along with the displays and other functions they house, and their corresponding exterior elevations, were the subject of intensive study by Clark and his associates, as is indicated by the large number of study models made of the various walls of the house.

The contrasts of the two pairs of living and dining room walls are complemented by the way in which the four corners of the room, where the walls of different character meet, are integrated in ways that enrich the experience, hinting at shadowed spaces within or inviting the inhabitation of window-seats cantilevered out into the landscape. The diversity of the four walls is counterpointed by the unity of the continuous horizontal planes of the wood floor underfoot and the plywood ceiling overhead. The integrative effect of the ceiling and floor is particularly evident at the thick plywood wall between the dining room and the kitchen below and loft study above. A double-height window of glass block, which runs from the kitchen to the loft study, floods the shadowed space within and behind the thick plywood wall with light. By allowing for the display of the African artifacts in both formal, designated places and in informal, almost casual arrangements in the threshold spaces of the house, the collection is skillfully integrated into the daily life of the inhabitants.

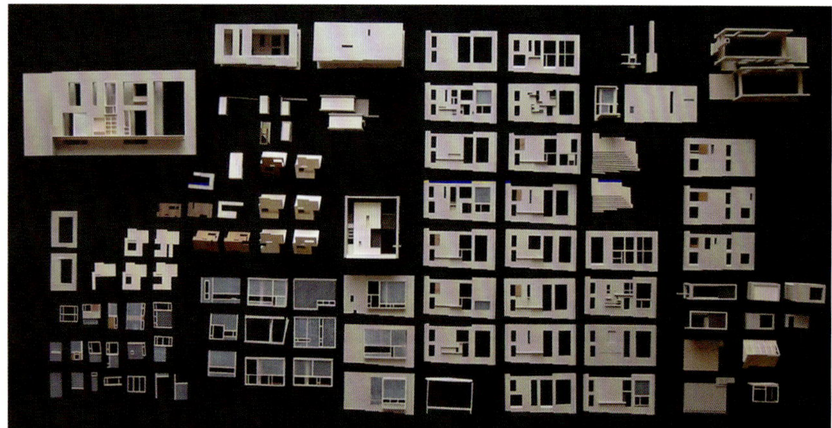

Study models of exterior and interior walls.

Site model.

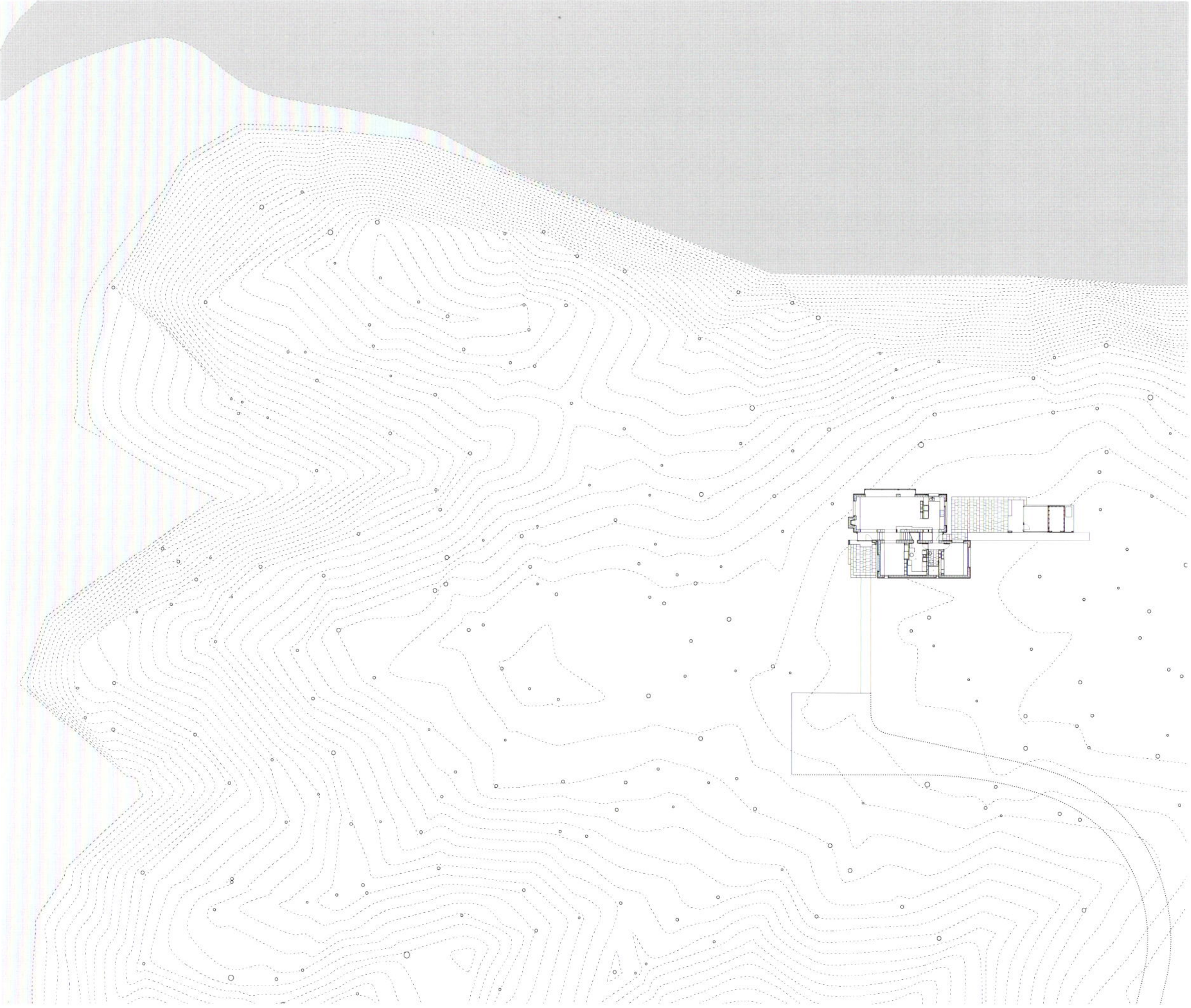

Site plan (north to upper left).

Folded interior wall housing artifacts.

A PRACTICE OF MAKING PLACES

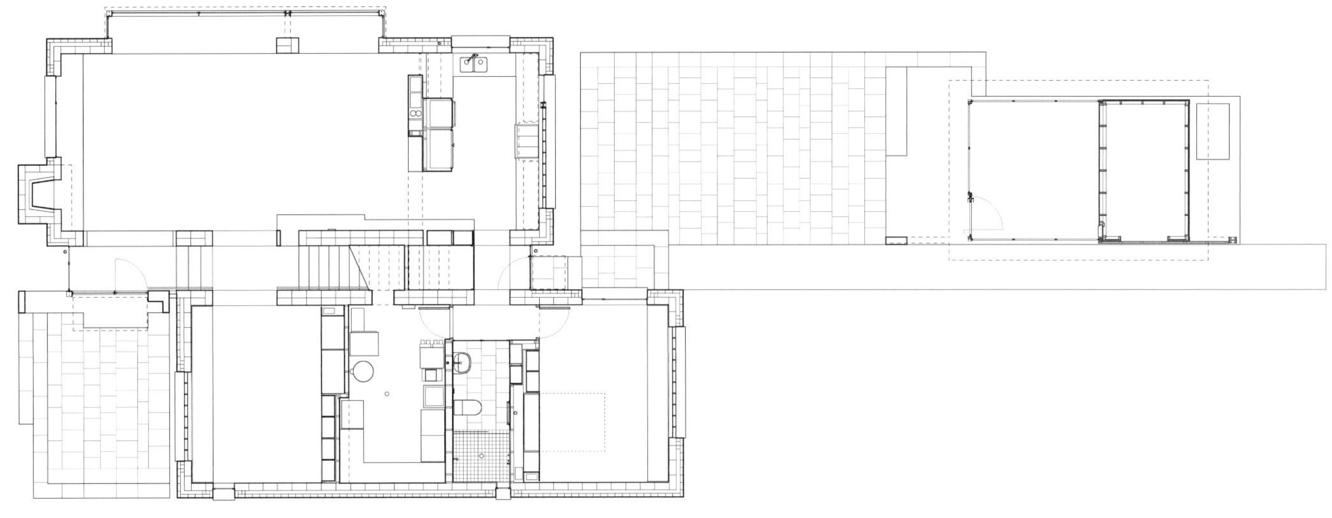

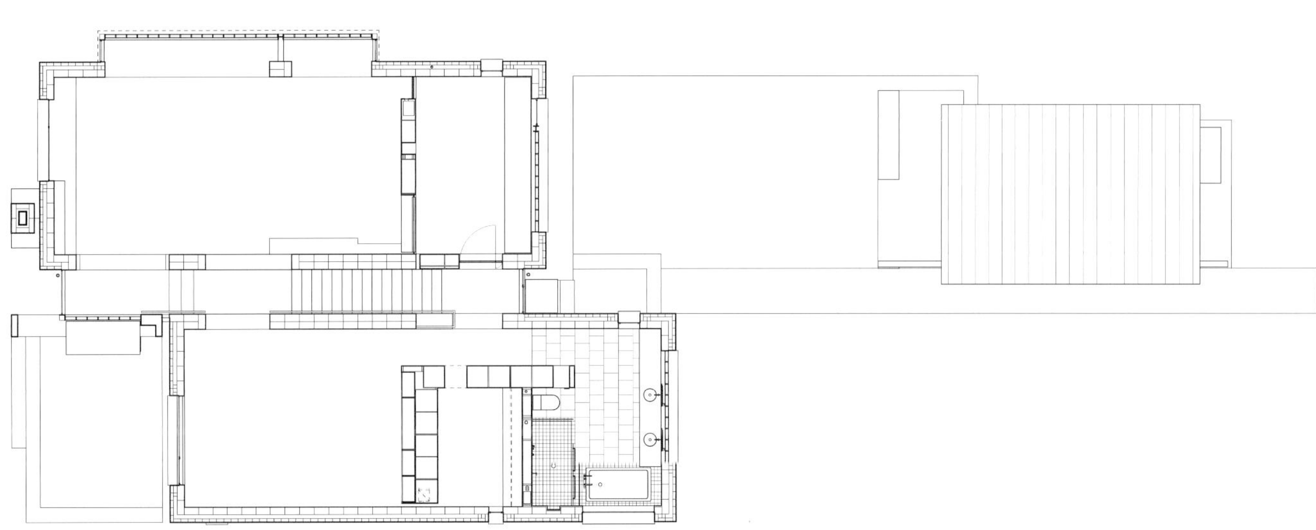

From top, main, ground-floor plan, and upper-floor plan.

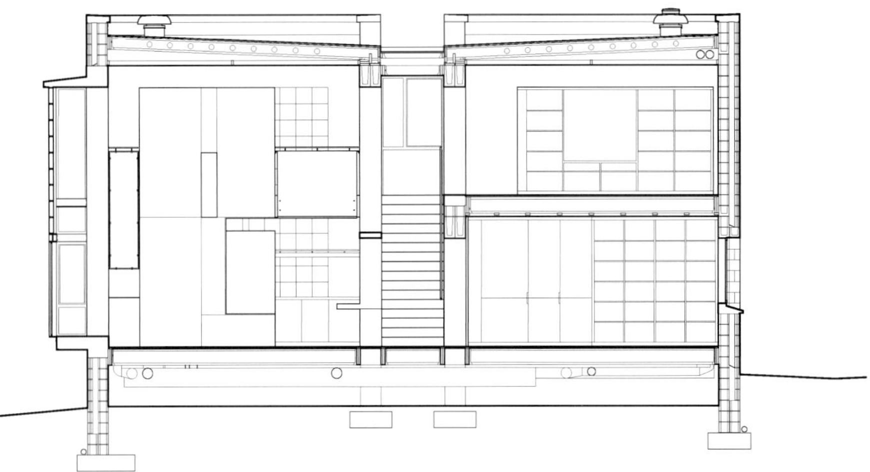

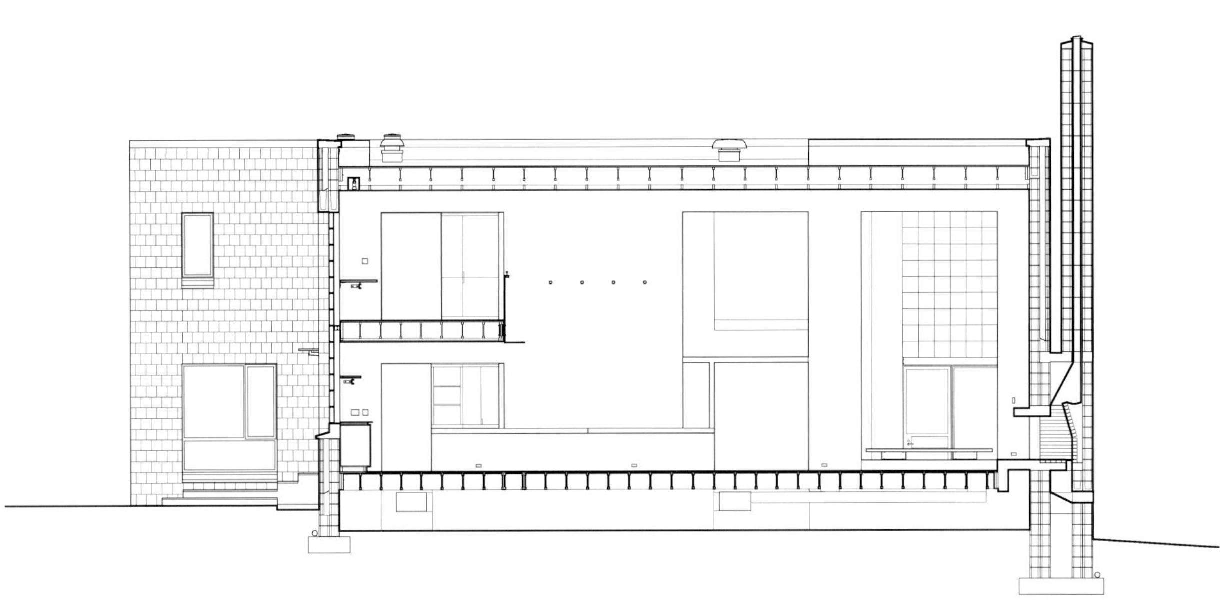

Section through two volumes (above), and section through living room volume (below).

   A PRACTICE OF MAKING PLACES

View of southwest façade (above) and detail of entry porch (below).

esigned in response to an invited competition with a very limited timeframe, the office building was to be built on a narrow, triangular "flat iron" site to the northwest of the Capital Building, on the southern side of the intersection of New Jersey Avenue MW and 1st Street NW. The building was required to be set back from the street-front so as to align with the existing buildings on the west side of New Jersey Avenue NW, framing the view down the avenue to the Capital. In Clark's design, the large program areas are accommodated within narrow, triangular plans on 12 floors, and the elevators, stairs, and services are organized into a triangular core at the center of the building, with bands of offices placed along the long east and west façades.

In describing the intentions of his design, Clark acknowledged that the necessarily narrow building surrounded by wide setbacks at the streets would inevitably result in what he called "a figural urban fragment seen prominently related to the Capital Building. Because of this relationship it is important that the New Jersey Avenue façade have monumentality of scale. This façade is designed as a glass block screen to provide that urban scale while being light and transparent in contrast to the Capitol's monolithic stone heaviness."[1]

The individual offices on the building's 1st Street façade, which faced due west, are articulated by vertical, solid, angled, cast concrete louver walls, intended to reduce the solar heat gain and glare. The vertical louver walls are angled outwards at each office to provide a north-facing window, each harboring a work carrel formed of built-in wood cabinetry. Together the vertical concrete louver-walls form a large, square, folded, and textured surface, strongly shadowed in the afternoon, which characterizes the building's west wall.

In contradistinction, the offices on the building's New Jersey Avenue side, facing east and framing the view of the Capital, are grouped together behind a continuous, flush, translucent glass-block screen-wall, which masks their individual scale, and which extends to cover the large conference rooms, executive offices, and other special functions placed in the narrow "prow" of the building to the north. The glass block screen on the east façade was intended to fill the spaces inside with diffused light as well as masking the scale of the individual floors in a similar way as the louver-walls on the west façade.

At the roof, a stone-paved terrace with a water channel and pergola extends the length of the building along the east, New Jersey Avenue side. The glass-block screen-wall and the volume behind it is notched on the southwest corner at the ninth floor to defer to the Capital, which can be seen from the small stone-paved terrace placed at the bottom of the notch, and the screen-wall is also carved open at its base to articulate the entrance at the street. Precast concrete tree planters on the paved plaza at the building's entrance are provided with light slots to bring natural light into the parking level below.

National Association of Realtors Headquarters Competition, Washington, DC, 2002 (unrealized)

WG Clark in association
with Wendy Redfield

THE SITE POSITION AND NARROWNESS WILL RESULT IN A BUILDING THAT IS A DISTINCTLY FIGURAL URBAN FRAGMENT SEEN PROMINENTLY RELATED TO THE CAPITOL BUILDING. BECAUSE OF THIS RELATIONSHIP IT IS IMPORTANT THAT THE NEW JERSEY AVENUE FACADE HAVE MONUMENTALITY OF SCALE. THIS FACADE IS DESIGNED AS A GLASS BLOCK SCREEN TO PROVIDE THAT URBAN SCALE WHILE BEING LIGHT AND TRANSPARENT IN CONTRAST TO THE CAPITOL'S MONOLITHIC STONE HEAVINESS. THE FIRST STREET FACADE WHICH FACES DUE WEST IS CONCRETE WITH VERTICAL LOUVERS TO REDUCE THE SUN LOAD AND GLARE.

THE UPPER FLOORS OF THE NAR ARE MARKED BY AN INCISION IN THE SOUTH EASTERN CORNER WHICH HOLDS A SMALL TERRACE FRAMING A VIEW TO THE CAPITOL. A SECOND STONE PAVED TERRACE WITH WATER CHANNEL AND PERGOLA IS ON THE ROOF OF THE BUILDING.

THE INTERIOR ON THE EASTERN SIDE OF THE BUILDING WOULD BE FILLED WITH DIFFUSED LIGHT THROUGH THE CLEAR GLASS BLOCK WALL. ON THE WESTERN SIDE THE LIGHT LOUVERS ARE FASHIONED INTO WORK CARRELS WITH CUSTOM WOOD CABINETRY

PRECAST CONCRETE TREE PLANTERS AT THE BUILDING'S ENTRANCE ARE DESIGNED WITH LIGHT SLITS TO BRING NATURAL LIGHT TO THE PARKING LEVEL BELOW

GROUND FLOOR PLAN

NATIONAL ASSOCIATION OF REALTORS COMPETITION

500 NEW JERSEY AVENUE NW · WASHINGTON DC   CLARK + REDFIELD ARCHITECTS ©

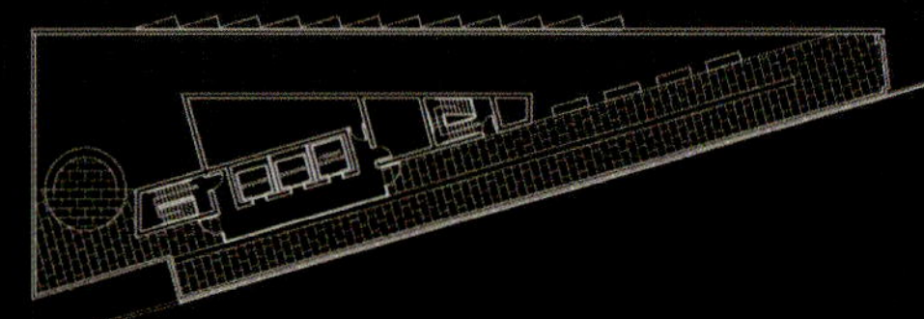

ROOF PLAN

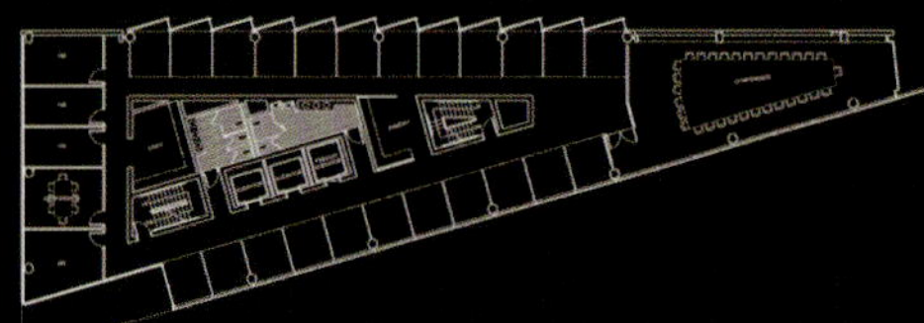

12TH FLOOR PLAN

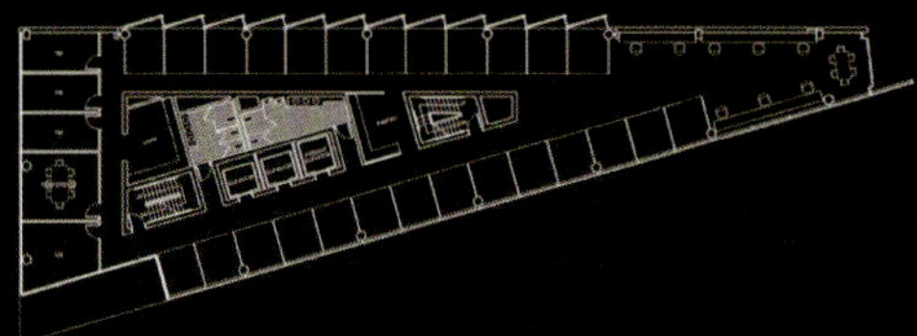

11TH FLOOR PLAN

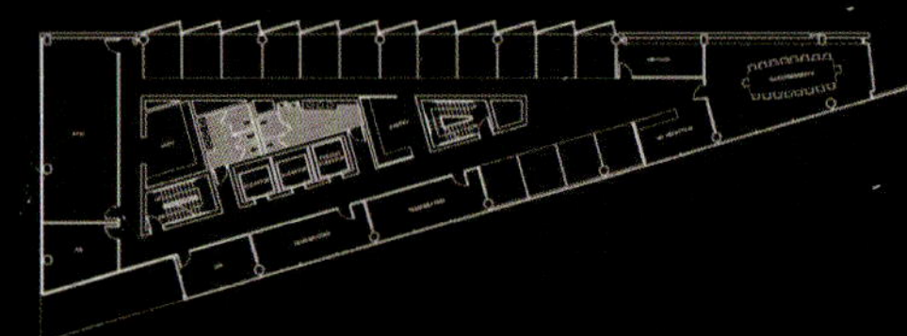

10TH FLOOR PLAN

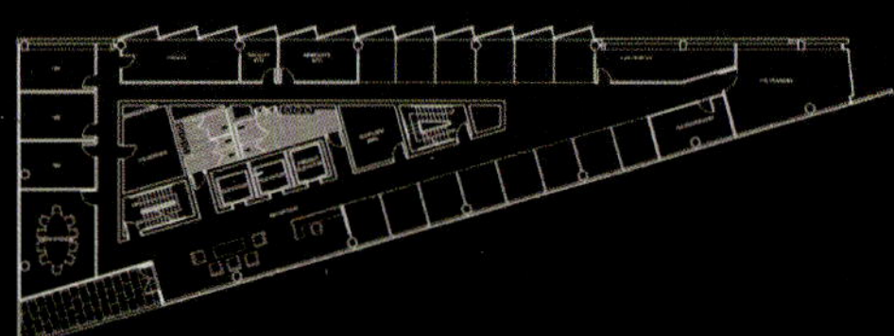

9TH FLOOR PLAN

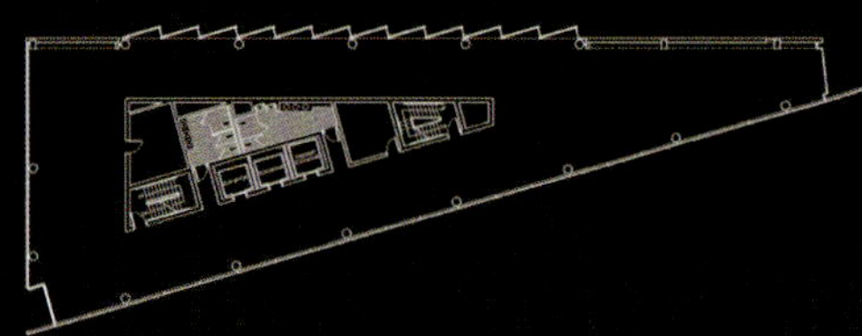

TYPICAL FLOOR PLAN

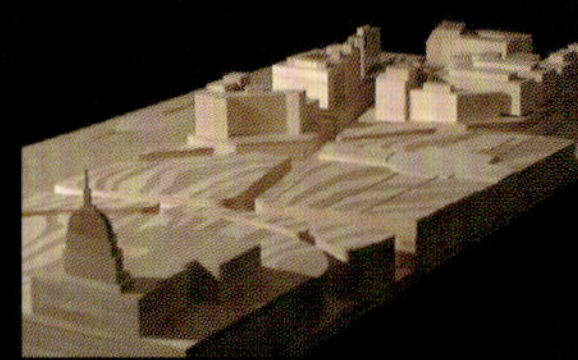

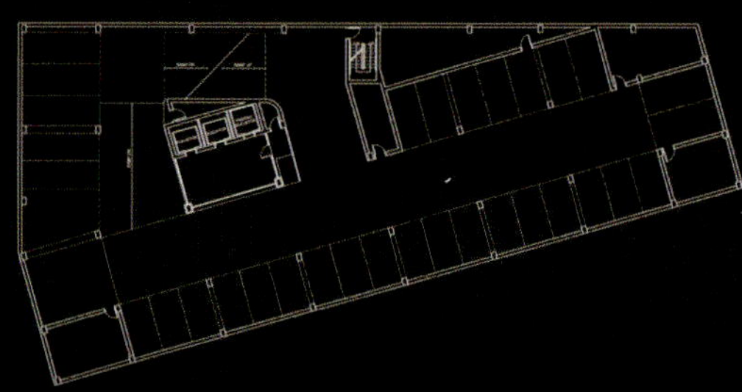

GARAGE LEVEL PLAN

NATIONAL ASSOCIATION OF REALTORS COMPETITION

500 NEW JERSEY AVENUE NW · WASHINGTON DC   CLARK + REDFIELD ARCHITECTS ©

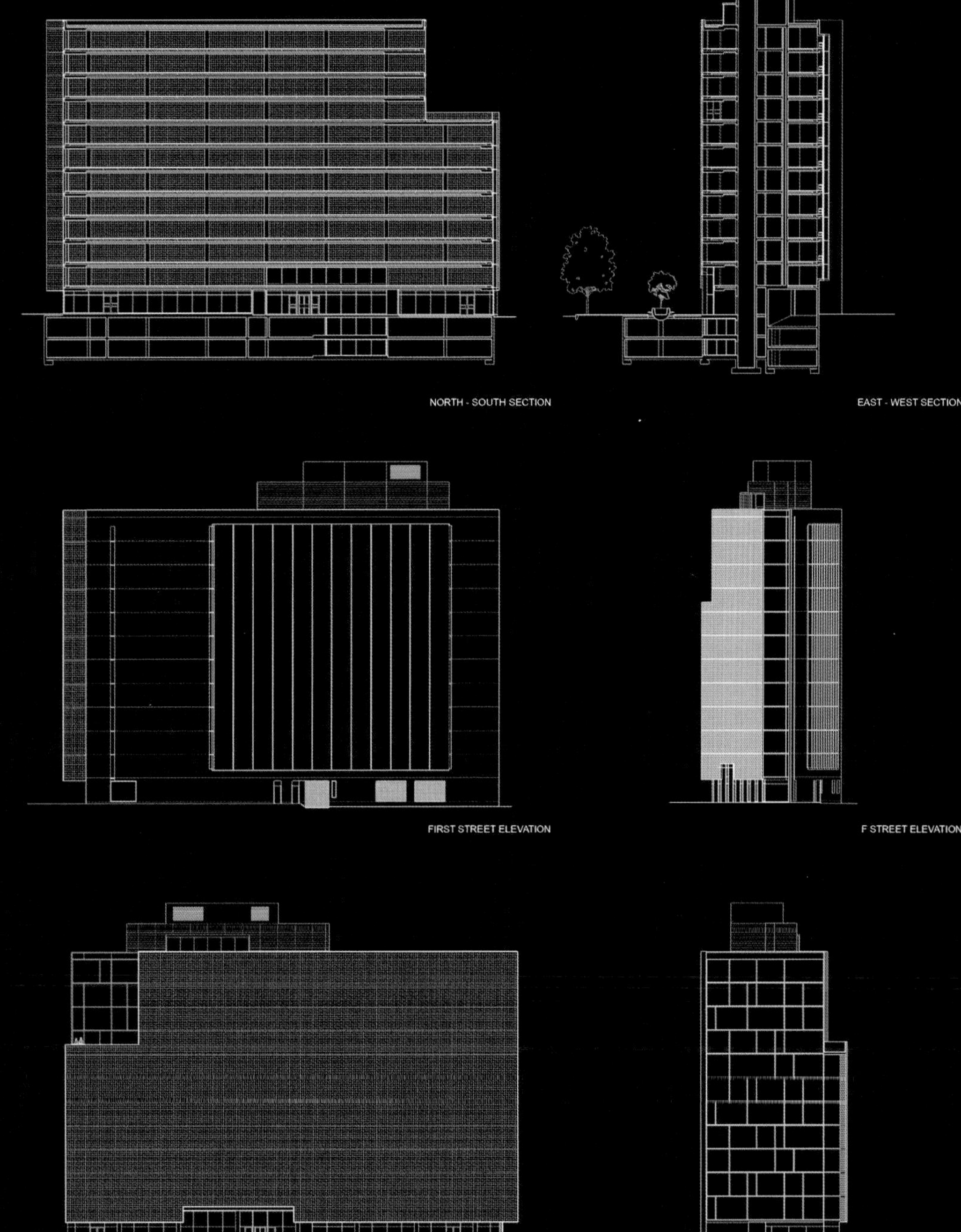

NORTH - SOUTH SECTION
EAST - WEST SECTION
FIRST STREET ELEVATION
F STREET ELEVATION
NEW JERSEY AVE. ELEVATION
E STREET ELEVATION
NATIONAL ASSOCIATION OF REALTORS COMPETITION
500 NEW JERSEY AVENUE NW · WASHINGTON DC
CLARK + REDFIELD ARCHITECTS ©

n responding to the assumptions underlying the competition brief, which was for the design of a prototypical suburban house to be constructed by Habitat for Humanity, Clark began with a declaration of the values underlying the design, recalling, "we decided that this was the right way to begin any design, with stated principles."[1] The competition was based on the premise that what was needed was a new prototype for the detached single-family house, to be built as a freestanding object surrounded by a grass lawn and fronting onto suburban streets. Rather than contribute to further suburban sprawl, Clark rejected the competition premise and proposed to design a settlement or community, not a single-family house. If the intention of Habitat for Humanity was to provide the most people housing for the least cost, Clark argued that building a community would result in a dramatically improved economy of land use, infrastructure, and unit cost. The design Clark proposed may be understood as a comprehensive critique of the failings of typical suburban development in the US.

Proposing a new prototype for suburban housing, the project clusters 12 single-family houses into to single structure, attaining a level of density, sustainability, engagement of the landscape, sense of community, and flexibility of adaption to changing life situations not possible with traditional suburban planning. The cubic, two-story houses are gathered to form an internal pedestrian street, connecting an entry court in front to the forest behind, and off of which all the houses are entered, allowing their opposite sides to open to the surrounding garden spaces. In emphasizing the importance of the central pedestrian street as a way to create community, rather than simply adding to the existing suburbs, which are scaled not to pedestrians but to the automobile, Clark is close to Louis Kahn, who stated; "The street is a room of human agreement," and that, in its essence, the street is "a community room."[2]

The 12 individual houses are shaded by a single large cable-supported roof canopy, which is covered with photovoltaic cells for electricity generation. The canopy is elevated above the tops of the individual houses to allow the heat from the sun to be evacuated, and it is sloped inwards to the central street to allow for the collection of rainwater in a large underground cistern. The density of the clustered form of the housing allows the majority of the site to be used not as lawns, but as vegetable gardens for food production. While Frank Lloyd Wright proposed similar productive vegetable gardens for the dwelling sites in his Broadacre City design, he was also committed to the deployment of single-family houses, each sited on its own one-acre lot. By comparison, Clark's design is both more radical and more comprehensive in its exemplification of the benefits of density over dispersal and sprawl.

The 24-foot-square floor plans of the two-story individual houses are structured by central columns that divide the space into four 12-foot squares, two of which are joined to form the living-dining room, and, along with the façades that open to the internal street and the external gardens, the narrow spaces between each house allows all the rooms to have cross-ventilation. Each house can be configured to accommodate single people, couples, and extended families, as well as being reconfigured as needed to accommodate changing family sizes and living arrangements among multiple generations. The modular "kit of parts" out of which each house is built not only allows flexibility in arranging the floor plans on two levels, but also allows client participation in determining the configuration of the four façades, in terms of openness to nature, publicity and privacy to the community, and solar orientation and prevailing breezes. As a result of the capacity to select from among a limited repertoire of building elements, client participation in determining their living arrangements is paralleled by a consistency of formal language and spatial generosity.

South Eastern Center for
Contemporary Art
Habitat for Humanity
Competition, First Prize,
2003 (unrealized)

Model.

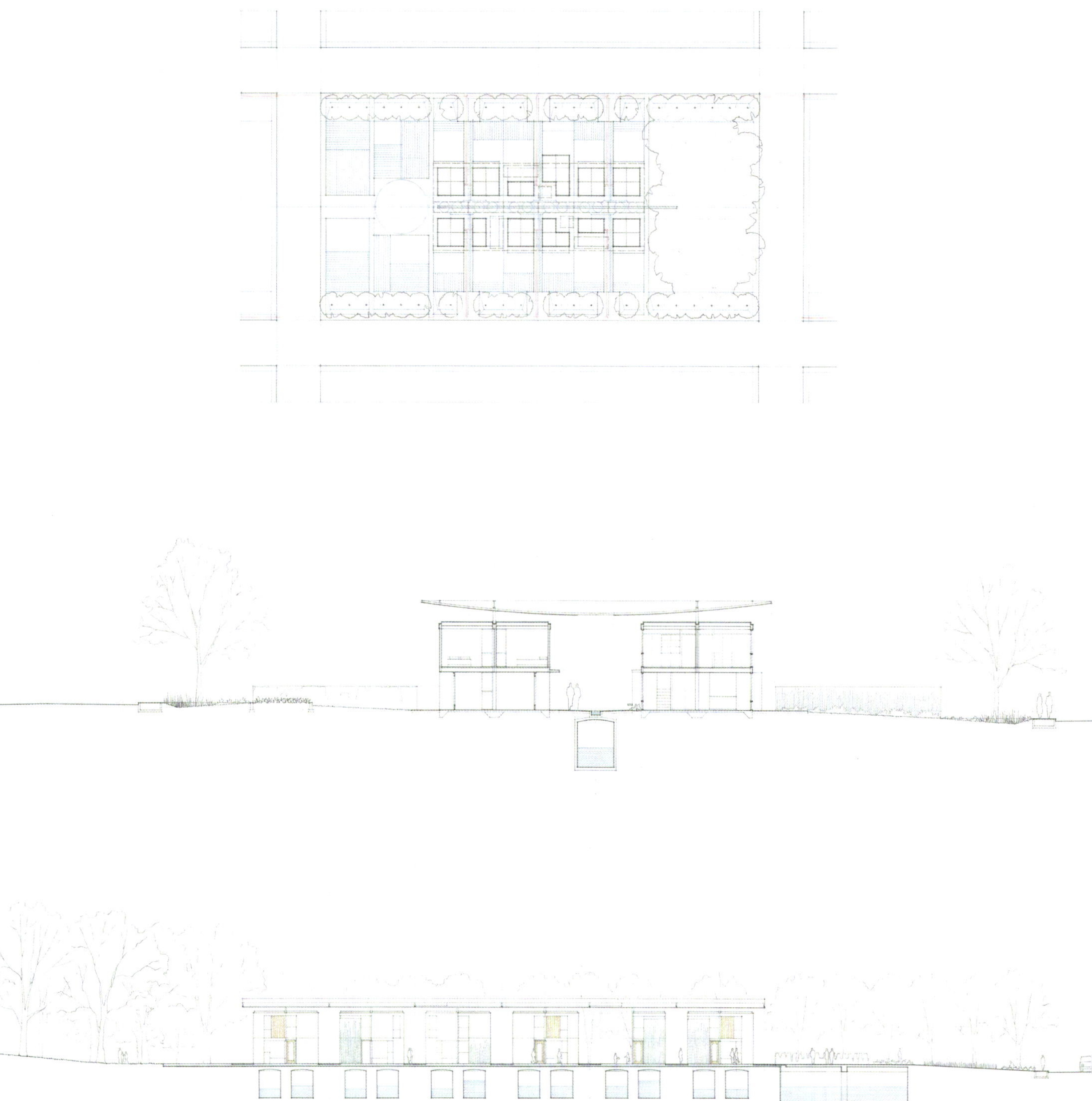

From top, site plan; section through buildings and central pedestrian street; section-elevation along central pedestrian street.

Perspective along central pedestrian street (left) and plans and elevation of unit variations (right).

Model, with underground water cistern.

I n response to the proposed site, a very remote location in the Sierra Nevada Mountains, the primary intentions of the prototypical design had to do with minimizing site work and utilities; maximal utilization of materials available on site; factory prefabrication and transportation by helicopter to the site of all non-site-sourced building materials; and final assembly construction by small crews with simple tools. Designed to provide shelter for hikers in a very remote area of the mountain park, the building comprises a linear series of minimal huts positioned along the mountainside. The line of huts connects to the upper level of a two-story, lodge-like structure that provides communal cooking, dining, and bathing facilities and spaces. The multiple private cells and single common room impart to the building the character of a monastery, the building type favored by Louis Kahn for its clear expression of individual spaces gathered to form a collective space. In this case, rather than forming a central courtyard, as is typical of monastic buildings, the line of private huts open to the upslope landscape while the common room opens to the downslope landscape.

The minimal huts are carefully structured and positioned on the hillside, aligned along the access walkway on the south-facing, upslope side, and set on parallel foundation walls, which carry utilities in the channel space formed between them. The huts employ an 8 x 8 x 8-foot prefabricated engineered wood frame to form the central cubic core element, which is infilled as needed with structural insulated panels. The wood structural frame forms the central, wood-floored cubic volume containing the bath, centered over the double foundation walls, and entered from the walkway on the upslope side. In its most minimal configuration, the cubic central volume is flanked on the downslope side by saddlebag-like volumes containing two bunk beds, one above the other, which are cantilevered from the central cubic volume. The huts can be configured to accommodate a varying number of people, from a minimum of two to a maximum of eight, by the addition of bunk bed volumes and the combination of multiple cubic central volumes. The metal roof of each hut is lifted above the walls to allow ventilation; tilted to shed snow; extended on the downslope side to cover a clerestory ventilation window; and extended on the upslope side to cover the wooden access walkway. The hut roofs collect rainwater and snowmelt that is stored in cisterns, and the roofs can also accommodate solar panels as needed. The façades of the huts can be varied to respond to local site conditions, and the entire front façades of the larger huts pivot upwards to form a canopy.

The line of huts is located on the upper, plinth level formed by the parallel foundation walls and utility channel, and they connect to the upper level of the two-story lodge-like structure, which provides staff spaces on the upper level and shared cooking, eating and bathing spaces on the larger, lower level. In counterpoint to the huts, which are elevated above the ground, the larger common room is partly embedded in the ground, with the bathing spaces set against the rear retaining wall and beneath the access walkway, with the kitchen placed between the bathing area and the dining room, which is framed on either side by retaining walls made from site-excavated stone. The communal dining room opens to the downslope landscape and is covered by a gently folding roof, supported on deep trusses, which is lifted above the walls to encourage airflow. The entire complex employs passive solar energy and prevailing breezes for heating and cooling, has a geothermal system for supplemental heat, and utilizes composting toilets throughout.

Palisade Glacier Mountain Hut, Competition, 2003 (unrealized)

WG Clark in association with Azadeh Rashidi, assisted by Joshua Stastny

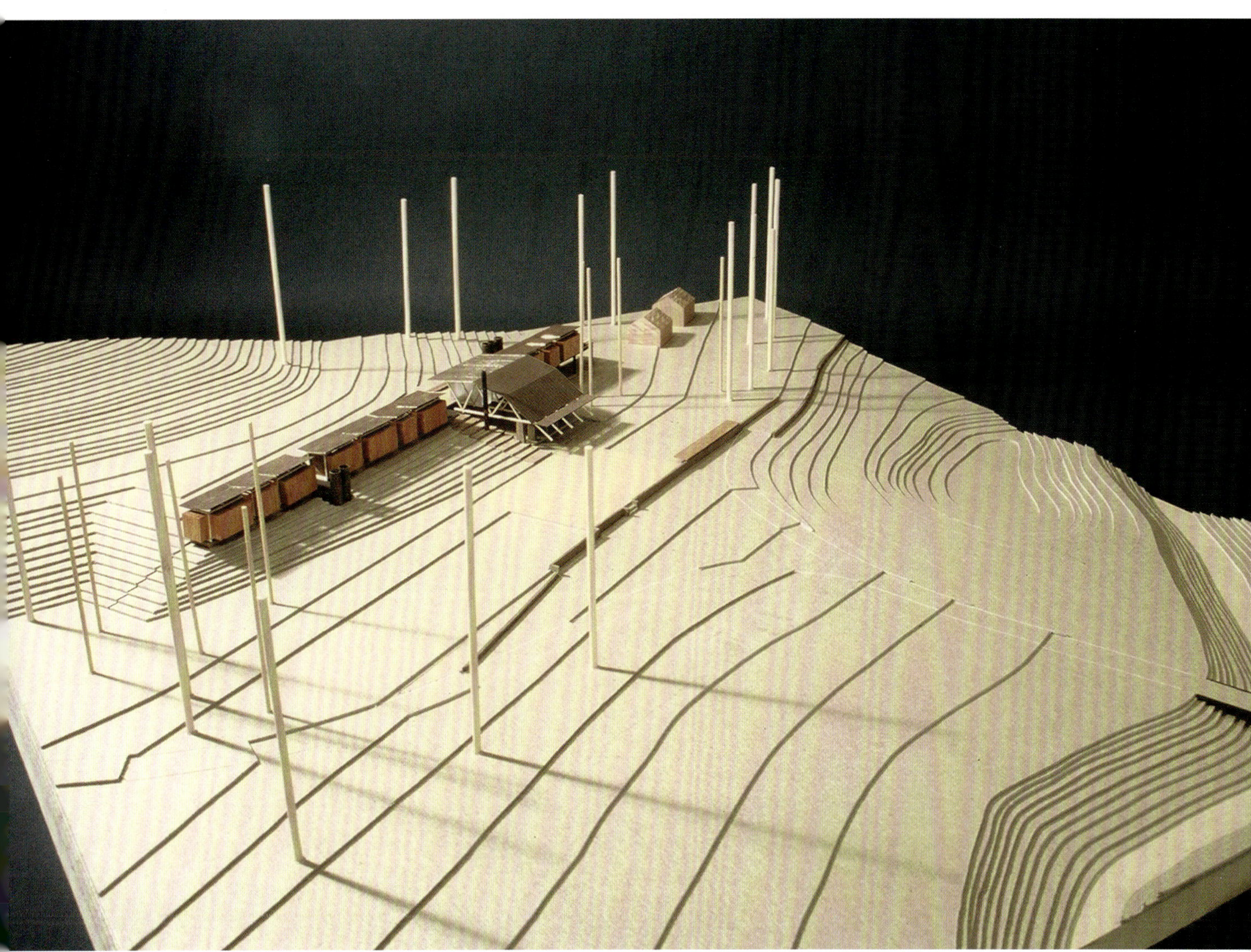

Site model, seen from the northeast.

DESIGN PRINCIPLES

LOCALIZED PROTOTYPE

THE MOUNTAIN HUT IS BOTH SITE SPECIFIC AND A PROTOTYPICAL DESIGN THAT CAN BE IMPLEMENTED WORLD WIDE. THIS DUALITY IS RECONCILED BY THE PROPOSAL OF A STRUCTURAL AND INFRASTRUCTUAL BASE THAT IS EARTHEN AND SITE SPECIFIC, CONSTRUCTED OF THE MATERIALS YIELDED BY THE EXCAVATION AND FOUND ON THE SITE. UPON THIS BASE ARE PLACED THE MODULAR CABIN / BUNK HOUSES WHICH ARE BUILT WITH AN 8'-0" x 8'-0" PREFABRICATED ENGINEERED LUMBER FRAME AND INCORPORATE STRUCTURAL INSULATED PANELS AS INFILL. THESE CABINS CAN SERVE AS A PROTOTYPE THAT CAN BE USED IN VARIOUS LOCATIONS. THE CLADDING CAN BE MODIFIED TO SUIT THE ORIENTATION ON THE SITE IN THE FORM OF ENERGY COLLECTING PANELS AND IN ORDER TO ALLOW FOR THE USE OF LOCAL MATERIALS.

ASSEMBLAGE

THE CHALLENGE OF CONSTRUCTING A HUT IN REMOTE LOCATIONS IS ADDRESSED THROUGH THE SAME PRINCIPLES AS STATED ABOVE. WHAT IS NOT YIELDED BY THE SITE IN TERMS OF MATERAILS IS LIMITED IN DIMENSION TO ENSURE TRANSPORTABILITY AND EASE OF ASSEMBLY. EVERYTHING FROM THE MODULE OF THE BUNK HOUSES TO THE SHAPE AND CONSTRUCTION OF THE TRUSSES AND ROOF OF THE DINING HALL ACCOUNT FOR THIS FACT AND IMAGINE A CONTRUCTION THAT INVOLVES A SMALL WORK CREW AND SIMPLE TOOLS.

MULTIPLE SCALES OF COMMUNITY

THE PROJECT ALLOWS FOR MULTIPLE SCALES OF COMMUNAL LIFE. THE BREAKDOWN OF THE SLEEPING QUARTERS INTO VARIOUS SIZED BUNK HOUSES ALLOWS FOR SMALLER GROUPS TO INTERACT. THE PLINTH WHICH THESE UNITS SHARE CREATES A LARGER COMMUNITY OF OVERNIGHT GUEST AND STAFF. THE MOST PUBLIC SPACES OF THE PROGRAM OCCUR ON THE GROUND LEVEL AND REPRESENT THE MORE INTENSELY COMMUNAL ASPECTS OF THE MOUNTAIN HUT. IT IS ON THIS LEVEL THAT THE ACTIVITIES OF THE DAY VISITORS AND THE OVERNIGHT GUESTS OVERLAP, CULMINATING IN THE DINING HALL AND THE OUTDOOR TERRACE THAT REPLACES THE OLD LODGE.

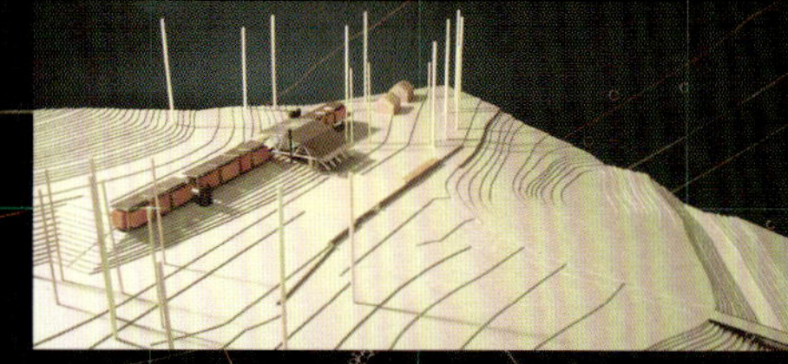

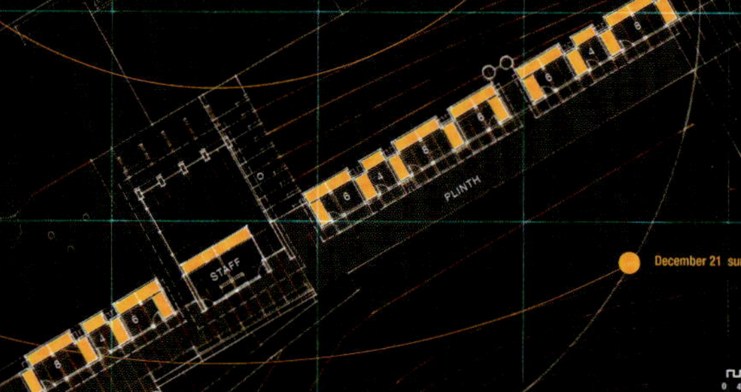

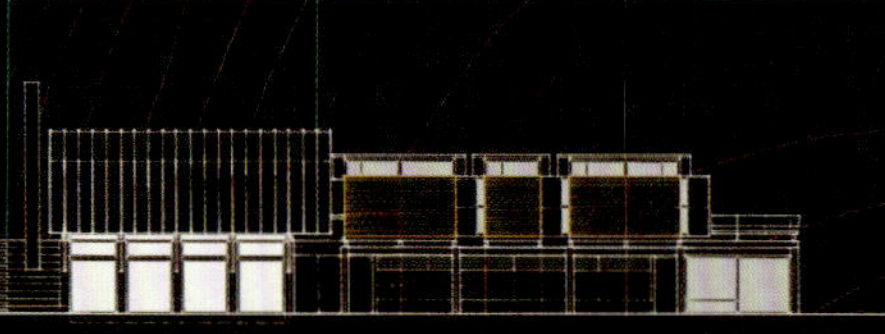

NORTH ELEVATION

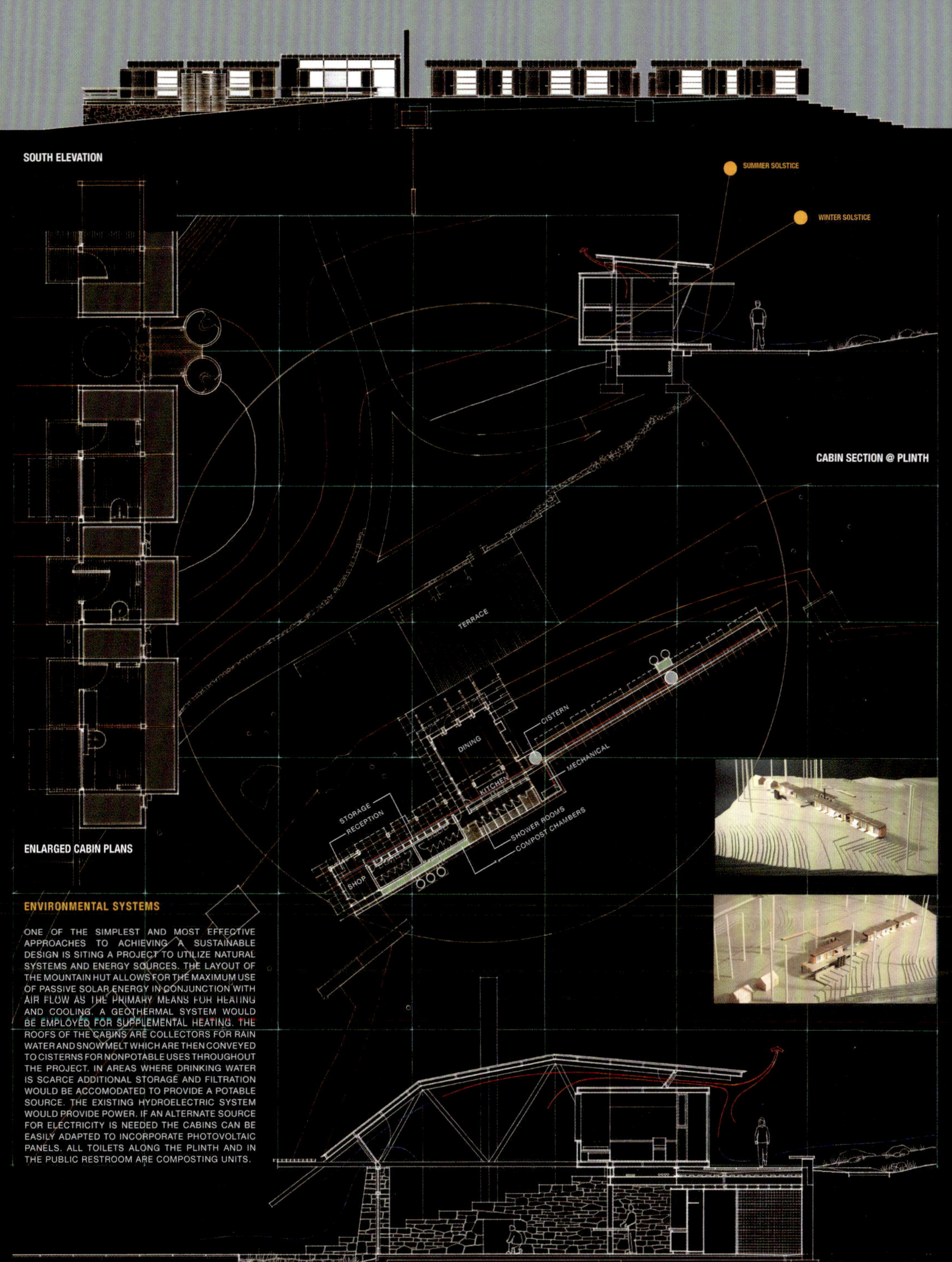

ENVIRONMENTAL SYSTEMS

ONE OF THE SIMPLEST AND MOST EFFECTIVE APPROACHES TO ACHIEVING A SUSTAINABLE DESIGN IS SITING A PROJECT TO UTILIZE NATURAL SYSTEMS AND ENERGY SOURCES. THE LAYOUT OF THE MOUNTAIN HUT ALLOWS FOR THE MAXIMUM USE OF PASSIVE SOLAR ENERGY IN CONJUNCTION WITH AIR FLOW AS THE PRIMARY MEANS FOR HEATING AND COOLING. A GEOTHERMAL SYSTEM WOULD BE EMPLOYED FOR SUPPLEMENTAL HEATING. THE ROOFS OF THE CABINS ARE COLLECTORS FOR RAIN WATER AND SNOW MELT WHICH ARE THEN CONVEYED TO CISTERNS FOR NONPOTABLE USES THROUGHOUT THE PROJECT. IN AREAS WHERE DRINKING WATER IS SCARCE ADDITIONAL STORAGE AND FILTRATION WOULD BE ACCOMODATED TO PROVIDE A POTABLE SOURCE. THE EXISTING HYDROELECTRIC SYSTEM WOULD PROVIDE POWER. IF AN ALTERNATE SOURCE FOR ELECTRICITY IS NEEDED THE CABINS CAN BE EASILY ADAPTED TO INCORPORATE PHOTOVOLTAIC PANELS. ALL TOILETS ALONG THE PLINTH AND IN THE PUBLIC RESTROOM ARE COMPOSTING UNITS.

esigned for a remote, rural site 25 miles southwest of Charlottesville, the house is positioned on the edge of a heavily wooded hillside overlooking the Rockfish River to the west. The house is composed of two rectangular volumes of the same length but differing widths, construction, and exterior materials, which are placed side-by-side and separated by a narrow recessed slot of space. The wider volume has concrete masonry walls, is set down the slope to the west, and contains the double-height living room, dining room, kitchen, and loft library above. The narrower volume, which has wood-frame structure clad on the exterior with wide vertical sheets of copper joined by standing seams, is set at the top of the hill to the east, and it contains the entry foyer, guest room, and utility room on the lower floor, the bedroom on the upper floor, and the staircase.

Like the Beckerdite-Scholley House, the Hillman House may be understood as a development of the Croffead House, in its composition as a "diptych," with two distinct but equal volumes, further divided into four smaller rectangles by a central pier, and having the daytime rooms in the double-height volume while the bedrooms are in the two-level volume. However, the Hillman House may also be understood as a development of the construction type of the Reid House, with its two differing volumes, in that one of the pair of volumes is built of concrete masonry walls exposed on the exterior and interior, while the other volume is built of wood-frame clad on the exterior with standing seam copper. The two volumes share wood-frame floor and roof structure, but have differing windows; the concrete masonry volume has steel-framed windows and the copper-clad volume has wood-framed windows. In addition, the concrete masonry volume is taller and wider than the copper-clad volume, and the shared roof slopes continuously downwards from the highpoint on the west wall of the concrete masonry volume to the east wall of the copper-clad volume, where a single large downspout drains the entire roof. Finally, the copper-clad volume has a concrete slab on grade at the ground floor, while the concrete masonry volume has wood-framed floor over crawlspace.

The house is approached on a gravel walkway along the top of the hillside, with a concrete masonry retaining wall forming an entry terrace at the front door, similar to the Menefee Mountain House. The northern, entry façade is an interwoven composition of overlapping L-shapes that joins the two volumes of concrete masonry and copper, while also subtly indicating the importance of the view downhill to the west. At the roof the two volumes read clearly, the complementary contrast of their materials articulated by the recessed slot of space between them, which is clad in wood, a third material, and opened with a window. The concrete masonry fireplace mass and chimney are offset towards the west, downhill side of the house, and the large steel-framed window is set off-center in the masonry volume, also towards the west and the view of the river valley. The cast concrete slab articulating the transition from fireplace mass to chimney carries across the joint between the concrete masonry and copper-clad volumes, towards the east, uphill side of the house, where it forms a roof over the front door, and then folds down and across to form the sidewall and floor of the entry porch. The concrete masonry of the fireplace steps back to align with the wood-framed glass entry door, which is set into the copper-clad volume. The large wood-framed window on the upper level is pushed to the western edge of the copper-clad volume, overlapping with the entry vestibule below.

Inside the entry door, the staircase leading up to the owners' bedroom is set into the corner to the left, and the low ceiling over the concrete-floored foyer and hallway opens out into the wood-floored double-height living room to the right, the transition from concrete to wood underfoot marking the joint between the two volumes. The

Hillman House,
Schuyler, Virginia,
2003–2005

Living room, looking south to dining room, below, and library, above.

concrete masonry-walled living volume is opened on all three sides by steel-framed windows, the largest opening to the forest downhill. The north-facing window takes the form of an L-shape, its upper glass extending in front of the exterior chimney, which interlocks with the L-shaped masonry fireplace, and the window and the fireplace share the cast concrete hearth-bench that runs the width of the room. The two west-facing windows, larger in the living room and smaller in the dining room and loft library above, extend from floor to ceiling and open towards the downhill river view. The double-height south-facing window runs from the kitchen below to the loft library above.

On the fourth, interior side of the living room volume, a central concrete masonry column divides the two, large double-height openings onto the bedroom volume, with solid masonry corners at either end. Steel I-beams carrying the upper level floor and roof loads run from north to south along the central wall dividing the two volumes, and the outer edges of the concrete masonry corners and central pier are notched to receive the steel beams, so that the piers step inwards as they rise, articulating the decreasing structural loads they carry from the first to second floor. At the outer, west wall, a steel beam integrated with the steel-framed window carries the floor loads of the loft library.

The kitchen is partly hidden from view, while remaining acoustically connected to the dining and living rooms, by a steel-framed frosted glass scrim, which glows with the strong light from the south window, and a plywood cabinet, which matches the plywood cabinets lining the inner wall of the dining room. Above the dining room, the loft library opens to the living room through a balcony screen of thin steel rods, while the owners' bedroom is protected from views by a solid plywood balcony wall. At the second floor, the bedroom and the library anchor the ends of the L-shaped plan, and the dressing room and spacious white-tiled bathroom, with the bathtub placed beneath a large window, are set in the southeast corner. The owners' bedroom, which opens to the staircase along the north wall, is given views across the top of the double-height living room to the west, down the hillside to the river below.

　　　　　　　　　　　　A PRACTICE OF MAKING PLACES

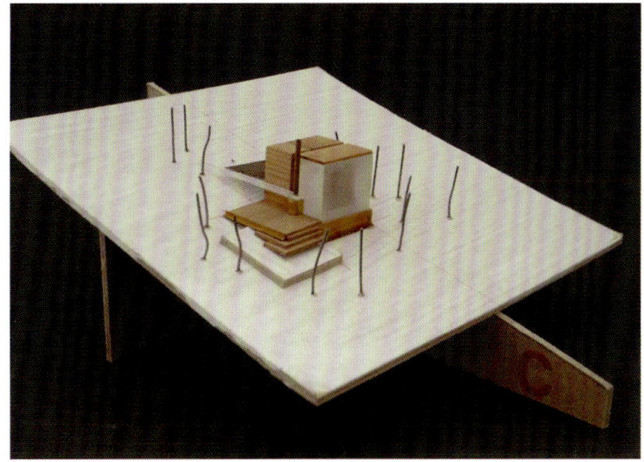

Site model design studies.

Site plan.

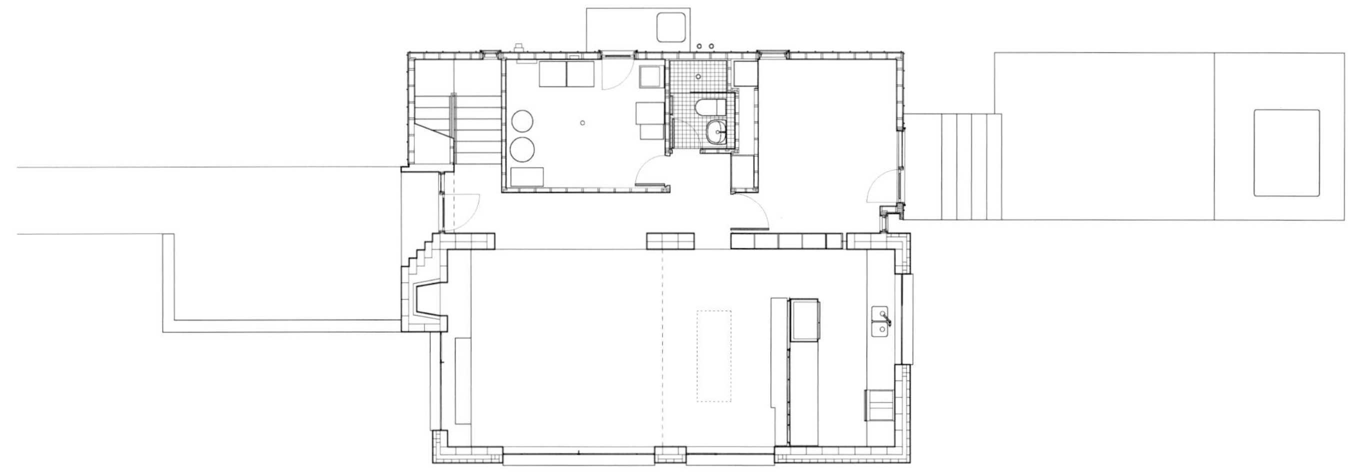

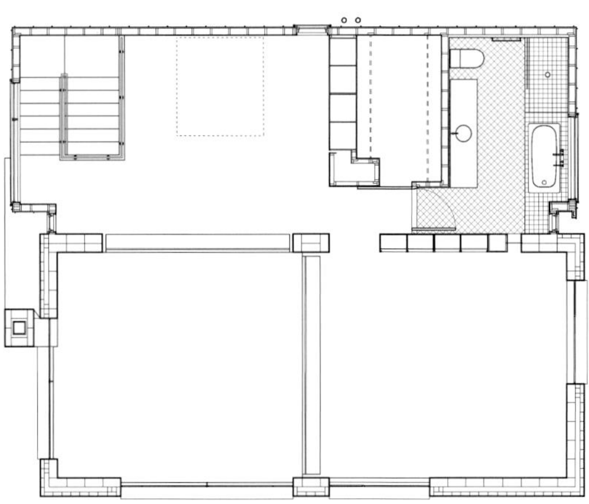

From top, lower, ground floor plan; upper floor plan.

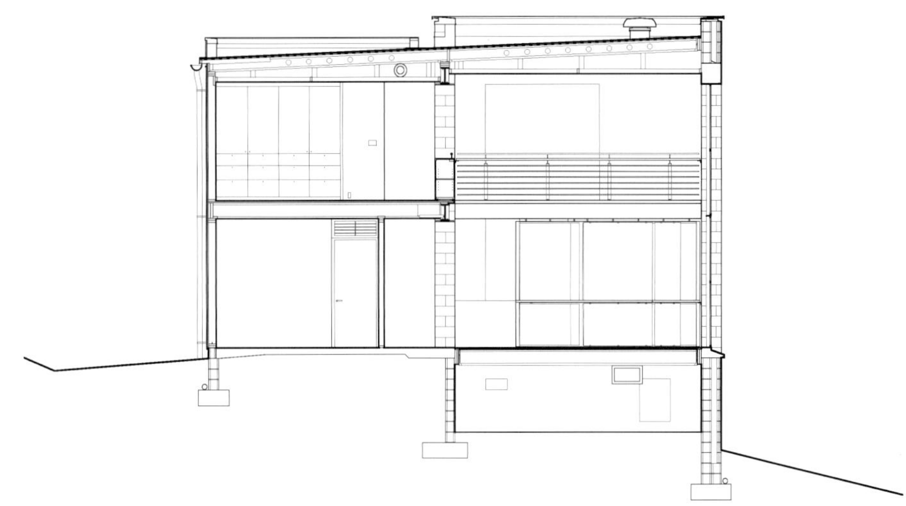

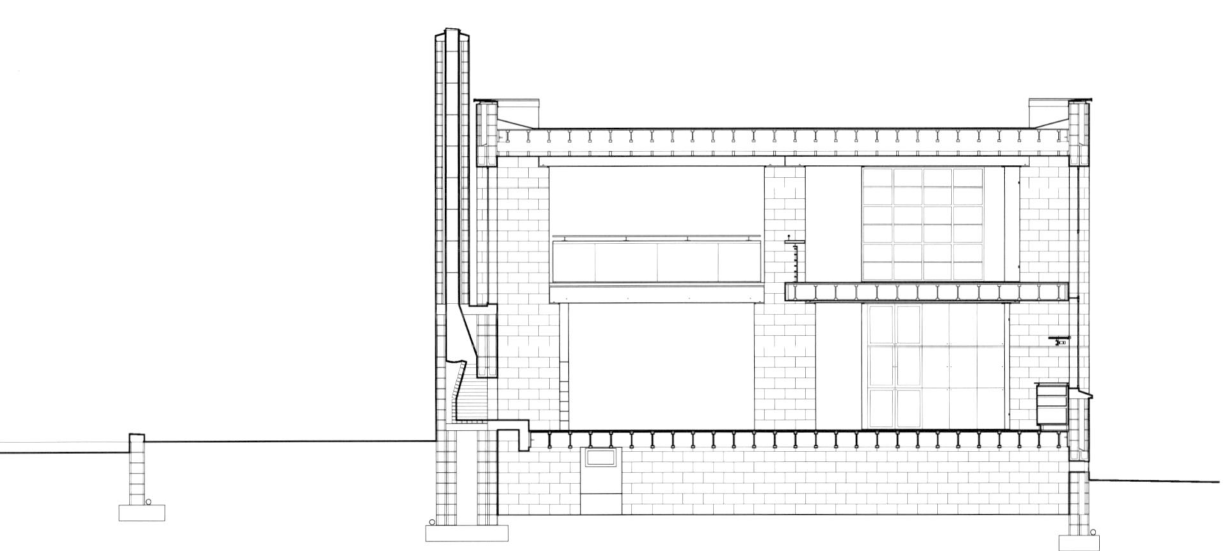

East-west section through two volumes (above) and north-south
section through living room, dining room and library (below).

View from northwest.

Study models of north wall at entry.

View of north façade on approach.

View from southwest.

Living room, looking south-southeast to dining room and library.

Living room, looking north-northeast to fireplace and entry.

Detail at living room fireplace.

View from dining room to living room (above) and view of dining room, with kitchen behind glass scrim to left (below).

The site is located to the southwest of Charleston, along the Atlantic coast, and within the low country landscape drained by tributaries of the Wadmalaw River, an area that has been dedicated to agriculture for many generations. The client, a close personal friend of the architect, owned a house in Charleston and a country house on Wadmalaw Island, situated on farmland that included extensive old tomato fields. In an interesting coincidence, the client named the land "Sheldon Farm," in homage to the ruins of the Sheldon Church – the same ruins that inspired Clark's design of Middleton Inn. The client wanted to build a "retreat," for use by his family, guests, and others, to be located near an existing irrigation pond that had been constructed for the farming operation.

Typical of the agricultural ponds in this coastal river delta farmland, the pond is a thin and extremely long channel of water, only 100 feet wide and almost a mile in length, which extends in an unwaveringly straight line across the landscape. The piles of earth that had been excavated in the making of the pond formed a massive berm along one side, which slowly increased in height towards the western end of the pond. After making a number of preliminary design studies, Clark proposed that the minimal dwelling be placed at the western end of the long, linear pond, and that it be anchored to the earth berm. Rather than make a freestanding object set against the enormous scale of the pond, berm, and flat agricultural landscape, the dwelling is embedded in earth carved from the berm, which encloses three sides of the building, the exception being the side opening to the view down the length of the pond.

The square, one-story volume of the dwelling is positioned on the central axis of the elongated pond, and earth taken from the existing berm is drawn up around its walls and over its roof to provide insulation from the hot summer sun. The new earth mound wraps around the north, west, and south sides of the dwelling, terminating on the east side in a retaining wall and stair to the roof. In plan, the earth mound enclosing the dwelling takes the form of a spiraling, shell-like shape opening and anchored to the larger landscape. The concrete roof structure of the dwelling carries the earth-covered terrace that is elevated above the surrounding fields, which are being planted as gridded orchards.

Within the new earth mound, the dwelling is formed by three massive retaining walls, and the fourth, east-facing side of the dwelling opens to the pond through a full-height window wall, in front of which stands a covered loggia. A single massive square concrete pier, its four sides sloped inwards as it rises, stands at the center of the square plan. The pier supports the heavy cruciform concrete roof structure, composed of a flat concrete slab carried by two beams that intersect above the central pier, which orders the space within the dwelling. The roof structure stops short of the sloped north retaining wall, where a linear skylight allows a band of south sun to play on the wall's inclined surface throughout the day, as well as forming a thermal chimney to exhaust hot air and enable through-ventilation for the interior. The monolithic, massive, heavy, and cool space formed by the concrete central pier, cruciform roof structure, and three outer retaining walls is complemented by the lightweight, warm, wooden cabinet-like rooms placed in front of the west and south walls. The kitchen and bath, illuminated by a cylindrical skylight, are set along the west wall. The wooden bedroom volumes are lifted above the floor, shielded by curtains, and illuminated by skylights along the south wall—the bedrooms are described by Clark as "wooden vessels to climb into at night."[1] As illustrated in one of Clark's evocative perspectives, the retreat was to be experienced as a complementary contrast of being at once enclosed and embedded deep within the earth, and at the same time sensing the space

A PRACTICE OF MAKING PLACES

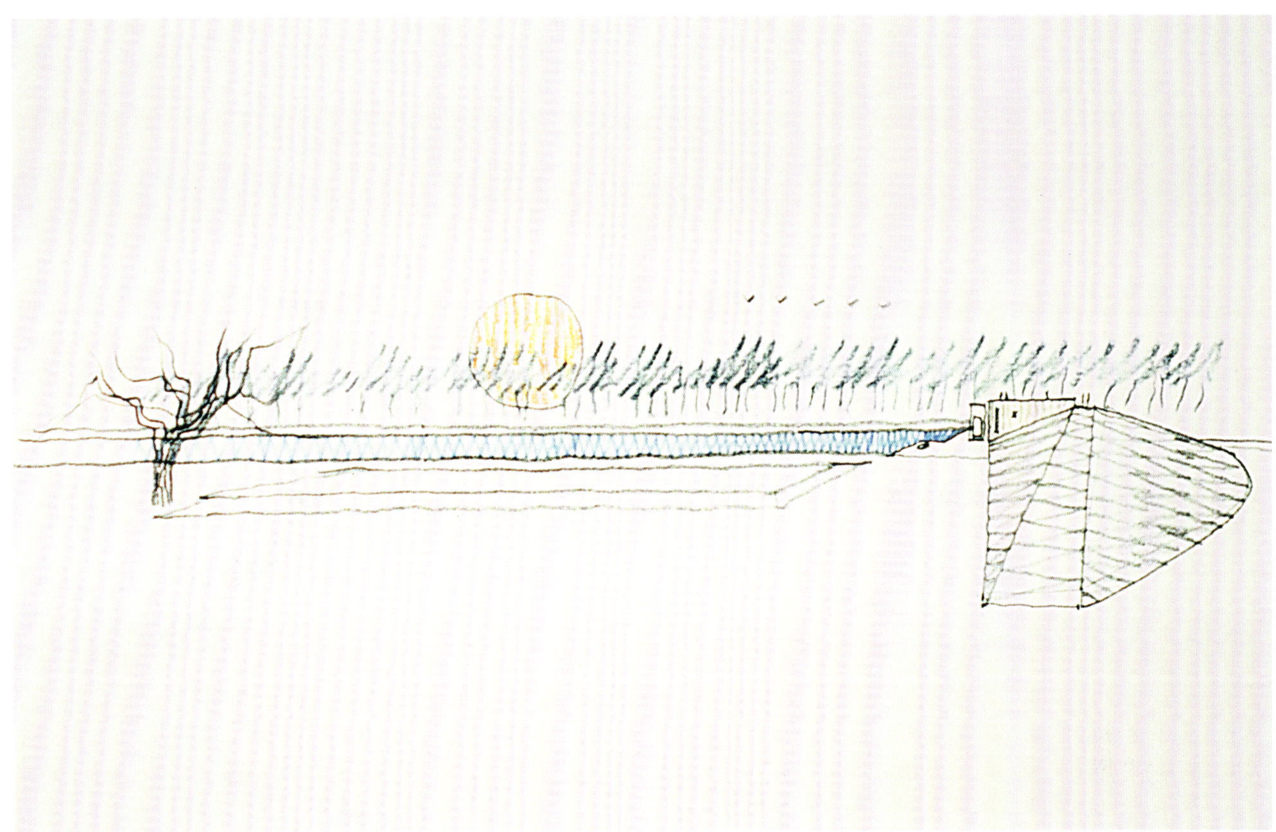

Perspective sketch from north.

within opening outwards and merging with the seemingly infinite extension of the pond into the distance.

In response to the monumental scale of the flat landscape of water and earth mounds, which assume the character of a ruin of some ancient civilization, the small house is articulated in tectonic contrasts of heavy anchoring walls and roof structure and levitating lightweight wooden vessels, the deep shadow of the underground opened by glazed planes and lines of sunlight. Clark's intention was to lock together the existing elements of earth, water, and sunlight, already part of the place, and transform them "into something habitable but reading as a landscape." As Clark wrote to his client, the retreat is intended to be at one and the same time a deeply spiritual place embedded in the landscape and a minimal dwelling; "Within the structure I have tried to make something that is spiritual while containing the program of a small house. I've always loved the fact that the pre-Anasazi pit houses were considered sacred places—that the sacredness was not removed to a special place of worship but retained in the home. The joining together of the spiritual and the everyday seems important to me."[2]

Aerial view of site.

A PRACTICE OF MAKING PLACES

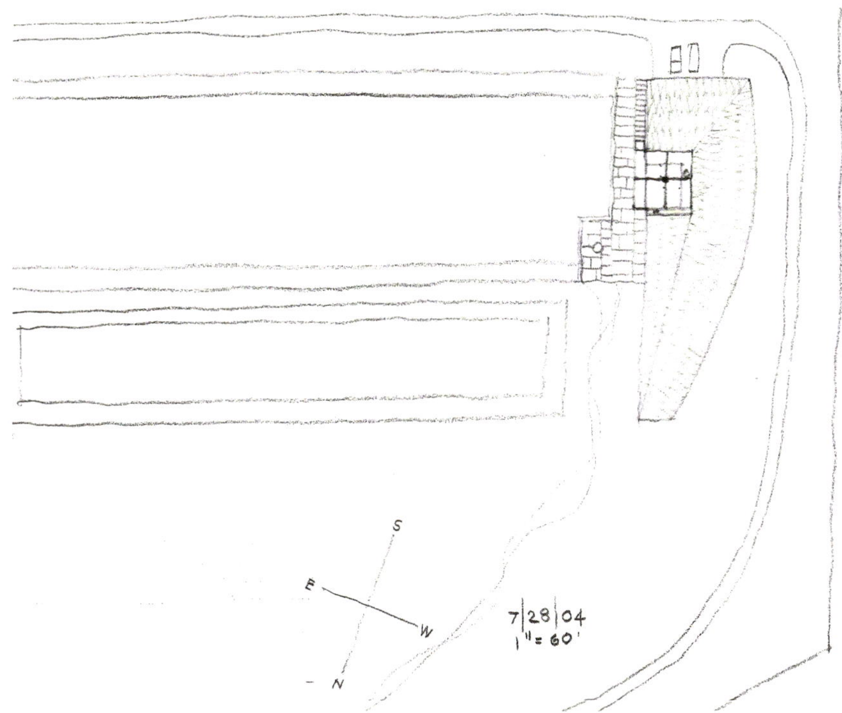

Site plan.

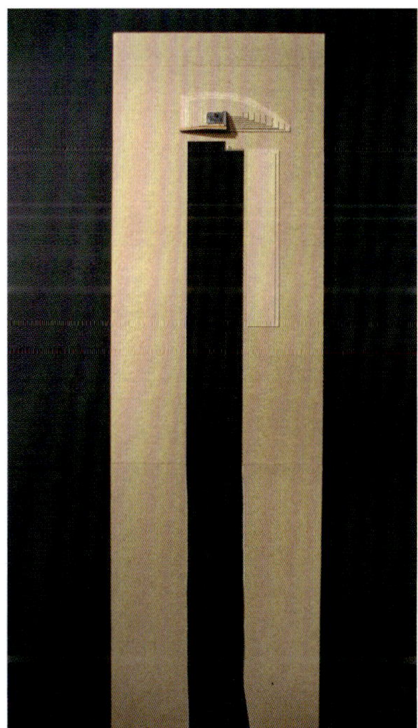

Site model, seen from above (left) and along axis of pond (right).

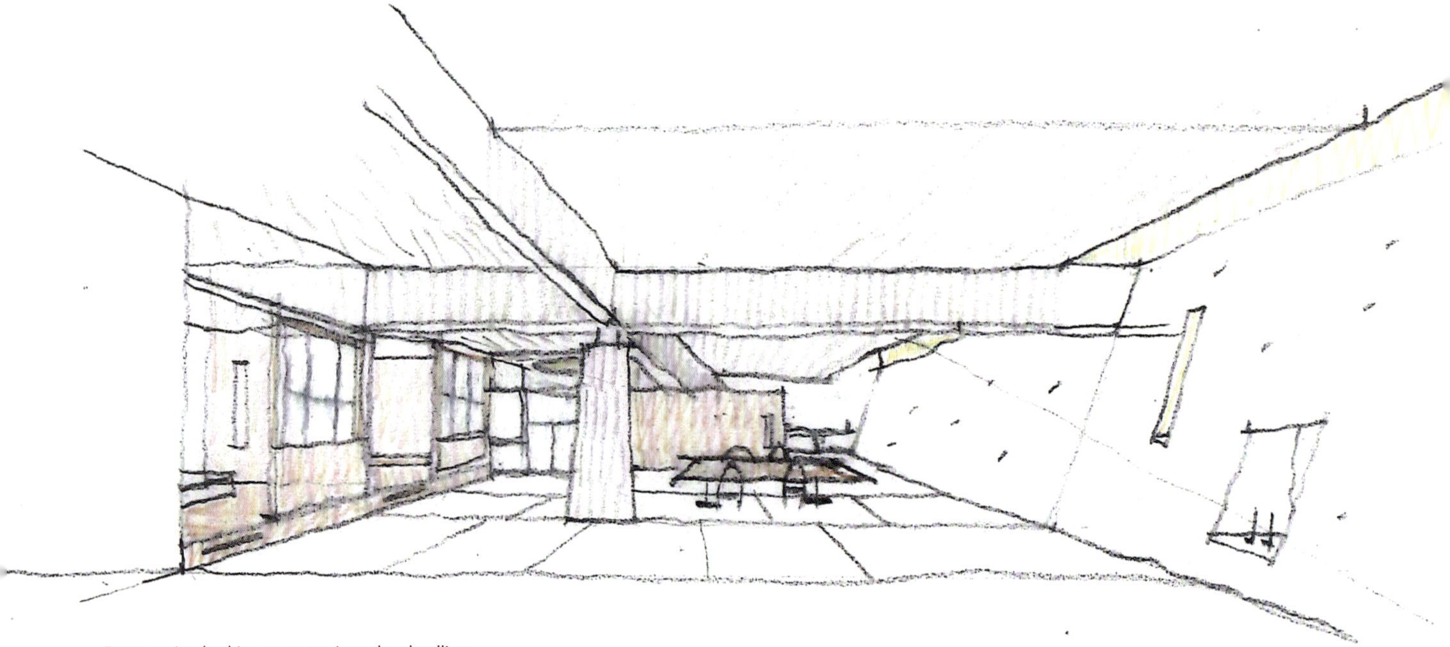

Perspective looking to west, into the dwelling.

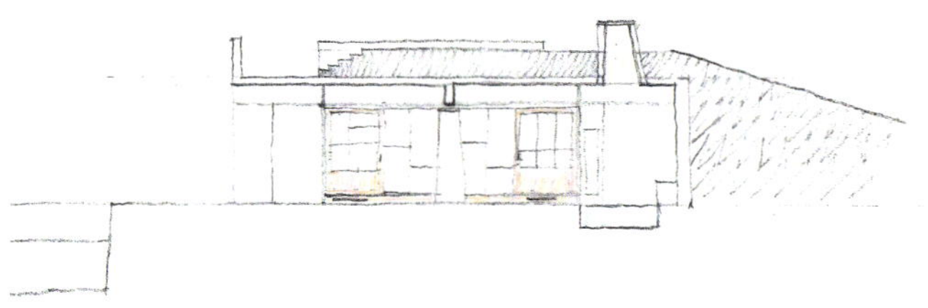

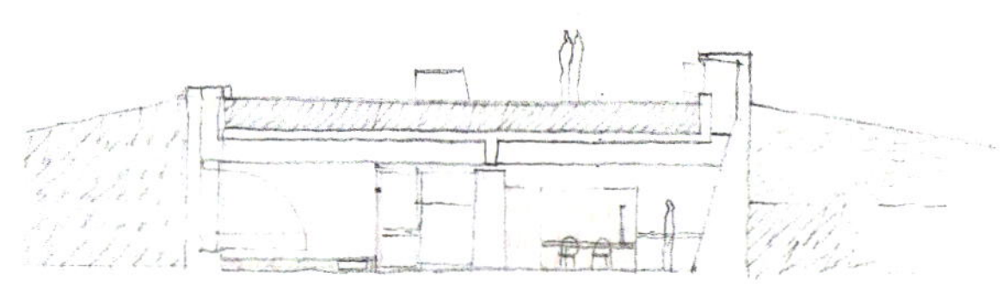

East-west section (above) and north-south section (below).

Perspective looking from within dwelling to east, towards the pond.

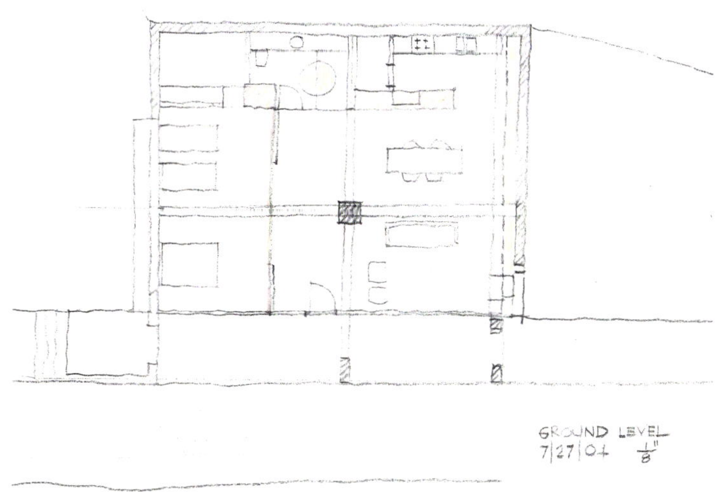

Ground-floor plan.

Clark's winning entry in the international competition for the design of a permanent building for the Clemson University Graduate Architecture program, which has been located in Charleston for many years, is a brilliant reinterpretation of the Charleston Single House type as the structure for a small institutional building. The competition site is located in central Charleston, a near-square double-lot on George Street, just off Meeting Street to the west, and one block south of Calhoun Street. The site, which is used for parking, is also located at a transition between neighborhoods, with long, narrow, and tall two-story traditional Charleston Single Houses on the east side, and larger four-story commercial buildings on the west side. The site is also across George Street from the historic Middleton-Pickney House, headquarters of the Spoleto Festival, considered to be America's premier performing arts festival, which takes place in public venues throughout Charleston for three weeks each spring.

The primary principle ordering the design was Clark's intention to make a building that would be appropriate to its place – a building that would be "at home" in Charleston. Responding to the transitional nature of the urban site, the program for the new school is divided into two buildings so as to be able to make each building narrow and tall to match the scale of the existing neighboring buildings. The design comprises two long narrow volumes, four-stories tall on the west side adjacent to the commercial building, and three-stories tall on the east side adjacent to the houses (whose height the lower building matches precisely). The two volumes are connected at the rear of the site by the main staircase and service block, and the two volumes form two outdoor spaces on their respective east sides, one comprising the entry and work courtyard, while the other is a parking court (with parking spaces beneath the building).

The taller western volume is set directly on the property line, abutting the existing parking lot, while the shorter eastern volume was set back from the property line so as not to shadow the side-yard garden of the nearest house. In addition, the narrow George Streets façades of the two buildings are stuccoed masonry, with simple minimal openings, and are proportioned to fit those typical throughout the city. Due to the use of the building by students both day and night, the façade of the east wall of the lower building is designed so that the windows face the street rather than towards the residential neighbors. The courtyard between the two volumes serves as the center of school activities, and it is oriented to the Spoleto Festival headquarters across George Street.

The life of the school is gathered around the stone-paved entry and work courtyard, which is also the primary light source for the rooms opening onto it on both sides. When entering the school, one walks towards the south across the courtyard, ascending the wide stairs to the stone-paved terrace at the second floor, off of which the entry doors open. In entering the building, one is introduced to the life of the school by views of the exhibition gallery, jury rooms, and studios, all of which may be seen through the windows opening onto the courtyard on the ground and second floor. The courtyard is the primary source of daylight and ventilation for both the western and eastern volumes, as well as providing the primary views into and across the central space, allowing the students and faculty to be visually and acoustically connected to the activities of the school at all times. Anchoring the south end of the courtyard is the glass-walled main staircase of the school, which provides views overlooking the courtyard and culminates at the fourth floor, where the student commons opens onto the roof terrace above the east building, providing views out over the city.

Clemson Architecture
Center in Charleston
Competition, First Prize,
2004–2005
(unrealized)

Perspective of central courtyard,
looking towards entry and stair.

The taller, western volume contains a jury room, gallery, and workshop on the ground floor; a double-height studio space on what functions as the school's *piano nobile*, the second floor; a faculty area overlooking the double-height studio on the third floor; and a studio on the fourth floor with north-facing skylights that carry photovoltaic cells on their south faces. The western building presents a solid wall to the adjacent existing parking lot and commercial building, and opens to the central courtyard and the vine-covered eastern wall through a full height glass wall – in both ways similar to the solid back walls and the open, garden-facing front walls of the Charleston Single House. The lower, eastern volume contains parking on the ground floor; the library, seminar rooms, offices, and meeting rooms on the second, entry floor; collaborator spaces on the third floor (for use by the public that are involved in the urban design activities of the center); and, at the roof, a terrace that wraps around a garden, and overlooks the courtyard. The eastern volume opens to the courtyard through a steel-framed screen wall on which jasmine vines are encouraged to grow and through which some of the rooms inside project. On the east side, the broad hallway running along the outer edge of the second and third floors is cantilevered out over the parking court below – similar to the long "piazzas," or porches running along the sides of the neighboring Charleston Single Houses. But, the way the eastern wall is fenestrated contrasts with the piazzas, in that it is opened with a series of pivoted, vertical, louver-like metal panel walls that give views only towards the street, protecting the privacy of the neighboring houses. At the end of the western, studio volume, a large window is opened onto the street at each floor, so that the school is connected to the city from within the building and without, through the entry court, the glass and vine-covered screen wall and roof garden of which serve as a reinterpretation of the tradition of the Charleston Single House side-yard garden as part of the contemporary city.

The school building is also intended to embody and exemplify sustainable design in action, utilizing both passive and active methods, such as the maximization of daylight and ventilation in order to minimize the use of electric lighting and air-conditioning; the vine-covered courtyard wall that shades the spaces within from the hot southwestern summer sun; the collection of rainwater in the cistern at the top of the main staircase that is used in the courtyard pool that waters the courtyard jasmine vines; the green roof above the eastern volume, which both retains rainwater and insulates the spaces below; the photovoltaic cells on the fourth-floor studio roof; and the heating and cooling by way of a radiant floor system that utilizes geothermal energy.

After Clark received first prize in the competition, Clemson University was unwilling to offer what Clark considered to be a fair contract, and the project was never realized. This was the last of five competitions in which Clark was awarded the first prize, only one of which was realized according to his design.

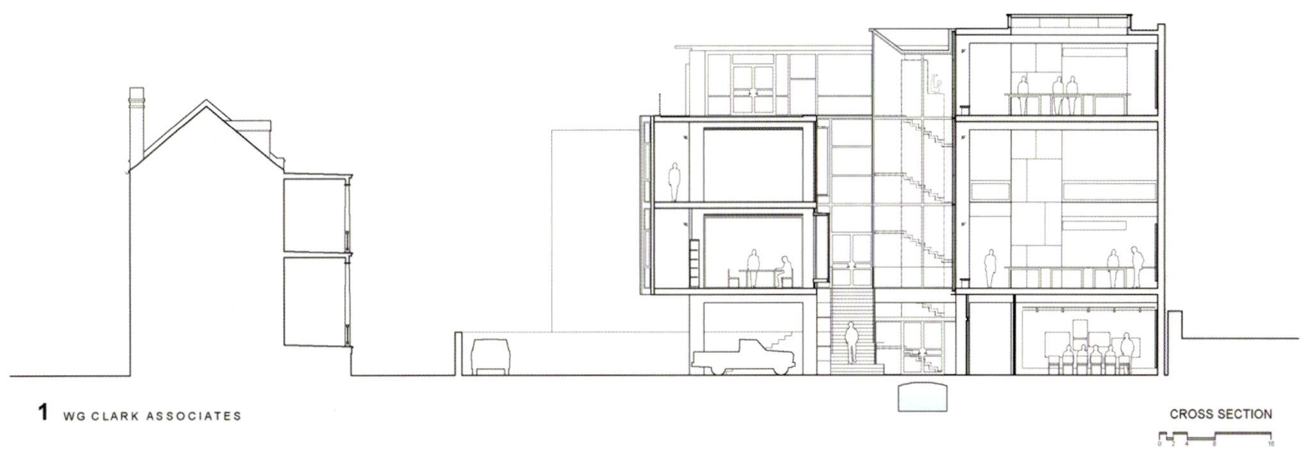

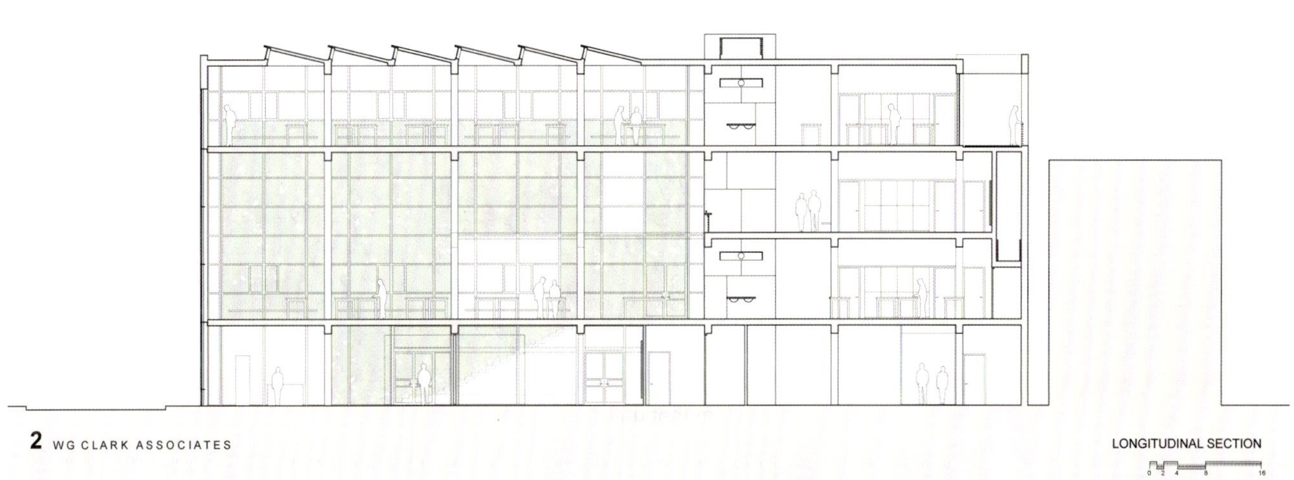

Cross section with central courtyard (above), and longitudinal section through studio building (below).

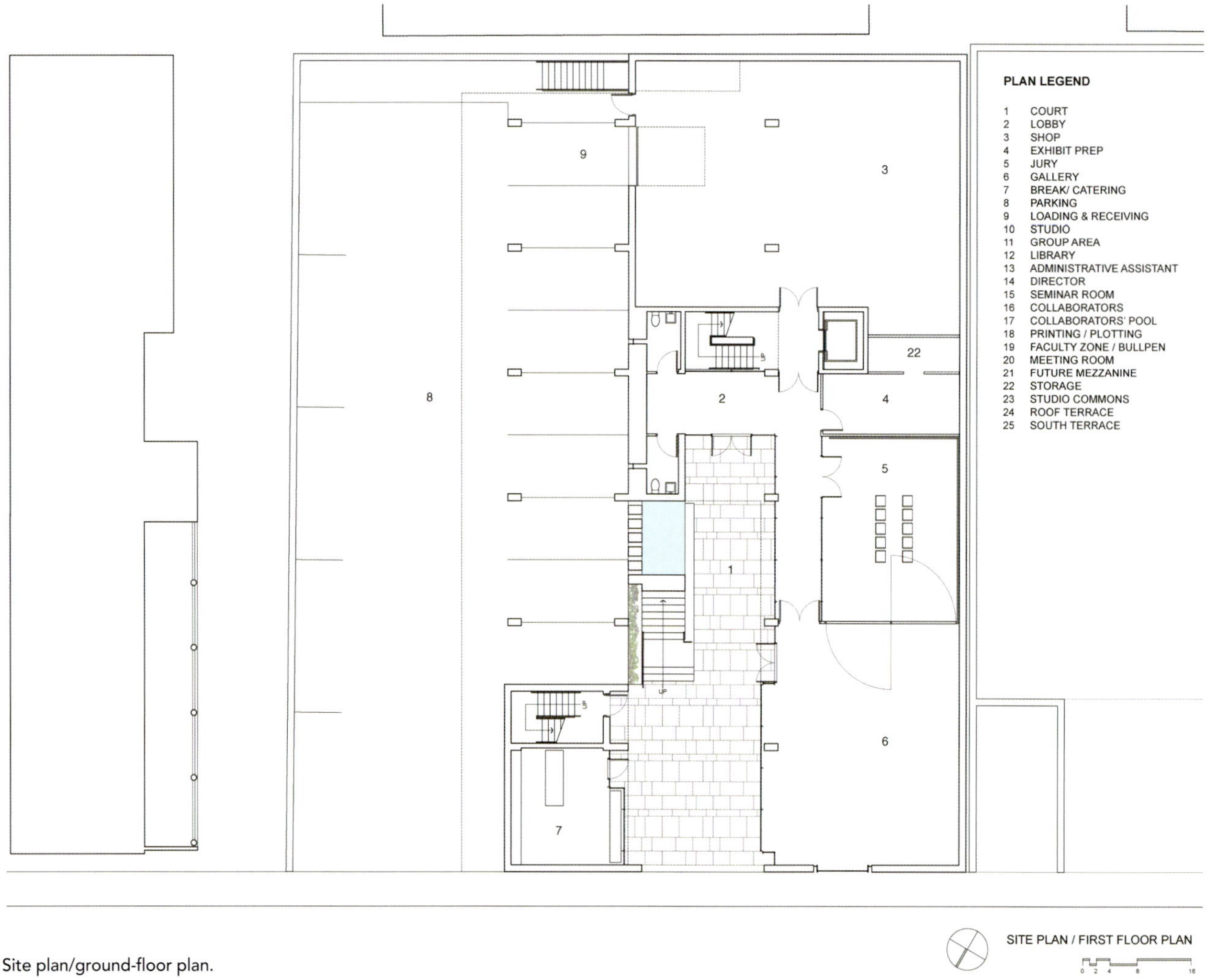

Site plan/ground-floor plan.

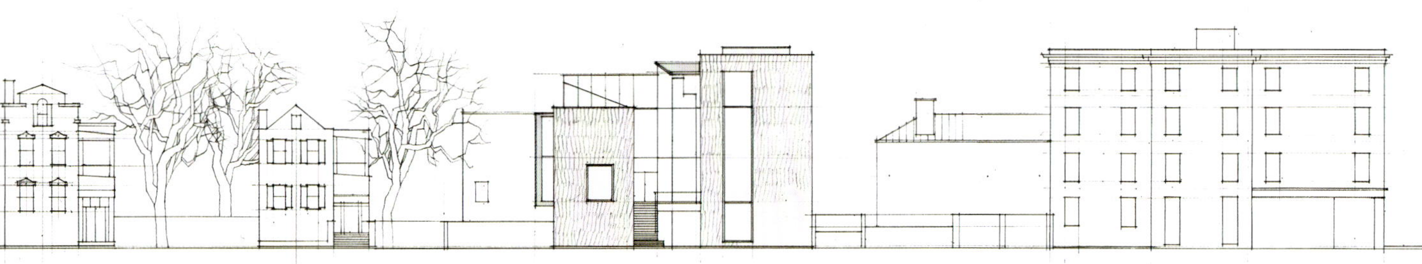

Elevation on George Street.

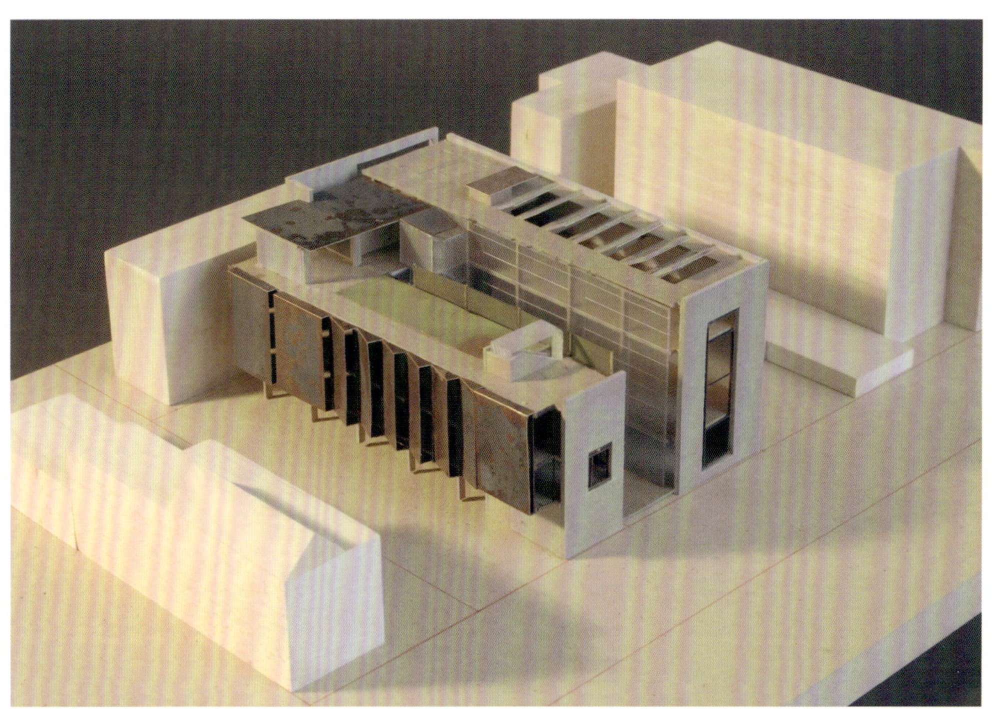

Two views of study and final models, seen from George Street.

Study model, view of courtyard walls of west wing (above) and east wing (below).

     A PRACTICE OF MAKING PLACES

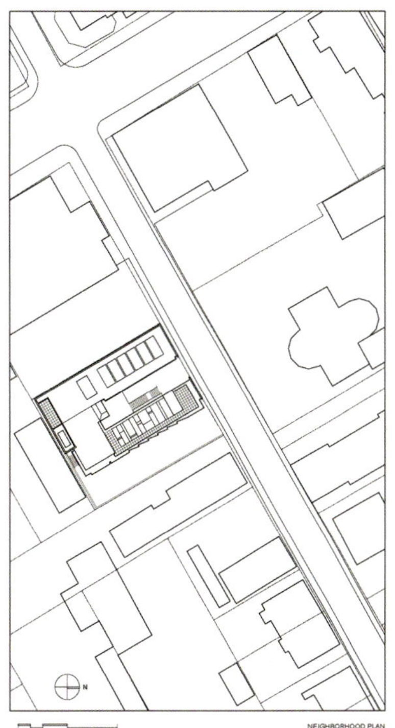

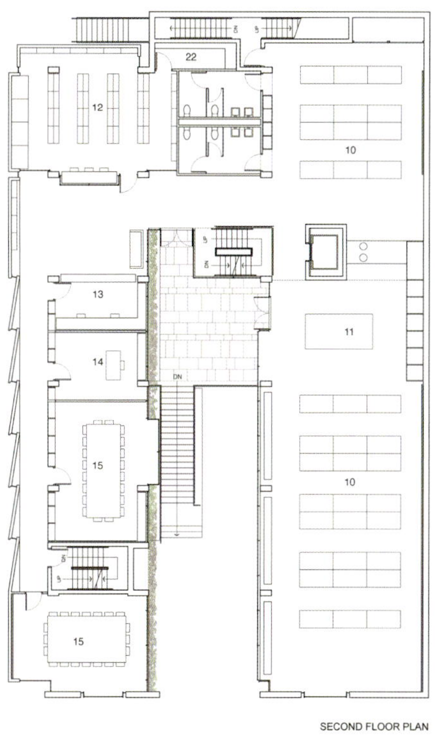

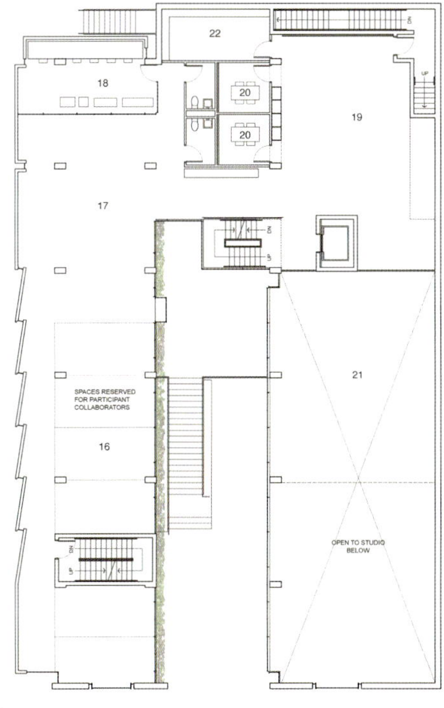

THIRD FLOOR PLAN

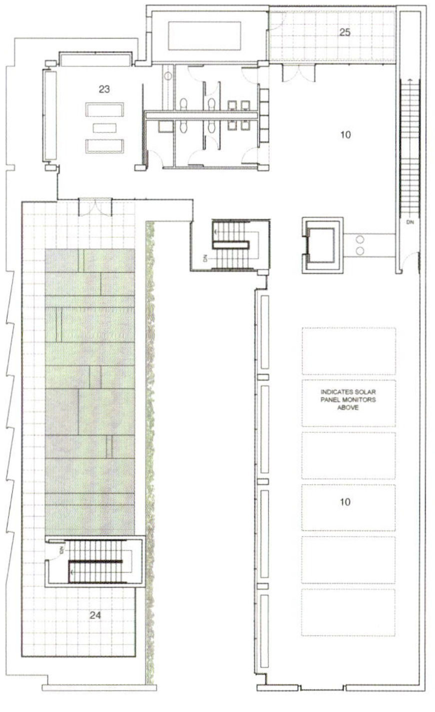

FOURTH FLOOR PLAN

Site plan (upper left); second-floor plan (upper right); third-floor plan (lower left); fourth-floor and roof plan (lower right).

The commission was for a new family room to be added to the rear yard of a 1933 gray rubble-stone walled and slate-roofed house designed by Milton Grigg and located in a neighborhood immediately to the northwest of the university campus. The existing gambrel-roofed house and the detached garage to the south are connected by a three-bay loggia that opens to the front and back yards. The client requested that the existing family room addition, which they characterized as dark and confining, be removed and replaced. The new addition was constructed largely within the footprint of the old addition so as not to encroach further into the rear yard of the house. The existing house fronts on the street to the west, and the new addition is invisible from the street, being placed in the rear yard to the east, directly behind the house and adjacent to the densely wooded area at the center of the suburban block.

The ground floor of the addition is a square in plan, bounded along its east and north sides by a thick, two-story tall, gray stucco-clad masonry wall, L-shaped in plan, which terminates at the edge of the concrete terrace floor to the south and in a semi-cylindrical enclosure for the spiral stair on the north side. The double-height family room, which is also a square in plan, is set in the northeast corner of the larger square plan. The family room is wrapped by an L-shaped space comprising a double-height concrete-floored exterior terrace on its south side, and a one-story entry foyer, hallway, and breakfast room that acts as a spatial joint connecting the addition to the existing house on its west side. A table is set in the northwest corner of the hallway space, forming the new breakfast room, which connects to the renovated kitchen through the new opening made in the rear wall of the existing house. An open mezzanine, containing a library and study, is set above the western half of the family room, and is accessed by the spiral stair embedded in the north wall.

The new addition can be entered either from within the existing house, through the hallway and new bath off the stairs, and through the kitchen, or from the new entry that opens to the garden. In the garden, a new stone-paved terrace extends from the entry to the addition, at its southwest corner, to the existing stone-floored loggia, terminating at the rubble-stone wall of the garage. Across from the existing loggia, a new landscape of tiered shallow grass terraces, held by stone riser walls, transitions from a lower grass terrace, at the level of the loggia and the new addition, to an upper grass terrace that runs across the back of the site, which is edged by the densely wooded area behind. The low retaining walls of the landscape terraces terminate in the thick, stucco-clad, double-height masonry east wall of the addition. This massive back wall is at one and the same time a part of the pavilion-like addition, and of the terraced garden; and, as an in-between element, it divides, frames, and anchors the exterior garden and the interior space, which are intertwined and overlapped in our experience.

The sense of interior and exterior space interpenetrating in the addition is reinforced by the complementary contrast of the solid thick east and north wall, and the transparent steel-framed double-height glazed south wall and delicate one-story glazed connector to the west. A thin roof with copper-clad soffit and fascia is cantilevered over the steel-framed glazing of the south wall of the family room, and over the west wall of the mezzanine, parallel to the existing house. The roof is anchored into the sides of the thick north and east walls of the addition, and is supported at its outer corner by a single concrete pier that stands away from the house. The transparent, porous, membrane-like quality of the glazed south wall is complemented by the translucent façade of the somewhat enigmatic, mahogany wood-clad cubic volume that projects out of the glazed wall to the right of the concrete pier.

Cameron Lane House
Addition, Charlottesville,
Virginia, 2005–2007

View of addition from new terrace garden.

The new steel-framed glass entry door is set between the double-height concrete pier and the rubble-stone wall of the existing house, and opens from the concrete-floored exterior terrace into the wood-floored interior hallway. The in-between, inside-outside character of the connecting hallway is accentuated by the full-height glazing at both ends of the space, and the views to the garden to south and north they provide. A plywood cabinet stands between the entry and the family room, framing the view of the breakfast room at the other end of the hallway. Above the cabinet, a steel I-beam runs between the concrete pier and the north end of the stucco-clad masonry wall, marking the edge of the double-height volume. At the breakfast room, the low ceiling of the hallway is carried out into the family room, where it creates more intimate spaces in front of the fireplace set into the wood cabinet at its center; over the cubic wood window seat that projects out through the glass wall to the south; and at the entry to the spiral stair that projects out of the stucco-clad masonry wall to the north.

The cubic, double-height volume of the family room is enclosed on its east and north sides by the thick L-shaped-in-plan wall, which orients the room towards the double-height steel-framed glass south wall and its views of the new garden and existing large cedar tree. The concrete masonry wall is finished on the interior in the same gray-colored stucco as on the exterior, reinforcing its character as being simultaneously part of the garden outside and part of the room inside. The thick wall is opened on its east side by a full-height steel-framed window admitting east daylight and allowing views of the forest at the rear of the garden. On its north side, the thick wall houses the steel spiral stair leading up to the mezzanine, which stands on a concrete landing at the floor and is opened at its top by a skylight. The red-painted interior surface of the semi-cylindrical spiral stair enclosure is struck by sunlight throughout the day, and its warm, glowing color complements the cool north light of the breakfast room window beside it, and parallels the warm color of the wood-walled window seat across the room. Called a "tokanoma" by Clark, to denote its character as a room-within-a room for spiritual and contemplative ritual, the cubic wood-walled window seat projects out from the steel-framed window wall towards the garden and the south sun, its frosted glass interior surface set behind the mahogany wood-slat exterior screen-wall, providing an ever-changing play of light and thin shadows for this cozy reading nook.

The inside-outside threshold quality of the steel-framed glazing of the south wall is emphasized by the concrete floor slab band that extends from the exterior terrace into the family room, and upon which the wood window seat is placed. The floor of the library and study on the mezzanine is supported by a steel I-beam at its outer edge, which bears into the stucco-clad masonry wall at the north and onto a freestanding column, made of two steel channels separated by a slot of light, standing next to the wood window seat at the south. At the front end of the mezzanine is a wood balcony wall, above which a continuous horizontal plane of wood forms tabletops and shelves. On the western, back wall of the library and study, wood shelves run beneath continuous clerestory windows, and a large window, giving a view of the roof of the existing house, opens next to the portal in the thick stucco-clad masonry wall that gives onto the red-walled volume at the top of the spiral stairs.

In our experience of the building, there is a complementary contrast between the old house and the new addition—between the solid, massive, rubble stone-walls of the existing house and the transparent steel-framed glass south wall of the addition, as well as a complementary contrast between elements of the addition—between the massive stucco-clad masonry walls and the steel-framed building structure, wood cabinets, and glass windows.

View of addition, existing house and loggia from elevated rear garden.

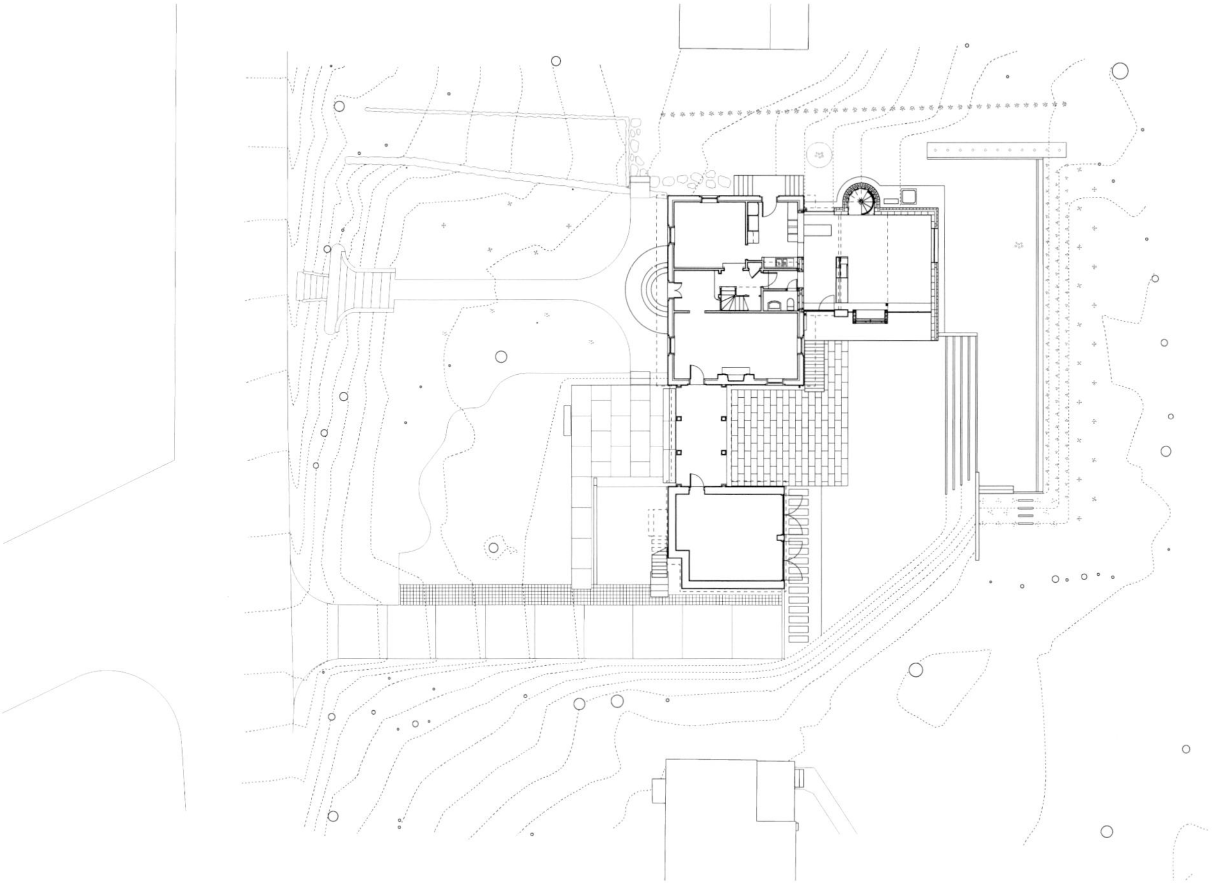

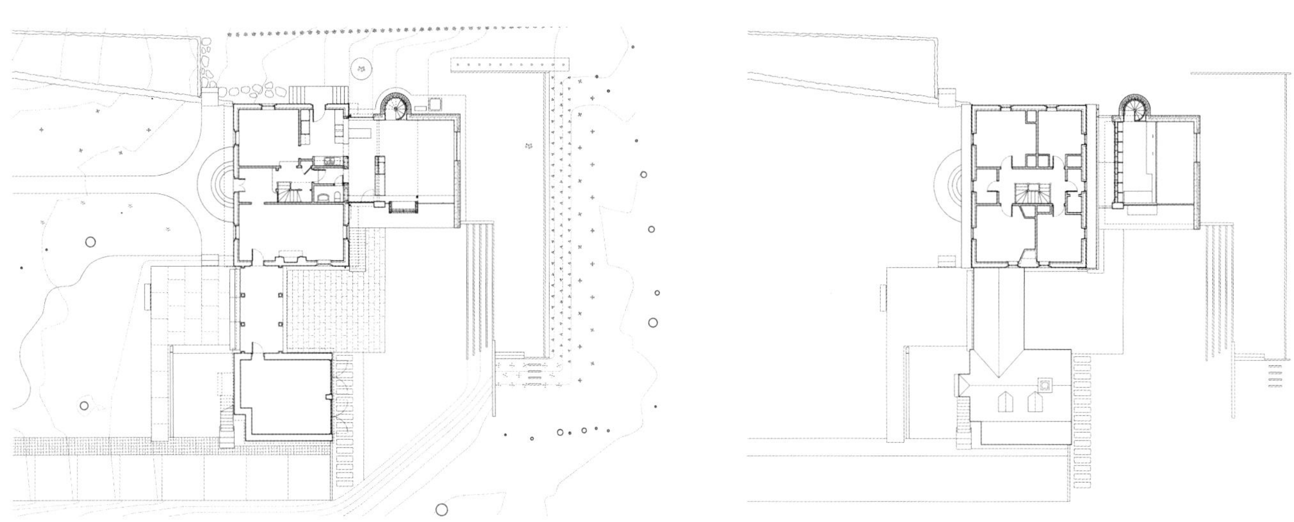

Site plan.

Ground-floor plan (left) and upper-floor plan (right).

View of addition, linking space and existing house.

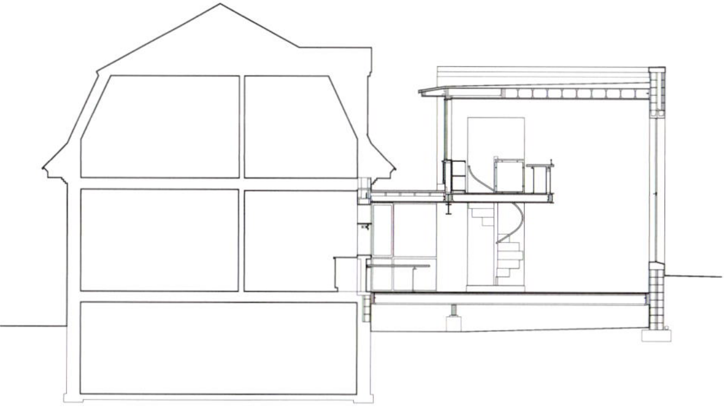

North-south section through addition (above) and east-west section through existing house and addition (below).

Exterior (above) and interior (below) views of wood-walled window seat.

View from renovated kitchen to breakfast room and family room.

View from breakfast room to family room and garden entry.

View of double-height family room, looking to garden.

View of lower-ceilinged area of family room, fireplace, and window seat.

View from upper-level study to garden.

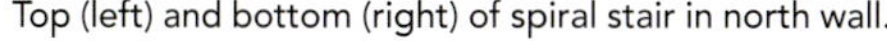

Top (left) and bottom (right) of spiral stair in north wall.

T he small commercial art gallery and artist's studio was built for the client and her artist husband adjacent to their existing house on a rural and heavily wooded hilltop northeast of Charlottesville. After a series of siting studies, Clark located the rectangular volume of the art gallery so that, together with the house and its freestanding garage, it shapes a loosely defined entry courtyard for the complex, not unlike the vernacular farm buildings in the rural area surrounding the site. The new gallery projects to the east, and is the first building visitors see upon arriving at the end of the steep approach drive. The gallery entry is on the west side, towards the house, so that visitors approach from the paved courtyard.

The building contains a commercial art gallery on the ground floor, an artist's studio on the upper, mezzanine floor, and a basement for storage and mechanical. The basement and foundation walls are cast concrete, the walls are wood frame, augmented by steel pipe columns, the floors and roof have wood joists, and the windows are framed with metal on the exterior and wood on the interior. In plan, the rectangular building is composed of four walls that are arranged to form two L-shaped walls, the north and east walls being primarily solid, clad on the exterior with Corten steel panels (a steel formulated so that its rust forms a protective coating) and on the interior with white stucco plaster; and the south and west walls being primarily glazed, with steel-framed windows outside, wood frames inside, and glass. Diagonal tension is thereby created between the open and glazed southwest corner, where the entry is located, and the more closed and solid northeast corner, at the back of the gallery and studio.

The pairs of walls shape the relationship between outside and inside, in that the solid, Corten steel-clad north and east walls are seen upon approach as one drives up the hill, and the open, glazed south and west walls are only seen after arriving to the court and approaching the entry. The four walls shape the interior by their arrangement in a pinwheel or rotating configuration, elevated off the ground and supported by the exposed concrete foundation walls. The ends of the solid north and east walls cantilever past the corners of the concrete foundation wall, and both walls are carried above the roof. The glazed south and west walls stand on the concrete foundation and terminate in, and are covered by, the over-sailing butterfly roof, which is folded along the east-west axis, and which cantilevers to the south and west. The roof overhang to the south is precisely calibrated to shade the glass wall from the high, summer sun and to allow the low, winter sun to enter and warm the interior.

The wall facing the entry court is made of glass block, with a section of Corten steel-clad wall at the east end (housing the bathroom), while the wall facing the house is composed of projecting and receding sections, perforated with vertical and horizontal glazing, that step back to form a re-entrant corner at the entry porch. The largest cantilever of the butterfly roof covers the entry porch, from which the concrete floor extends out to form the raised entry walkway that runs along the north edge of the entry court. Stepping inside, the white stucco soffit of the entry porch continues inside to become the white plaster ceiling of the double-height space, the floor changes from concrete to wood, and ahead is a staircase giving access to the upper, mezzanine level. The staircase has wood treads and open risers, and is set between the glass block wall on the outside and a solid, white plaster wall on the inside. Two thin, cylindrical steel columns stand just behind the non-load-bearing glass-block wall to the right, and two matching steel columns emerge from the top of the solid wall on the left, where they rise to

Les Yeux des Monde Art Gallery, Albemarle County, Virginia, 2007–2009

   A PRACTICE OF MAKING PLACES

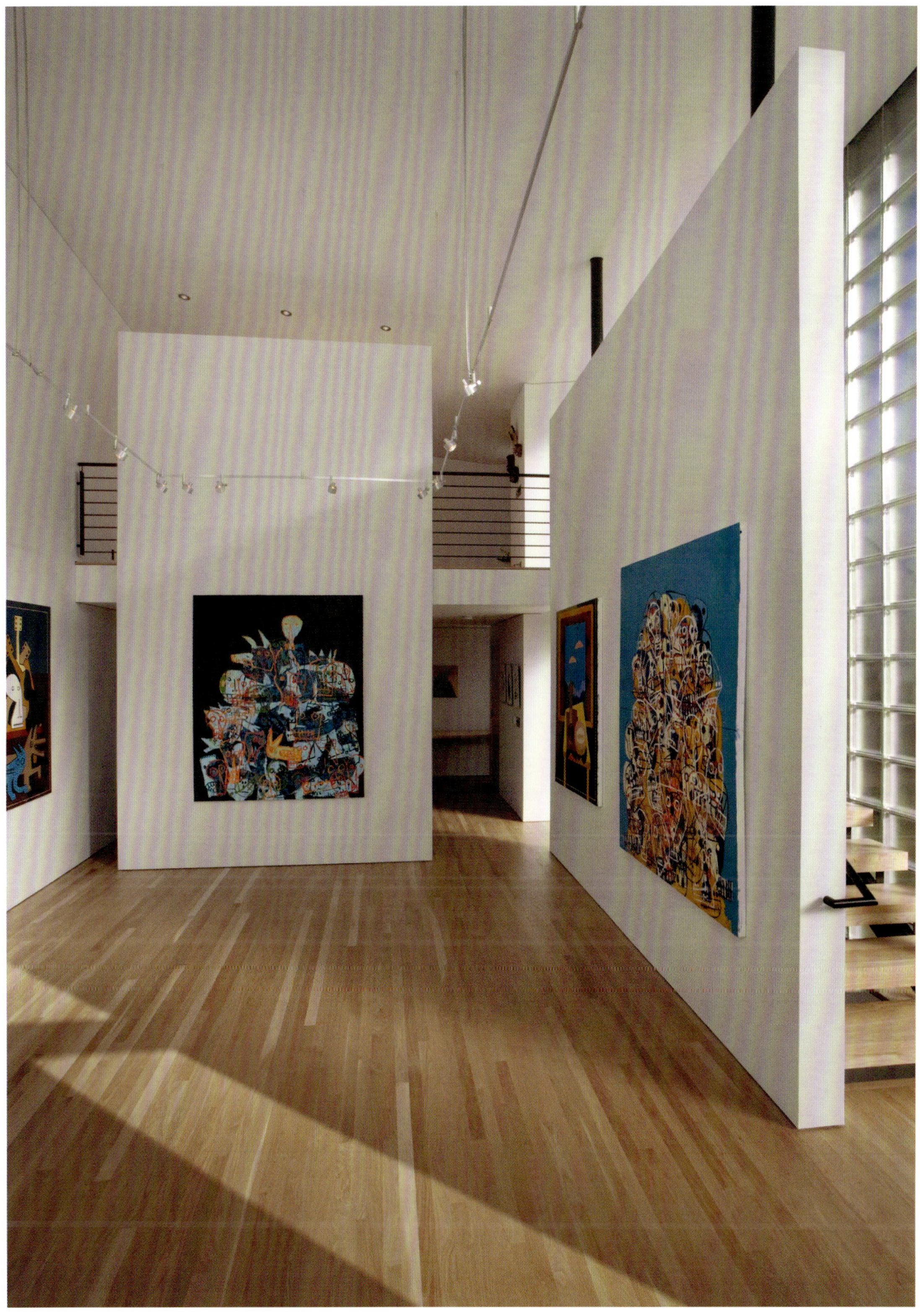
View from gallery towards office, below, and studio, above, with stair to right.

meet the fold at the valley of the ceiling beneath the butterfly roof. The butterfly roof is asymmetrical, supported off-center in the room, so that the narrower section of ceiling slopes upwards to the right, over the staircase, while the wider and higher section of the ceiling slopes upwards to the left, spanning across the main gallery space.

Inside the gallery, the majority of the artworks are hung on three large white plaster walls. The solid north outer wall rises from floor to ceiling, while the inset wall to the east, behind which is the office below and the studio above, is set away from the walls to either side as well as from the ceiling, and the inset wall to the south, behind which are the staircase and the glass block wall, is the shortest. In the office and studio behind the east wall, light enters at the northeast and southeast corners of the building, and the walls are separated and articulated by joints of light. In each corner, one of the solid Corten-clad walls is projected while the other wall is retracted, forming a recessed niche opened by a vertical glazed slot, through which daylight washes along the white stucco interior surface of the projecting wall. In addition, as north light is considered the ideal light for painting, the office and studio are illuminated by the large, projecting steel-framed window opened in the otherwise solid north wall.

The west wall of the gallery is a complex folded plane perforated with windows of varying dimensions and proportions, above which the folded white plaster ceiling continues from inside to outside, cantilevering outwards. At the southwest corner, the interior face of the recessed entry is a fully glazed vertical band, adjacent to which is a solid outward-projecting wall aligning with the wall on the inside of the stair and with the valley of the folded ceiling. The projecting, bay-like central volume, which is largely solid above (allowing paintings to be hung among the varied windows), is only opened by a long narrow window in the left corner, and by a wide window set at the ground that gives a view down to the ground and lawn (as in a Japanese tea house). The southeast corner, where the outer edges of the solid north wall and glazed west wall meet, is opened from ceiling to floor by the largest window in the gallery, through which one can see the white surface of the solid north wall continuing from inside to outside, through the glass, and cantilevering out over the grass lawn.

During the day, the light enters the gallery from all sides, each in a different way: in broad geometric blocks that wash across the floor, in thin slicing lines that demarcate the joints between surfaces, and in a general luminous, diffused glow that suffuses the space. In contrast, in the evening the building glows like a Japanese lantern, and the white stucco surfaces of the cantilevered walls and roof are washed with light, forming a white frame around the glowing volume, setting it off from the darkness surrounding it.

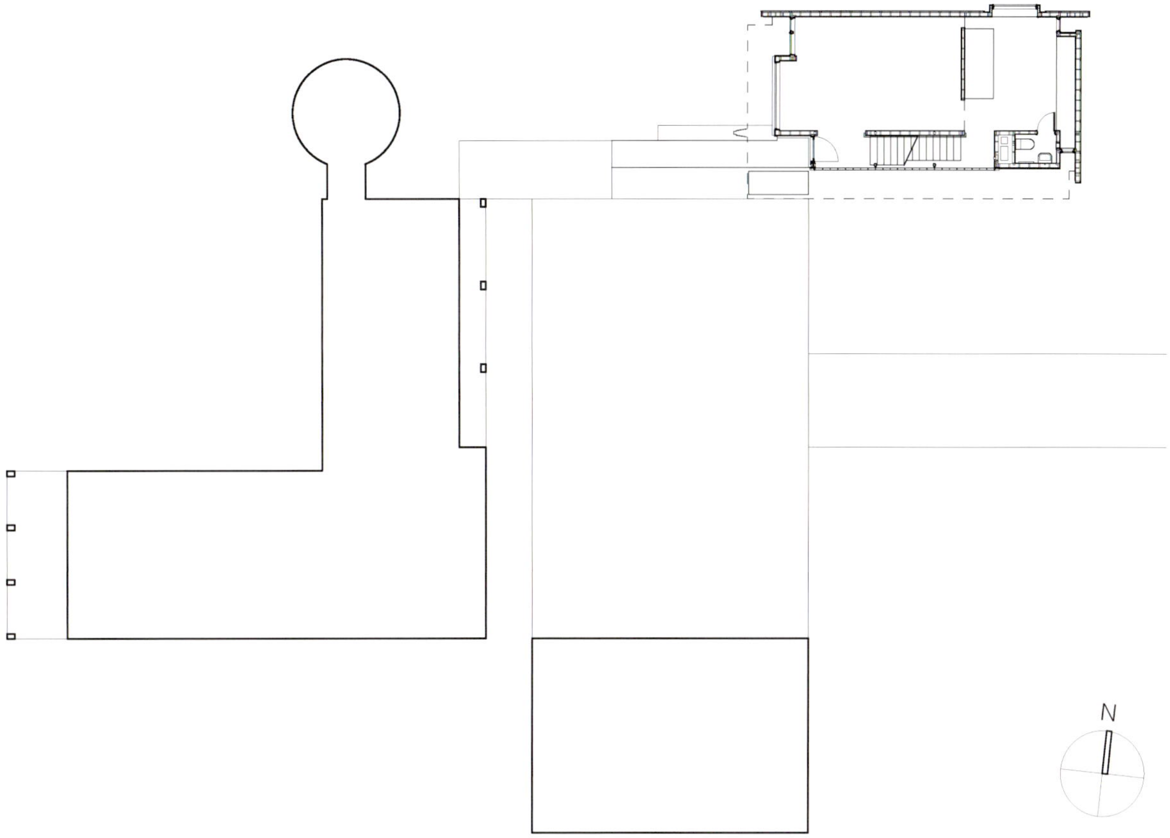

Site plan.

Site model.

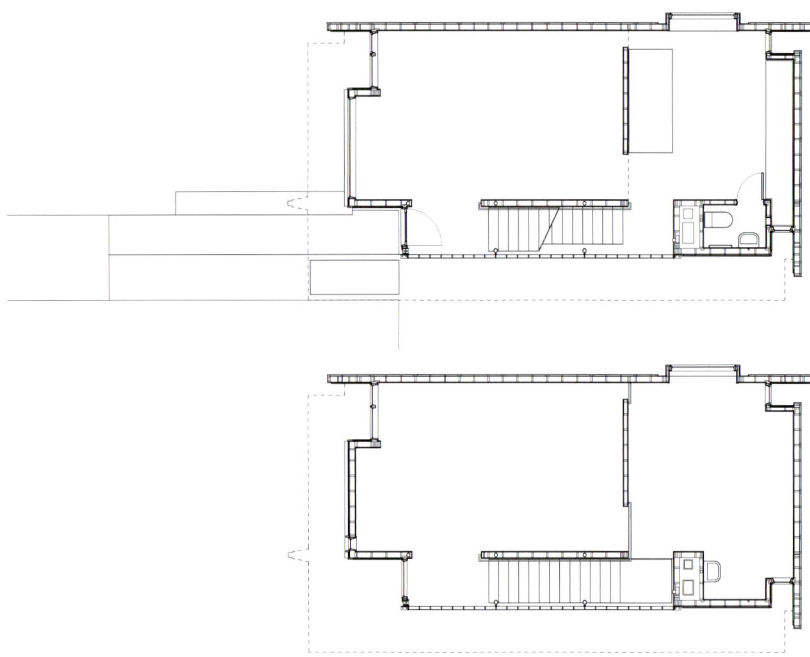

View from northwest.

Ground-level plan (above) and upper-level plan (below).

A PRACTICE OF MAKING PLACES

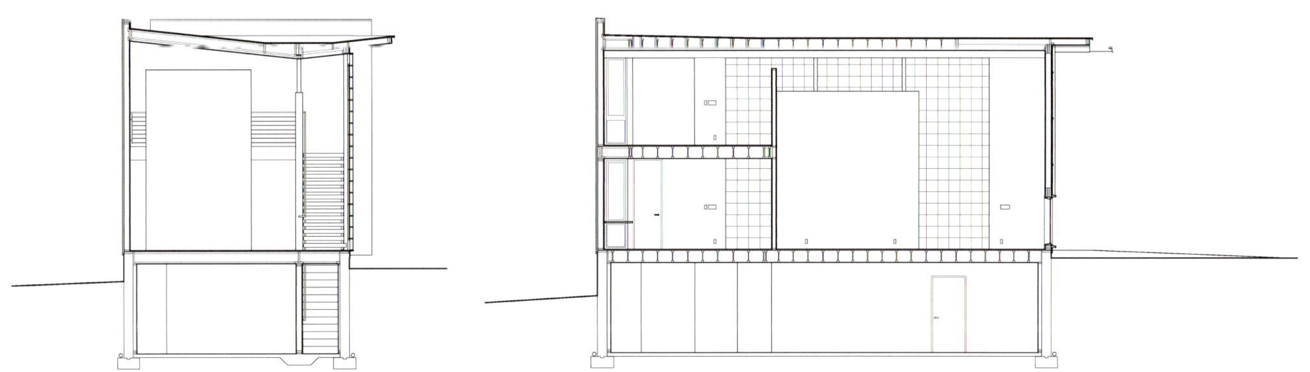

View from southeast.

North-south section (left) and east-west section (right).

View of entry from southwest.

View on approach, seen from west.

      A PRACTICE OF MAKING PLACES

Stair up to studio, seen from entry foyer.

View of gallery looking west.

View of gallery looking east.

Evening view from southwest.

The commission for Clark's most recently realized works came from the monks of the Mepkin Abbey, a monastery of the Order of Cistercians of the Strict Observance (better known as Trappist), who requested a design for a retreat or guest house for visitors to the monastery, as well as consultation on a series of smaller projects. Mepkin Abbey, founded in 1949 by monks from the Abbey of Our Lady of Gethsemani in Bardstown, Kentucky, was built on a beautiful site along the Cooper River, 30 miles north of Charleston, on 3,132 acres of land that was donated to the Diocese of Charleston by Henry and Clare Boothe Luce.

By the code of their order, Cistercian monks are committed to prayer, seclusion, work, poverty, and chastity, and to a life of withdrawal, solitude and silence. Their daily rituals include seven prayer services, the first at 3:20 am and the last at 7:35 pm, interspersed with work on the Abbey farm, reading, and private meditation. They do not actively recruit new members, believing that their way of life is a vocation, wherein the individual responds to a call from Jesus. Yet, hospitality is also central to the daily lives of Cistercian monks, and the atmospheric beauty of their land, bordering the Cooper River to the west and south, with its enormous live oak trees hung with Spanish moss, draws visitors who often would like to stay for longer periods at the Abbey.

In 2006 the land of the Abbey, along with several neighboring properties, were placed under a conservation easement to protect the natural environment. In a 2018 interview, Father Stan Gumula, Abbot of Mepkin Abbey, indicated how much the monks value the landscape of their Abbey – and the degree to which they and Clark share ethical principles of building: "In everything we do here, we try to respect the land, the ecology, the environment. The main architecture is the trees. All the buildings have been built around the trees."[1]

Prior to commencing work on the design of the guesthouse, Clark was commissioned to design a new set of gates and a sign for the entrance to the Abbey from the state road, which is separated from the Abbey buildings and gardens by a dense forest. Due to the monks' desire to encourage visitors to the Abbey grounds, Clark's intention was to detail the gate in such a way that it could be welcoming even when closed. Set between the existing brick walls and piers, the new entry gates are composed of steel sections, bronze plates and mahogany railings. The two low, Z-shaped steel frames are supported from pivot-hinges, which are in turn anchored to low, L-shaped concrete foundation walls, with bronze panels at the inner ends and cylindrical counterweights at the outer ends – these last can be adjusted as needed to counteract any deflection or sagging over time. When opened, the gates nest into the space provided above the L-shaped concrete foundation walls, and when closed they present to the street a cross that is carved from one of the pair of bronze plates at the center, with a slotted lock at the rear. The wide oval section of the mahogany railing at the top of each gate invites the touch of the hand.

The Abbey sign, which is set outside and to the south of the new gate and the existing brick piers, serves as a counterpoint to the horizontal gates: a vertical L-shape of gray powder-coat-finished steel plate, anchored to a small concrete footing. The sign, with vertically-stacked letters carved out so as to read as being made of light, fills the left side of a cross formed by a vertical plate and a pair of horizontal square bars that intersect by threading through rather than abutting, leaving the joint between them as a void, charging the space around it. Due to only the left side of the cross, nearest the road, being filled by the solid steel plate carrying the sign, the right arm of the cross appears to point towards the Abbey

View of chapel, courtyard and surrounding cloister-loggia-porch.

entrance gates. The sign is first seen from the south side, calling attention to the entrance for those coming from Charleston, but the letters can be read only from its north side, after making the turn onto Mepkin Abbey Road.

The guesthouse and meditation chapel, formally named the Saint Francis Retreat Center and Father Francis Kline Memorial Chapel, continues the Cistercian tradition of welcoming to the Abbey and its gardens visitors who stay varying lengths of time, and who participate in some aspects of monastic life. The guesthouse and chapel are located a short distance from the existing Abbey buildings on a peninsula framed by a series of ponds to the north and the broad expanse of the Cooper River to the west. The building is placed close to the ponds, and the 16 guest rooms form an L-shaped exterior space, with 10 guestrooms in the north wing and six guestrooms in the east wing. The larger commons building, with living room and library, kitchen, conference room, and offices, is placed to the west of the end of smaller guestroom wing, turning the corner so as to form a J-shaped plan, enclosing a courtyard space on three sides. The freestanding meditation chapel, which is the tallest of the buildings, is placed to the south of the longer guestroom wing, a position that allows the chapel to both hint at the missing fourth side of a traditional closed courtyard, as well as to stand in the courtyard's open end. The courtyard opens to the west, to the Cooper River, which is visible through the live oak wood.

Clark's design for the guesthouse and chapel may be understood as a reference to and transformation of the classic monastic plan-form, as exemplified in the Certosa di Galluzzo, just south of Florence. The plan of the monastery, where a cloister courtyard is enclosed by the monastic cells on three sides, with the larger mass of the common rooms and church set along the courtyard's fourth side, as well as the plan of the individual monk's cells, inspired many of the works of Le Corbusier, who first visited Galluzzo at age 17 and thereafter considered the typical monk's cell to be the ideal house type. Louis Kahn considered the monastery to be the ideal plan-type for all institutional buildings, employing it in his designs for the Indian Institute of Management and the Salk Institute (where the monastic courtyard at Assisi inspired the paved court at the center of the Institute), among other projects.

Yet Clark's interpretation of the monastic plan type in the guesthouse is subtle, informal, and intentionally incomplete, the courtyard more implied or suggested than actualized in the open-ended J-shaped plan. This informal approach to the formal monastic precedent plan-type is also evident in the way the chapel and the north wing of 10 guestrooms are aligned precisely on the cardinal directions, while the shorter wing of six guestrooms and the commons building are rotated slightly to the east, as if the inner corner of the L-shape of guestrooms was a hinge, opening the courtyard to the river. Informal also is the fact that the four elements defining the courtyard—the two guestroom wings, the commons building, and the chapel—do not meet at the corners, with the resulting open corners accentuated by 45-degree-angled walls that direct the view out into the woods. But, in a mark of the carefully calibrated balance of formality and informality of the design, the open reading of the plan is contrasted and counterpointed by the roof, which spans across the open corners, re-asserting the J-shape of the larger plan by the shape of the shadow it casts on the ground.

In the end, the literally open-ended and informal quality of Clark's plan can also be understood as a response to the institutional and architectural context—to the fact that the existing Abbey buildings comprise a low, L-shaped volume with wings on the north and east sides, and a taller, freestanding chapel that anchors the southwest corner of the square courtyard subtly implied by the L-shaped volume. This reading is reinforced when one realizes that Clark has employed the same construction materials as were used in the existing monastery buildings: concrete floors, stucco-clad masonry walls, and copper-clad roofs with the wood framing exposed beneath.

The guesthouse is entered along a straight walkway that cuts across the parking area to connect the Abbey entrance to the roofed entry porch at the southeast corner of the guesthouse, set between the commons building and the east wing of guestrooms. The importance of the entry porch is subtly denoted by the bronze cladding applied to the exterior wall of the conference room to the left, while the diagonal wall on the right directs the view inwards to the courtyard, at the inner corner of which is the entry to the commons building. The guest rooms are sheltered beneath and shaded by the deeply overhanging copper-clad roof, which slopes downwards towards the courtyard. Where it covers exterior spaces, the roof structure is exposed beneath, with wood tongue-and-groove boards carried by wood joists, which in turn bear on steel beams that are carried on widely-spaced steel columns. The entries of the guest rooms are recessed into the stucco-clad concrete masonry walls, and they open onto a paved walkway space that is framed at its outer edge by a low and wide concrete wall, onto which the steel columns bear and on which we are invited to sit. Beyond the low concrete wall, a wide band of stones frames the inner edge of the courtyard in front of the two guest room wings. The center of the courtyard is defined by a field of small gravel, with a line of five trees along the north side. The gravel terminates against the stone paved terrace at the center of the courtyard, off of which a long thin walkway extends to the chapel entry.

The 16 single guest rooms have concrete floors, stucco-clad masonry walls, and full-height steel-framed glass walls on the forest side. Each guest room is unified by the plywood ceiling that slopes down from its highpoint over the window wall on the forest side to the entry foyer on the courtyard side, where it folds down and forms the low, flat ceiling that also covers the toilet and shower. The bathroom and dressing area are visually separated from the bedroom by a plywood closet cabinet and wall behind the sink, the top of which aligns with the low ceiling over the entry. On the other side of the plywood wall, a plywood platform holds the bed, and the plywood plane then turns the corner and folds up to form the desk by the window. The stucco-clad masonry walls, concrete floor slab, and sloping wood-framed roof all continue out past the steel-framed window wall, opening the guest room to the forest and pond outside.

Along the south side of the courtyard, the paved terrace wraps around the glass-walled commons building, and, diagonally across the courtyard from the chapel, the entry to the commons building opens off the covered entry porch. Like those over the guestroom wings, the roof of the larger commons building slopes downward towards the inner courtyard and upwards towards the outer edge. The entry foyer of the commons building has a flat plywood ceiling (similar to the guest rooms), a concrete floor, plywood tabletop, and cabinets on the walls of the offices to the left, and long plywood benches set between massive concrete piers and in front of the full-height steel-framed windows on the right, which looks out to the courtyard. The plywood ceiling of the large living room and library slopes upwards towards the south, and the room is opened on three sides by full-height steel-framed windows, the tallest on the south side, opening towards the existing Abbey.

The continuous, low, inward-sloping copper-clad roofs of the guest rooms and the common rooms, and the deep shadows they cast throughout the day, reinforce the fundamentally horizontal character of the cloister-like courtyard. The horizontal layering of material and shadow of the courtyard is counterpointed by the vertical character of the freestanding chapel, which is given by its roof, which takes a diagonal butterfly form that slopes upwards and outwards on all sides, exposing the wood and steel structure beneath, as well as by its tall walls of stucco-clad masonry and steel-framed frosted glass, which glow brightly when struck by sunlight throughout the day.

The chapel is approached across the paved terrace at the center of the courtyard, at the edge of which a low, wide concrete wall, like a continuous bench, anchors and frames the south side of the paved walkway that extends from the terrace to the chapel. To the right of the walkway is the gravel floor of the courtyard garden, and the chapel walls stand in a narrow band of stones, which extends out on the northeast corner to receive the rainwater spilling from the single large scupper draining the entire chapel roof – this likely a nod to Le Corbusier's Ronchamp Chapel, the roof of which is similarly drained through one scupper. The entry is at the far, western end of the chapel, closest to the river, so that one walks in front the south façade, past the steel-framed frosted glass window, and beneath the wood-framed roof, which is supported by a steel beam bearing on a single, tall, steel column, which in turn bears on the low concrete wall adjacent to the walkway – a single elongated counterpoint to the repeating rhythm of the steel columns carrying the roof along the perimeter cloister walk.

At the end of the walkway, the roof structure overhead and the concrete wall and walkway underfoot terminate in the solid stucco-clad chapel wall which folds out at a 45-degree angle in plan, forming the entry where the bronze entry doors, one wide and one narrow, open into the chapel. Three stucco-clad masonry walls, to the east, north, and west, and one steel-framed frosted glass window wall to the south, together form the space. Along the west and north walls the concrete floor is folded up to form low concrete walls that serve as benches. The fact that the interior bench-walls match the concrete bench-wall that parallels the entry walkway outside, which forms the foundation for the steel column, suggests that the benches are extrusions of the foundations below.

The rectangular plan of the chapel has been charged with diagonal tension by the disengagement of the four walls from each other, and the opened corners that result are highlighted by lines of light. The solid north wall slides past the solid west wall, which is slightly pulled away, and a sliver of glass is set into the joint. In a similar way, the solid east wall slides past the frosted glass south wall, which is slightly pulled away, and a sliver of clear glass is set in the joint. The other two corners of the chapel are more dramatically opened: at the southwest, entry corner, the frosted glass wall is folded outwards to form the entry foyer, and the frosted glazing above the bronze entry doors is projected outwards, opening a thin slot of clear glass over the door; while at the northeast corner, housing the minimal altar, the solid north and east walls are pulled apart, and into the space opened between the ends of the walls is set a concrete pier rotated to 45-degree angle and flanked by a wide window on the right, and a narrow, slot-like window on the left, so that here too the corner is sliced open with a line of light.

Reinforcing the diagonal emphasis on these two corners, the plywood ceiling overhead is folded into triangular sections, reflecting the diagonal butterfly roof above, and the center fold where the two inward-sloping planes meet slopes

Abbey sign, seen from road.

downwards from its high-point in the southwest corner, above the angled entry foyer, to its low-point in the northeast corner, above the altar, where the diagonal concrete pier supports the center fold of the plywood ceiling. Looking through the window next to the diagonal pier, the single scupper that drains the chapel roof can be seen hanging below the outer corner of the butterfly roof, where the cascade of rainwater falls into the gravel beds outside.

The degree to which the guest house and chapel serve their intended purpose as a retreat for those who wish to experience the contemplative character of monastic life, and the dedication of some part of one's life to a spiritual journey of renewal, has been proven by fact that the monks have begun to offer, in addition to the traditional short-term overnight or weekly stays, a month-long monastic institute as well as a year-long residency at the Guest House and Chapel, which is now, only five years after its opening, often fully booked months in advance.[2]

From top, view of right section of gate in open position, meeting of two sections of gate when closed, and detail of end of gate.

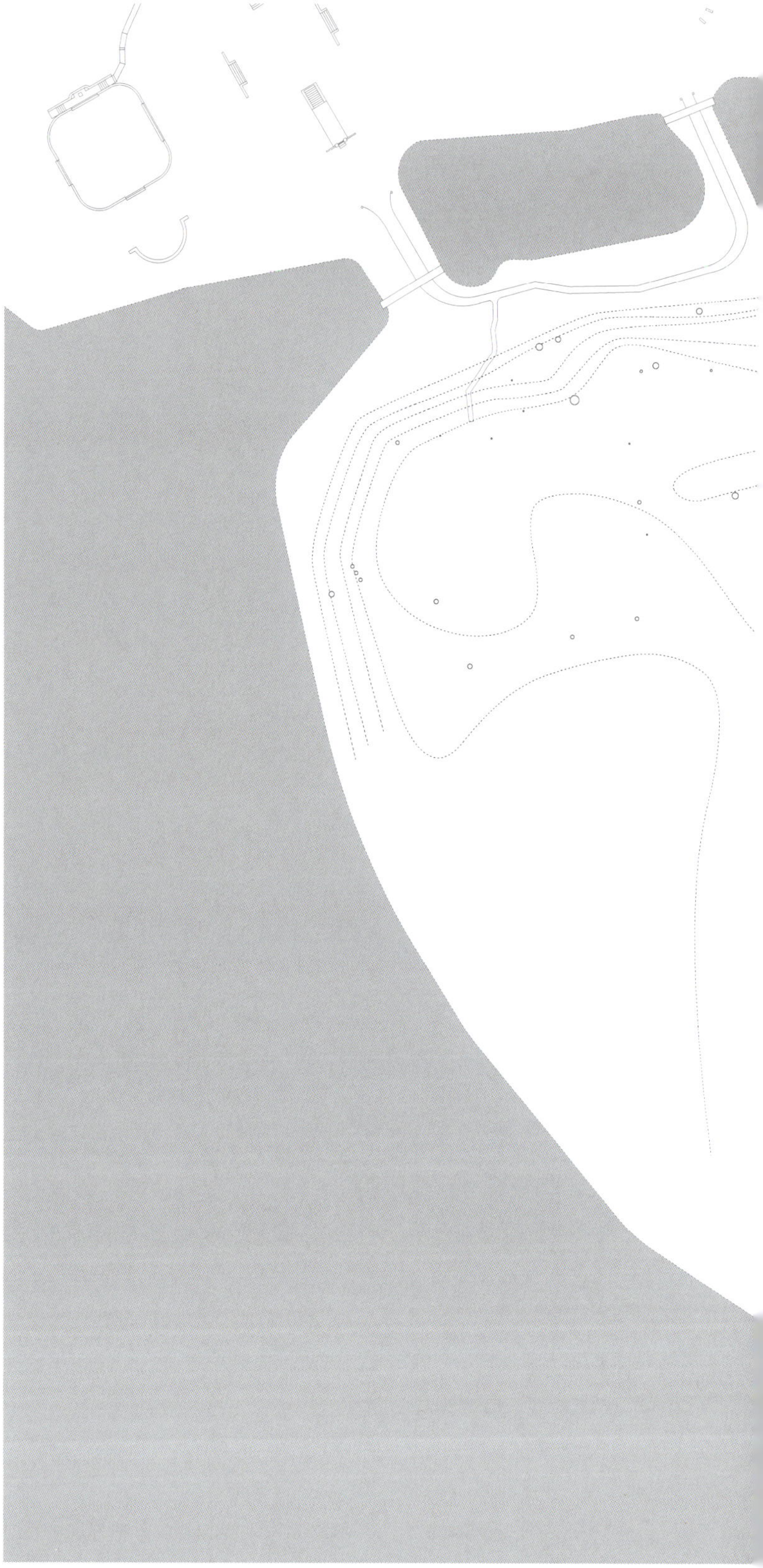

Site plan, with existing buildings at bottom.

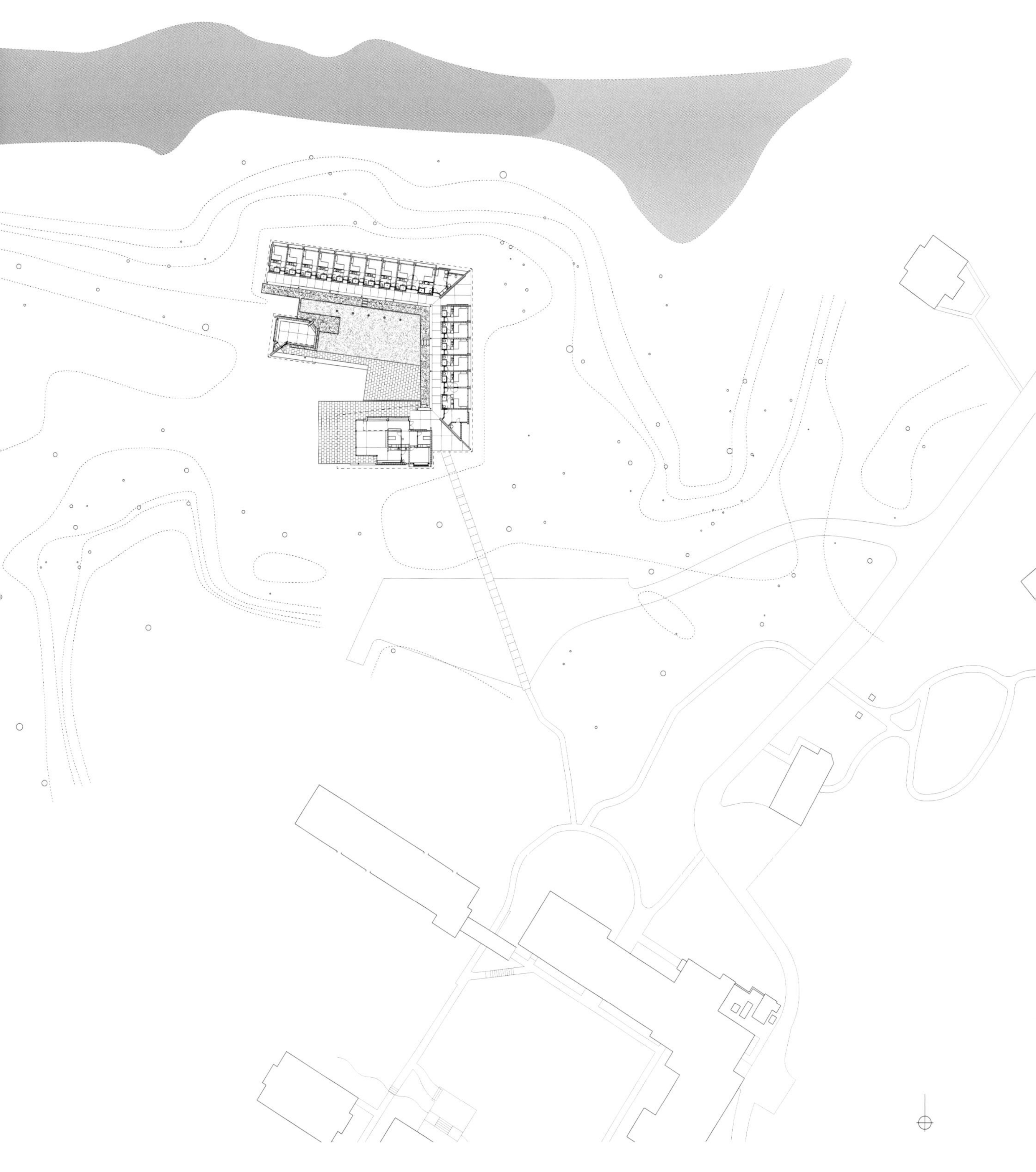

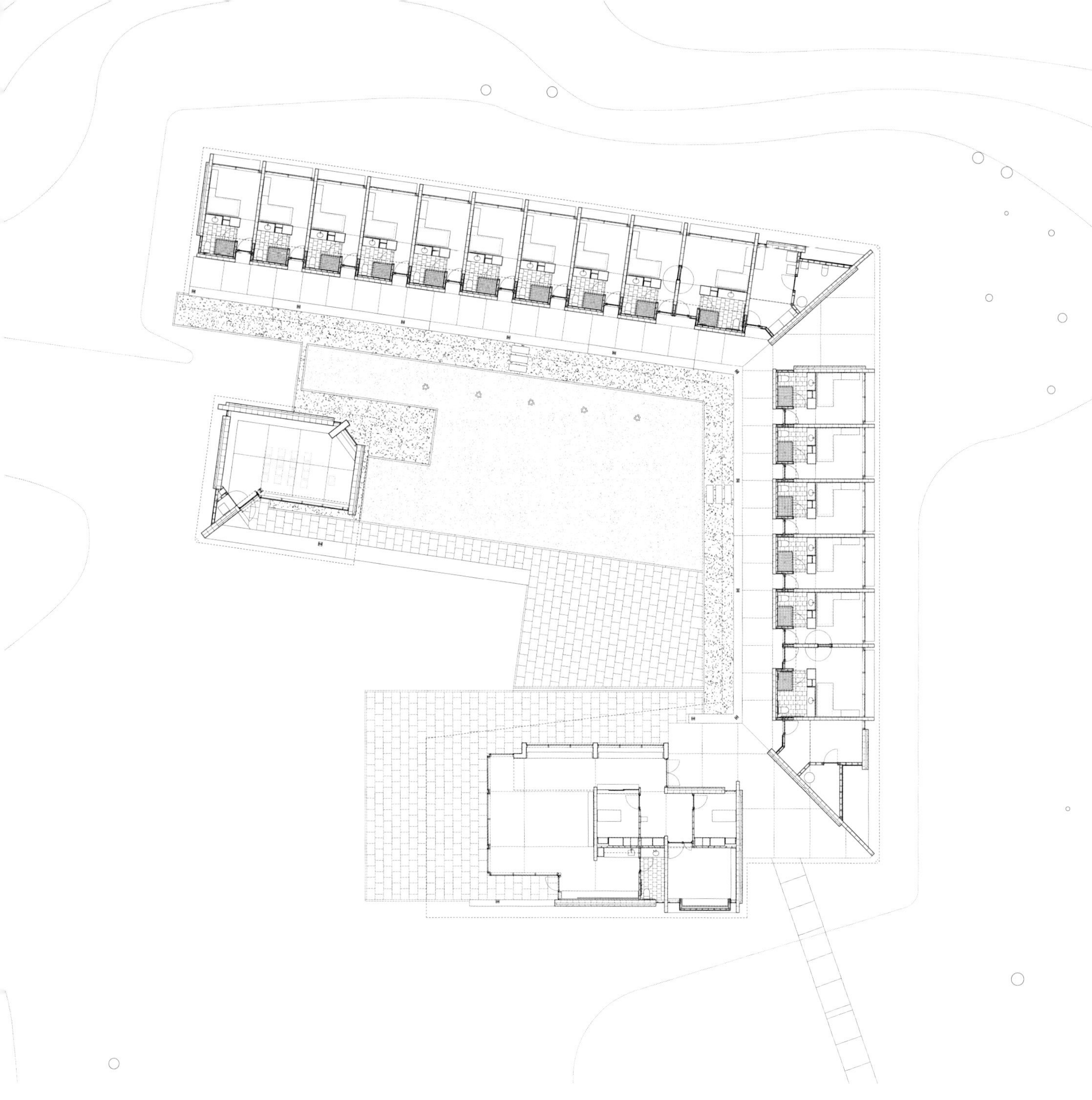

Floor plan.

    A PRACTICE OF MAKING PLACES

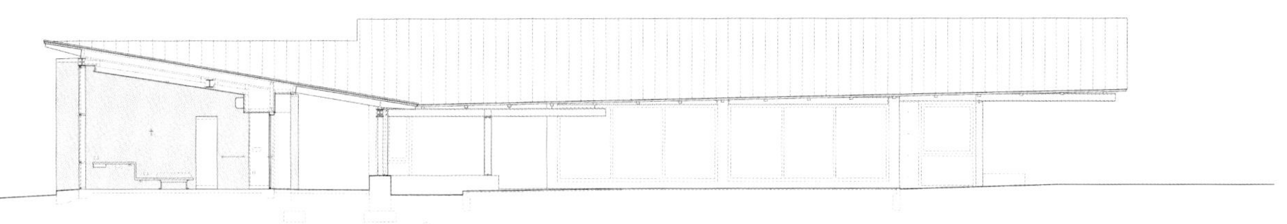

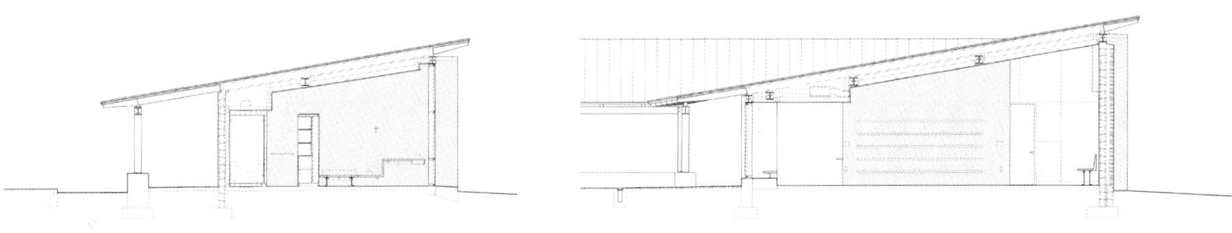

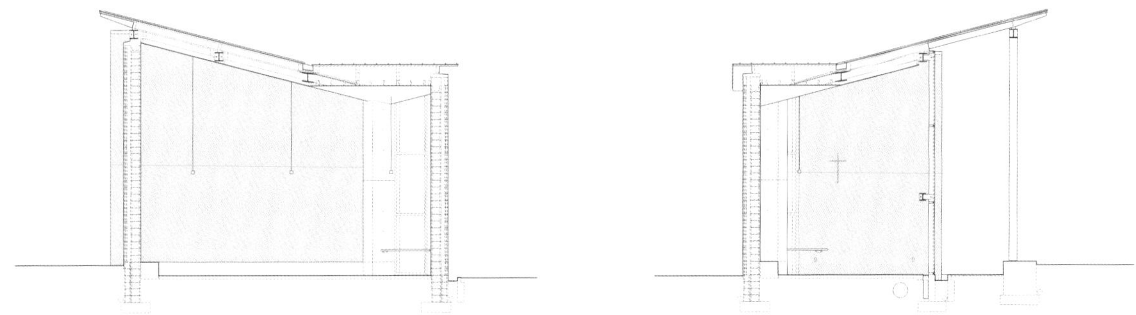

Sections of guesthouse, above, and chapel, below.

View from entry porch, with commons building (left),
chapel and court (center) and guest rooms (right).

View of guest room from entry, with dressing and bath to left (above), and bedroom and window (below).

 A PRACTICE OF MAKING PLACES

View into commons rooms from entry.

View along porch-loggia of guest rooms, looking towards chapel to the west.

View of chapel entry walkway (left) and chapel interior (right).

View from commons room covered terrace across court to chapel and guest rooms.

Chapel interior.

The architecture school at the University of Virginia is housed in Campbell Hall, a concrete and brick building dating from the 1960s, which is connected by an entry court and upper level bridge to the Fine Arts Library. The architecture buildings are sited on a hillside to the north of Jefferson's original university buildings, which with its central rotunda and its ten academic pavilions and student houses arrayed along the east and west sides of the Lawn, remains one of the most important precedents in American academic architecture. While the architecture school and library are oriented and positioned on an urban planning grid that was generated from Jefferson's buildings on the Lawn, the architecture school is not visible from the original campus.

The architecture school had outgrown its existing buildings by the 1990s, and the school commissioned designs for a substantial addition, first from Steven Holl, then from Brad Cloepfil of Allied Works, both of which were rejected by the university trustees as being too modern and insufficiently "classical" in their language. The idea that the late 20th-century addition to Campbell Hall, a modern design typical of the 1960s, should be classical, presumably in reference to Jefferson's original campus of 1817–25, rather than being a building of its own, contemporary time, is patently absurd, and indicates the University trustees' lack of understanding of Jefferson's design for University of Virginia, which was considered at the time to be highly innovative, and which was intended by Jefferson to be the most advanced building of its kind in the world.

Clark and the other architecture faculty believed as a matter of principle that students of architecture should learn about their future profession in buildings that reflected the time and place in which they were built, and that the mimicking of classical forms in buildings that are built with contemporary construction materials and methods, as was proposed by the trustees, was fundamentally unethical. In order to be able to realize the much-needed additions to the architecture school, a long-standing ban on university faculty being commissioned for work by the university was waived in this case, and several architecture faculty were commissioned to make the needed additional spaces as a series of interventions into the fabric of Campbell Hall.

Clark's design for the addition to the east of Campbell Hall, housing three new design review or jury rooms, along with a new stair and elevator, takes the form of a freestanding pavilion or tower, which is a tall, thin, and vertical complement to the horizontal composition, massing, and articulation of the much larger Campbell Hall and Library. Due to its prominent position at the east end of Campbell Hall, the addition now frames the entry sequence to the architecture school, which consists of a series of three stepped terraces leading from a larger plaza at the top of the hill (accessible by car), down a wide set of stairs to a pedestrian court adjacent to the review room tower, down another set of stairs and, after passing under a bridge joining the school and library, arriving to the entry terrace along the north side of Campbell Hall.

In plan, the review room tower takes the form of a rectangle that is elongated along the east-west axis, with wide, square façades on the south and north sides, and tall, narrow elevations on its east and west sides. The addition is built with cast concrete structural frame and floor slabs, with aluminium-framed windows opening to the west, north, and east of the jury rooms and a solid wall, with brick cladding (matching the brick in the existing buildings) on a concrete structural wall, on the south side. The complementary contrast of the solid, "mute" south wall—which blocks the intense south sun, provides structural bracing, and

View of jury room tower from the northwest.

provides privacy for the university president's house to the south—and the glazed, "active" north wall—which admits as much north light as possible, provides a new front façade for the school, and reveals the activities of the school on the north— was the inspiration for the design. As Clark notes, "It's interesting how place and purpose often conspire to make a room. The major façades of the addition face north and south. The design became that of a room made of two walls in opposition, one toward the south opaque to obviate glare, one facing north, translucent, gathering that gentle, ambient light."

The sequence of designs for the north façade of the review room tower involved the layering of transparent, translucent and opaque surfaces, attempting to balance the need to introduce the maximum amount of north light into the room with the need for sufficient wall space for the mounting of student project presentations. An early design for the façade, which included a substantial area of bronze panels that imparted a "brooding" character to the design, was inspired by the cast bronze façade of the American Folk Art Museum in New York, designed by Tod Williams and Billie Tsien.

The north façade as built is almost entirely glazed, and the square surface is framed at its edges by deep concrete piers on both sides and a deep beam across the top. The concrete piers are L-shaped in plan, with the legs turned outwards to east and west, so that when seen from an angle, the north façade is framed by a thin concrete edge, with a recess separating it from the glazed corners of the projecting east and west façades. The north façade is given a frame of a consistent depth, while the east and west façades have wider concrete frames on their south edges, and thinner frames on their north edges, so that the asymmetrically framed east and west façades defer to the symmetrically framed north façade.

Within the concrete frame of the north façade, the aluminium-framed glazing is set in three layers, the largest layer is set flush with the inner edge of the concrete frame, and consists of translucent glazing with narrow bands of clear glazing at the top and along the right side; a vertical recessed clear glass section towards the left side; and a deeply recessed, L-shaped section at the lower right, framed by a concrete slab and wall, within which a glazed vitrine to hold student models is set, adjacent to the descending staircase. The only solid portion of the façade is the projecting bronze-clad panel to the right of the glass vitrine, which houses air intakes and exhausts for the ventilation equipment. When seen from the exterior during the day, the translucent glazing becomes opaque white and the clear glazing is black, while at night the translucent glazing glows and the shadow patterns reveal both the layers of the façade materials as well as the inner layers formed by the presentation panels that stand behind the glass.

The new review room tower frames the south side of the brick-paved entry court, imparting to the space a distinctly urban quality. A concrete staircase descends in front of the review room tower, past the glazed vitrine, and arriving to the new stone-paved entry court at the first floor, where a new glass-walled lobby, flanked by new restrooms, provides access to the existing auditorium beneath the court, to the other rooms on the first floor of Campbell Hall, and to the new stairs and elevator in the addition. The jury room tower can also be entered at the three upper levels from the south side of the building: at the second floor, from the paved terrace, at the level of the entry court, which wraps around the east end of the building to access the doorway that aligns with the new stair; at the third floor, from the staircase that ascends from the upper plaza along the face of the retaining wall to reach the entry door behind the concrete elevator tower; and at the fourth floor, from the stair that ascends from the sculpture terrace at the top of the hill to the south. These three intertwining staircases and passages set against the steep hillside transform the daily movements of students and faculty into a kind of spatial choreography.

On the three upper floors of Campbell Hall, a glass-walled hallway, with symmetrical glazing framing a view across the entry court, connects the existing studios to the new jury rooms. The new stair, elevator, and mechanical shafts are housed in a concrete-walled vertical tower set on the south side, nearest the existing building, and the larger rectangular tower of the jury rooms is set on the north side, projecting out towards the east. The new four-story stair is a concrete masterwork, a continuous Z-shaped series of treads and risers cantilevering off the edge next to the hallway, from which it is separated by a steel-framed screen of frosted glass panels. The Z-shaped treads and risers reveal the stepping of the stair from below, and cast changing shadow patterns on the frosted glass scrim. The stair is slightly different in configuration at each level, from the first floor where the stair opens off the sunken entry court, to the fourth floor, where an exterior stair spans out to the sculpture terrace and views open in all directions. The views out of the building and the play of sunlight within the staircase changes at each floor, complementing the subtle variations in character of each of the three jury rooms.

The three jury rooms, stacked one above the other, are held within the massive concrete frame that bounds and defines the northern façade, infilled with sections of clear glazing and translucent, Opalux insulating glazing, which fronts onto the entry court. The end walls of the jury rooms are opened with clear glazing that runs vertically from the bottom to the top, full width on the east side and a narrower band on the west side, both of which fold inwards to form small glazed corners on their north sides. While similar in plan, the three jury rooms are subtly articulated in relation to their place in section, and how that relates to the original building and the surrounding campus. The second-floor studio engages its position at the ground level of the entry court, its translucent glass section shifted to the eastern edge to provide privacy from passers-by, which is complemented by the large glass vitrine set into the other end of the room, in which student models are displayed. The upper two jury rooms are given matching north elevations, with large translucent glass panels framed by a narrower clear-glass band at the west end, with recessed clear glass set within the field of translucent glass near the east end. The difference between the two upper jury rooms is not in plan or elevation, but in height, with the third-floor jury room being the same height as that on the second floor, while the fourth-floor jury room is one and half times taller, so that its short section is a square in proportion.

Inside the jury rooms, the concrete floor slabs turn up along the solid south side, and this stepped floor can be read as composing a frame with the concrete piers at either end, as well as being folded out from the concrete wall above it. Both readings are reinforced by the thin slot of space opened in the L-shaped concrete pier at the end of the room, which bounces south light around the corner, creating a slot of light that cuts the concrete pier away from the concrete wall. In the taller top-floor studio, this reading of light cutting the structure apart is continued across the ceiling, where the concrete beam is similarly cut away from the concrete back wall by the south light from the narrow clerestory opening above the roof. The lines of south light are introduced through recessed slots of space formed by the L-shaped-in-plan piers at the corners of the south façade, which separate the brick wall from the concrete frame on the exterior at the corners and across the top at the roof. In counterpoint to the exposed structural piers and beams at the edges of the room, the smooth plywood ceiling at the center of the room (which conceals ventilation ducts and wiring, and from which the lighting fixtures are hung) is set flush to the bottom of the concrete beams.

The east wall of each jury room is fully glazed, passing in front of the floor slabs to join all three jury rooms in section. At the eastern end of each jury room a wooden bench is set, accommodating students attending their colleague's jury. The west wall adjacent to the existing building is glazed only in the outside corner, while the inner corner is a concrete wall that accommodates the entry, which is accomplished by a large, pivoting, wooden door that opens against the solid wall. The north wall is brilliantly illuminated by the light coming through the translucent glass panels, and provides the majority of the room's generous natural light, which is constantly changing throughout the day. In the varied use of natural light in these rooms, Clark is again close in spirit to Louis Kahn, who held that daylight gave each room its mood and atmosphere, and that a room is not a room unless it is given natural light, so that the occupants can perceive by the angle and intensity of the sunlight the change of the hour, the day, and the season. In addition to being anchored in place and time by the play of daylight, Clark also notes, "Natural light allows longer juries."

Wooden panels are affixed to the solid concrete south walls to allow drawings to be pinned up, while on the glazed north wall a series of ingenious pivoting wooden panels, which can be rotated to lock in three positions, with the inner and outer faces of panels parallel to the glass wall, and, with the panels at 90 degrees to the glass wall, allow use of both panel faces to accommodate twice the number of students. A large fold-down table is set in front of the clear glass panel in the north wall of the two upper studios, allowing the jury rooms to also be used for seminars and meetings. When the table is folded down, those gathered around it are given an expansive view to the north. At night, the pivoting wood panels and fold-down table play their part in revealing the layering of the north façade through the shadows they cast on the translucent glass panels.

The small vitrine for displaying student models in the second-floor façade may be said to be complemented by the continuous clear glass bay-window-like curtain wall of the jury rooms that projects slightly on the east façade, facing the approach from the main campus, which reads like three large, room-sized vitrines, which both display the students' work and present the students at work. The principle underlying the design of the jury rooms is that of putting rooms in service of architectural education, and in this Clark believes the transparency of the windows, particularly on the east side facing the campus, is of critical importance: "Transparency is a necessary characteristic of design education. We learn from seeing the work of others. Wishing to extend this transparency to the outside, the east end of the building is clear glass so that what we do, the beautiful student work, is visible to passers by." This was proved true soon after the building was completed, when the president of the university, whose residence is just up hill to the south of the architecture school, was walking his dog one evening near dark. The president stopped on the upper plaza, across from the east façade of the review room tower, where the activity of the design jury that was taking place within the brightly illuminated room could be seen clearly through the large windows, and said, "You can see education taking place here – maybe the whole campus should be built this way."

In a sentiment shared by Clark, Kahn believed that review rooms are the most important room in the architecture school, and that therefore they should be made in a way that honors architectural education. Of the jury room, Kahn said, "There should be something wonderful about it, and it should always be a friendly room. It's always a sanctuary, you see … It is the sacred space in the school of architecture."[6] The final design juries, the most important pedagogic event in the life of the school, now take place in rooms that hold innumerable lessons for architects and students of architecture. Like Kahn teaching for 10 years in the top-floor studios of his Yale Art Gallery, Clark is teaching students not only through his inspiring words and constructive criticism, but by way of the students inhabiting the spaces he has made.

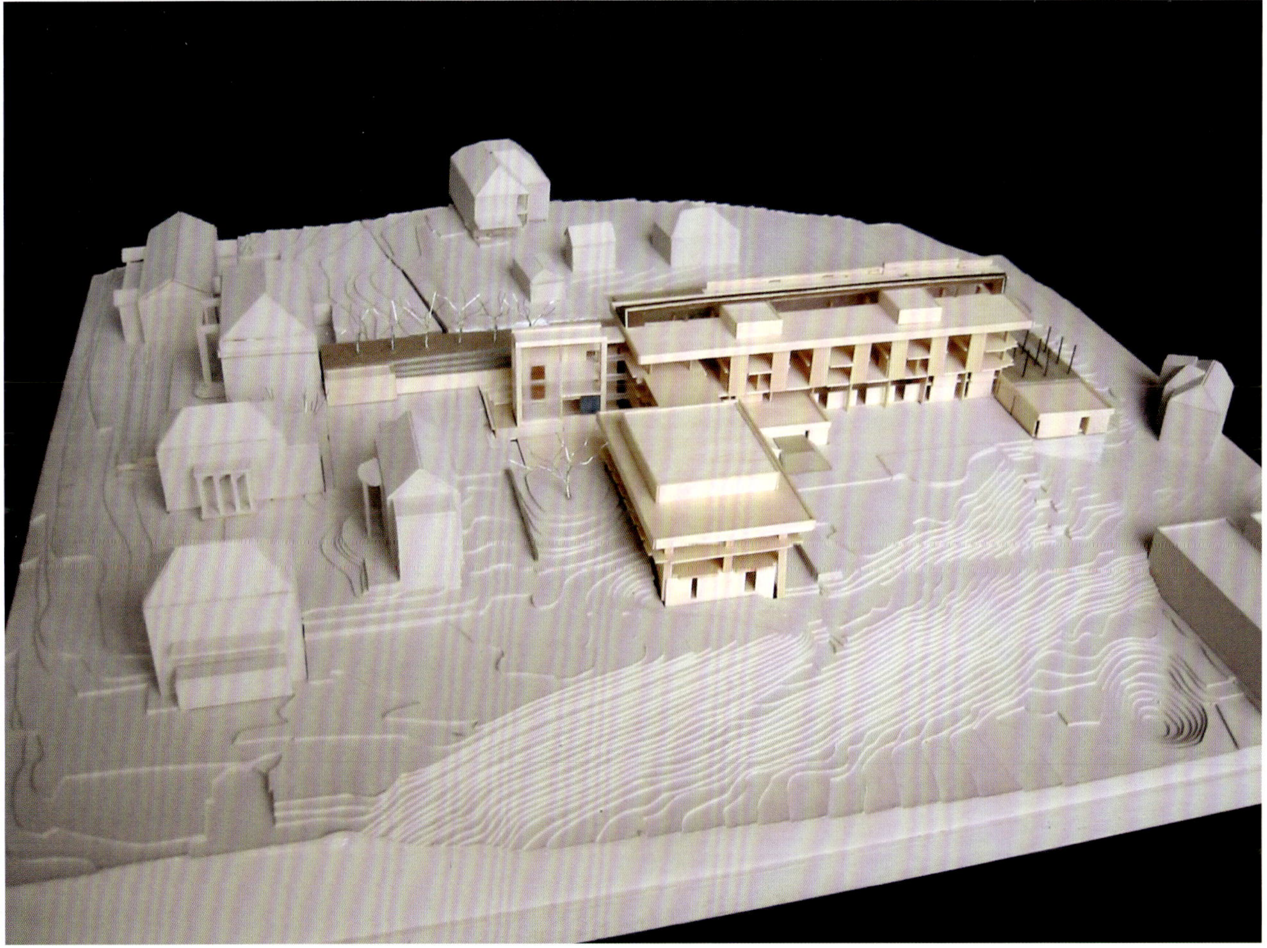

Site model.

Design study models.

Perspective sketch from north.

Perspective sketch from east.

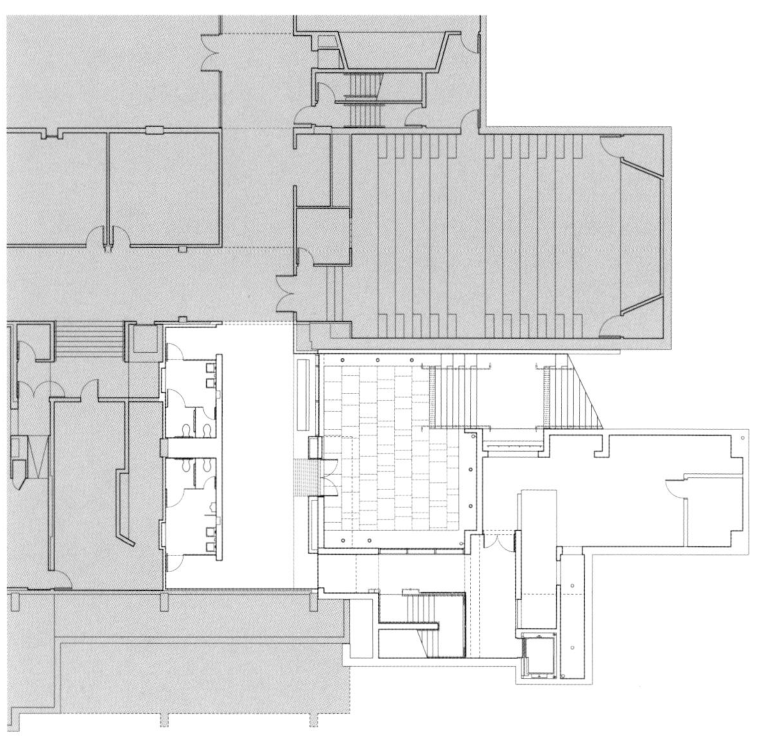

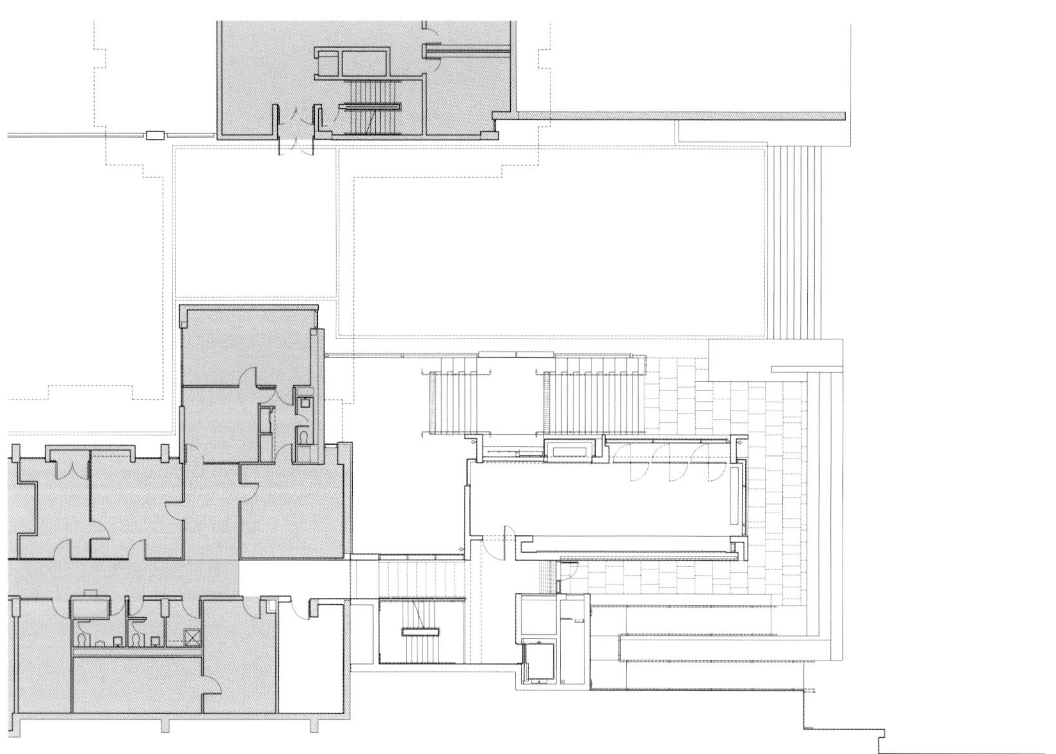

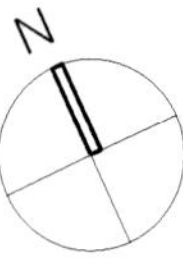

Lower, first-floor plan (above) and second-floor plan (below).

 A PRACTICE OF MAKING PLACES

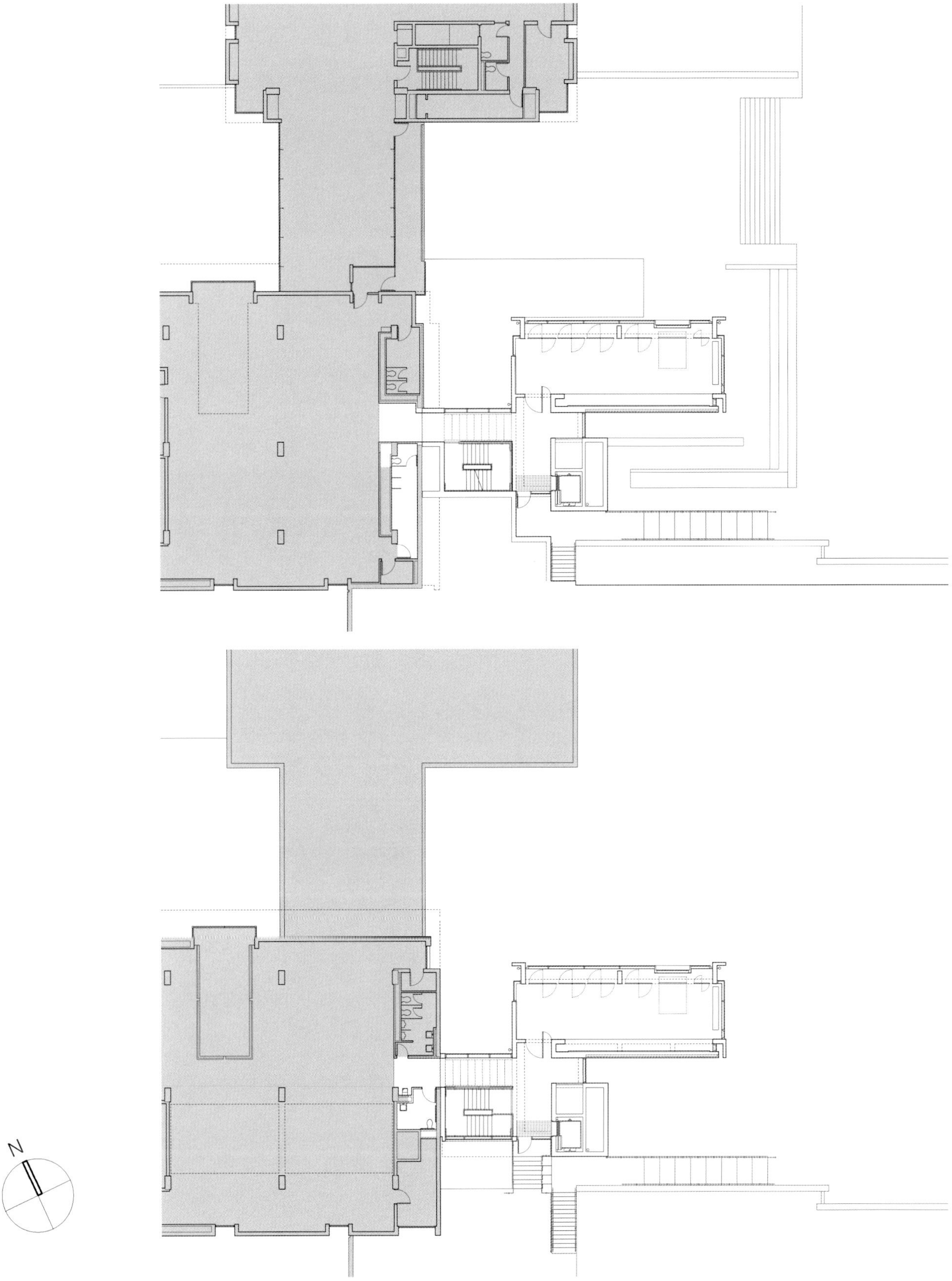

Third-floor plan (above) and fourth-floor plan (below).

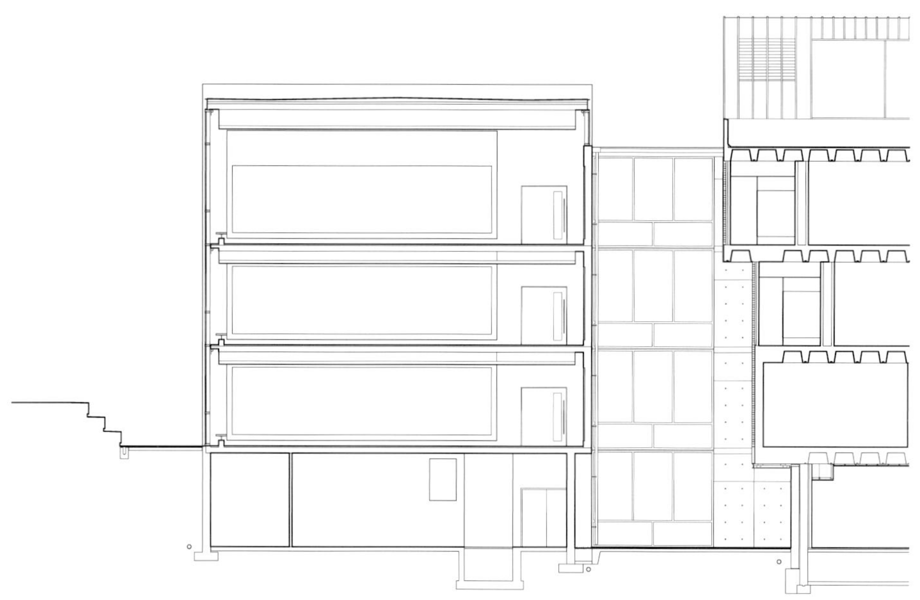

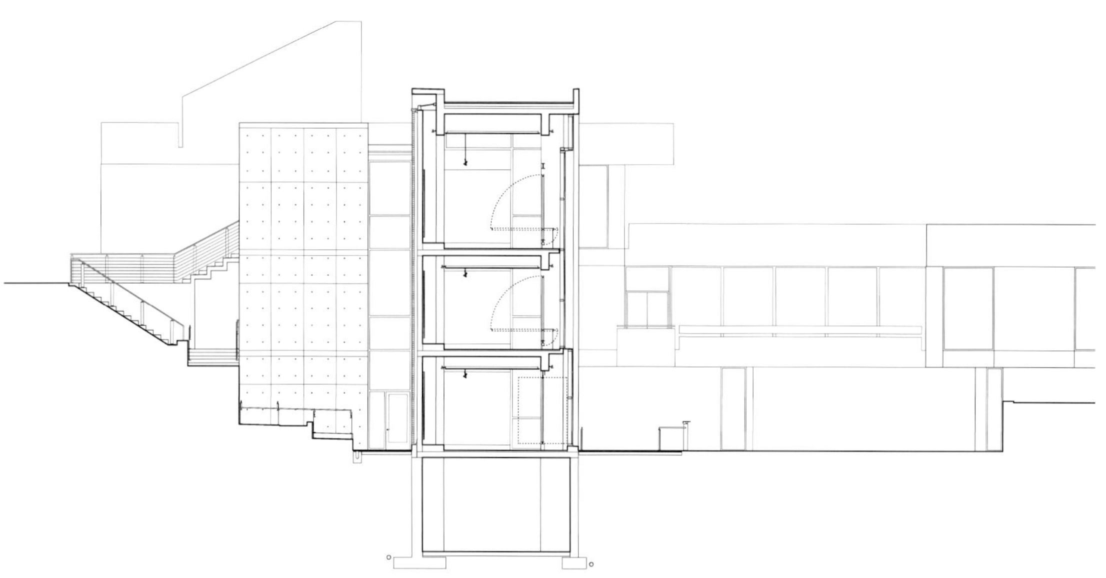

East-west section (above) and north-south section (below).

View of tower and entry court from northeast.

View of north elevation.

View from southeast of tower and hillside terraces and stairs.

View of display vitrine and bronze panel at entry stair.

View of top-floor entry bridge from hillside to south.

View from existing pedestrian bridge to northwest.

View of concrete stair from foyer.

View of stair from landing (left) and detail of frosted glass scrim wall (right).

Views of the top floor jury room set up for reviews (above), with display panels pivoted (below left), and with pivoting table lowered for meetings (below right).

Evening view of new tower, existing building and entry court.

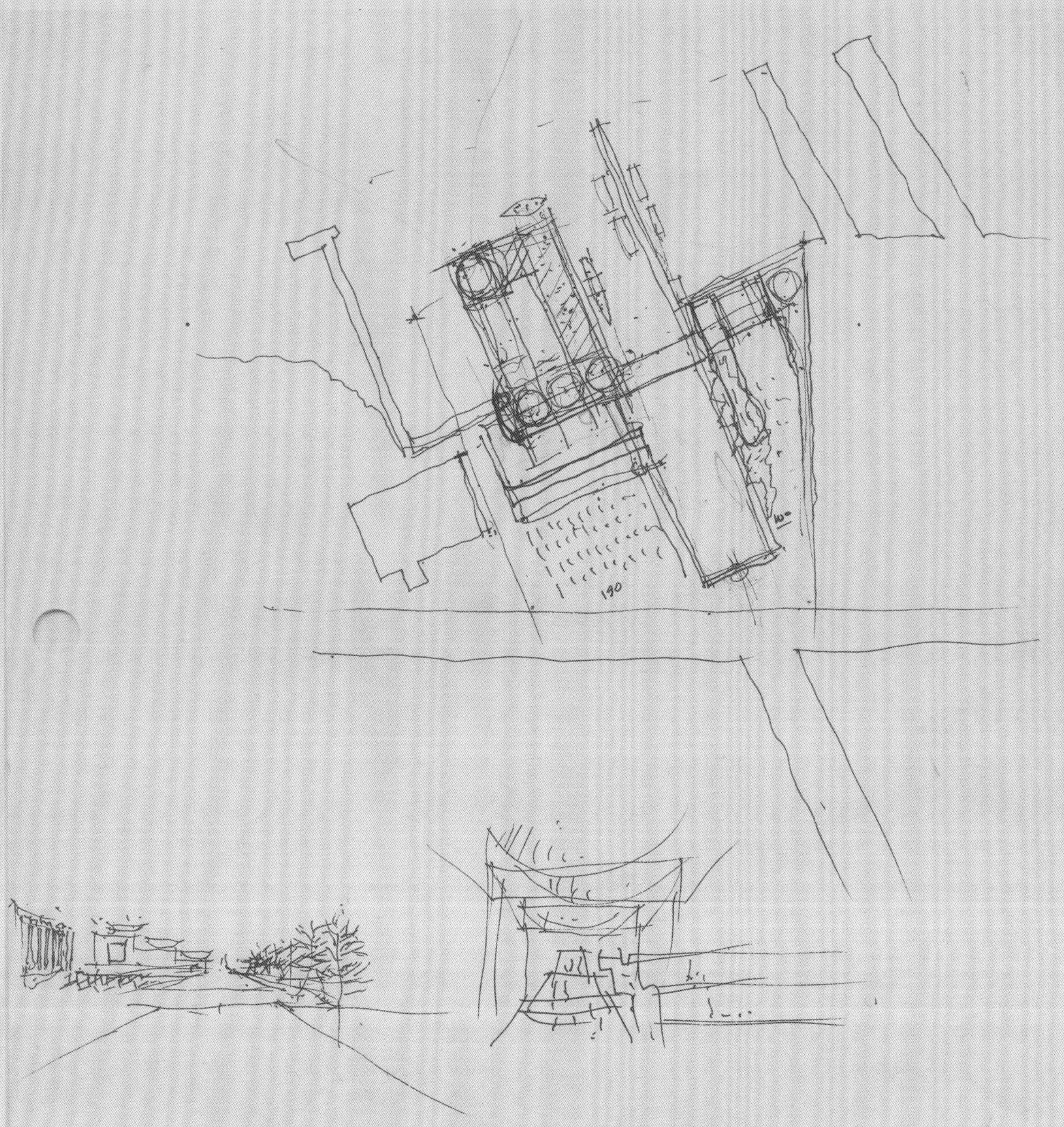

Design sketches for South Carolina Aquarium competition; plan, above, and perspectives, below.

I n a lecture that WG Clark gives annually to architecture students at the University of Virginia, in which he employs his own works as examples of the process of thinking and making in architecture, he often concludes by presenting the jury room addition to Campbell Hall. He describes how, from the first day of their program of study in architecture, the students will present their design work in the new jury rooms on two to three occasions each semester, four to six times a year, and that during the design review they will each receive at least one half-hour of criticism from the four senior professors who are sitting as the jury. Clark concludes by making the simple observation that while anywhere else in the university, the only students who would receive such generous and sustained attention from senior professors would be PhD doctoral students, architecture students benefit from this level of commitment on the part of the faculty from their first day at school until the conclusion of their course of study.

Any discussion of Clark's university teaching has to be paralleled by a discussion of his architectural practice, for they are inextricably intertwined in the work of practitioner-teachers such as Clark. He began his practice in 1974 in Charleston, and shortly thereafter, in academic years 1976 to 1978, during the time he was working on the Middleton Inn, he was appointed as a visiting design studio critic at the University of Virginia. In 1988, 10 years later, Clark was appointed as a visiting design studio critic at the Graduate School of Design at Harvard University. That same year he was appointed Professor and Chair of the Architecture program at the University of Virginia, moving his practice from Charleston, South Carolina to Charlottesville, Virginia. He was Chair of Architecture at the University of Virginia from 1988 to 1990, and for the last 30 years he has been the Edmund S. Campbell Professor of Architecture at the University of Virginia, his teaching paralleled by his practice in Charlottesville.

It often comes as a surprise to non-architects to learn that many university professors of architecture do not practice—and in some cases have never practiced—the discipline that they teach. While we expect our doctor who teaches in the university medical school to practice what he or she teaches, in architecture schools this is often not the case. This disengagement of practice and teaching, almost always accompanied by the rise of so-called "theory" disconnected from practice, and described as "thinking without making," is something that can only occur inside the university. Standing directly opposite this tendency are those such as Clark, whose parallel careers as architect and professor is similar to that of Louis Kahn, who practiced continually while teaching at Yale University and the University of Pennsylvania from 1947 until his death in 1974, or Carlo Scarpa, who practiced continually while teaching at the Instituto Universitario di Architettura Venezia from 1926 (the year it opened) until his death in 1978, as well as serving as Dean of the IUAV from 1972–78. Practitioner-teachers such as Clark are also able to employ their own work as examples in teaching, a long-standing tradition in the studio design disciplines, including Paul Klee's use of his own paintings to exemplify the principles he was imparting in the basic design course at the Bauhaus; Josef Albers's similar use of his own paintings to demonstrate ideas at both Black Mountain College and Yale University; and, most pertinently for this discussion, Louis Kahn's use of his office projects as the programs for his studios at the University of Pennsylvania.

Design sketch model for house project.

The degree to which the disengagement of theory and practice in architecture schools has alienated practitioners from the disciplinary discourse over the last two decades of the 20th century is reflected in Clark's 1997 statement, made in response to a request from the editors of *Perspecta* 28: "We have been asked to comment on our theory and methodology. I am not aware that we have either. I don't believe that either is necessary. We do know that all building involves the use of a place and that all architecture, regardless of program or cost, must become that place. The things that we admire most accomplish this either through an architecture of innocence or through an architecture of emplacement which seeks to make the building and the place one thing. This makes the job quite difficult since it is probably impossible for an architect to achieve innocence, and just as unlikely that one can achieve that profound engagement of building and land, which is so maddeningly easy for primitive man. But I think we all crave an ancientness, which we never had, and an innocence which we have lost, desperately, if futilely, seeking their realization."[1] This statement of Clark's first principles begins and ends with place, and the idea that the fundamental ethical obligation of architecture is to become its place; that a building should improve its place; and that architecture is an act of adoration for the place – for WG Clark, place matters.

In his more than 30 years of teaching architecture, almost all of which has taken place at the University of Virginia, Clark has endeavored to present the ordering principles and insights into design he has evolved in his 50-year practice. More recently this effort has found a new focus in the construction of his seminar on "how to design," which he calls *Thinking and Making*. The seminar syllabus, which constitutes a statement of Clark's ordering principles, is distilled almost entirely from his practice, so that students understand that theory is drawn from practice, that practice is not drawn from theory, and that thinking and making form an inseparable whole in architectural design: "Design is thinking and making. Thought is both generative and self-critical. Making is both experiment and determinate."[2] As a way to begin the seminar, Clark has employed as the epigraph on the course syllabus a quote from E.E. Viollet-le-Duc's *Entretiens sur l'architecture* (Lessons on Architecture) of 1872: "The first condition of design is to know what we have to do; to know what we have to do is to have had an idea; and to express this idea we must have principles and a form, that is, grammar and a language."

The first of three primary ordering principles that Clark sets out for the *Thinking and Making* seminar is: "A building should improve its place; architecture is an act of adoration for the place." The tradition of practice, shared with Wright and Kahn, in which Clark engages daily, is one that recognizes, as Viollet-le-Duc noted: "We must endeavor to proceed like the Greeks; they invented nothing, but they transformed everything."[3] This has more recently been paraphrased by Alvaro Siza: "Architects do not invent anything – they transform reality."[4] Such transformation begins with the place where one is asked to build, and the definition of architecture as making the place better after one works there than it was before. The architect begins with the

Design sketch plan and elevation, Telluride House.

history of the site, from its "original" natural condition through all the permutations of its inhabitation and use over time. This leads directly to the recognition that all new building are additions to pre-existing places, whether urban, suburban, or rural; as Clark states, "Every building is an addition; define to what it is an addition."

For Clark, place matters, and it follows that the most important design document is the site plan. It is the task of the architect to construct additions that make their locations, and the larger world, a better place. He encourages his students to make their own site plans, and to endeavor to document the history of the land, showing the changes it has undergone over time, and to draw what was there before. This also extends to the ethical principle of always designing on the site plan, so as to always keep the context in view, and to understand that the new building and its site are only a fragment of a larger order, which the students should endeavor to draw into their design. Though it seems a matter of common sense, Clark urges his students to never draw or present their building without its landscape or urban context, and to remember that every building occupies an ancient part of the earth, which should be honored in the design.

Clark's second primary ordering principle is that design and craft are inseparable, and that the architect must seek an economy of both gesture and material in their buildings. The tradition of practice in which Clark participates begins with the understanding that architecture is a discipline with a history from which lessons may be drawn, and that architects (and students of architecture) only learn from the work of other architects, past and present. Parallel to this is the realization that "we only know what we make," as Carlo Scarpa translated Giambattista Vico's *Verum Ipsum Factum*, and that the conception and construction of architecture are inextricably intertwined. Vico's aphorism can also be translated as "truth is in the made," an idea that is intimately engaged with a profoundly ethical pedagogical concept of edification. As Gianni Vattimo noted, "Edification has two principle meanings – to build and to be morally uplifting. That is, edification must be ethical, entailing the communication of value choices. In the present situation, the only possibility of edifying in the sense of building is to edify in the sense of 'rendering ethical,' that is, to encourage an ethical life; to work with the recollections of traditions, with the traces of the past, with expectations of meaning in the future."[5]

For Clark, architectural ordering principles invariably have aesthetic, ethical, and constructional implications. In this, the craft of construction is critical, and Clark has developed a close relationship between structure and light, using light to separate masses and materials, as well as to articulate the constituent elements of a building through the revelation of the joints between. Following Kahn, Clark reminds his students that as architects, they have to take their un-measurable ideas and make them measurable in the act of building, and the resulting designs must be spatially, materially, structurally, and functionally resolved. In this crafting of the essential, the models Clark most often references are the result of a local material culture, such as vernacular buildings, Shaker buildings and traditional Japanese houses. The emphasis is on how economy and the use of minimal materials and resources can result in maximal experiential enrichment for the inhabitant of architecture. In this Clark is close to Gaston Bachelard's concept of the "material imagination," which recognizes the degree to which the materials of which a building is made affect our experience.

Clark holds the word economy in high esteem, parallel to Kahn's idea of "the poetry of economy"; economy of gesture and conciseness, when applied to materials, results in the absolute essential, unfolded as the most rigorous yet restrained relationship of parts within a structure. Clark believes that constraints make architecture better, noting they can be a source not of frustration, but of inspiration. In this he is paralleled by the modern composer Igor Stravinsky, who pointed out the fundamental truth that without limitations there can be no freedom: "Human activity must impose limits on itself. The more art is controlled, limited, worked over, the more it is free."[6] Wright argued that without limitations, there could also be no exercise of the imagination in architecture: "The human race built most nobly when limitations were greatest and, therefore, when most was required of imagination in order to build at all. Limitations seem to have always been the best friends of architecture."[7] As Clark notes in his essay on the lessons of constraints and the inspirations arising from limitations: "The importance of constraints on architecture cannot be overstated," going on to note, "their profound necessity [and] their ability to inspire design."[8]

In the third ordering principle that is drawn from his practice, Clark argues that the first step in the design process is often to question and critique the building program given by the client, which has generally been conceived only in terms of private agendas, and not with the larger public good in mind. In particular, it is essential for students and architects to question the program as regards its appropriateness to the place in which it is proposed to be built, and its appropriateness as regards the economy it will require to be realized. Louis Kahn, who late in life said, "I teach appropriateness. I don't teach anything else,"[9] also argued that architects must, as he said, become "the philosopher" for their clients, who usually do not recognize the importance of the institution of which they have been given responsibility. Rather than unthinkingly following the program, the architect must act on behalf of the larger culture and society of which both he or she and the client are a part. This principle and the concern regarding appropriateness that generates it are part of the tradition of practice, as evidenced by Viollet-le-Duc's 1872 statement, "When an architect is called upon to erect a building, a confused scheme is probably laid before him—for written programs are generally such—and it rests with him to bring these elementary instructions into something like order."[10]

Design sketch model for house project.

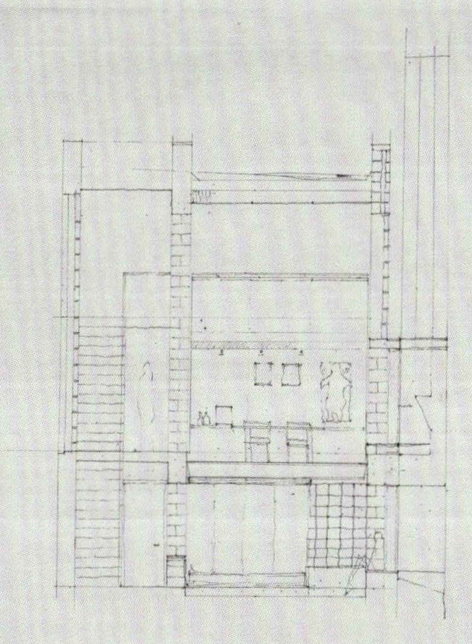

Design sketch section, Clark House.

THINKING AND MAKING

Design model of interior, Hillman House.

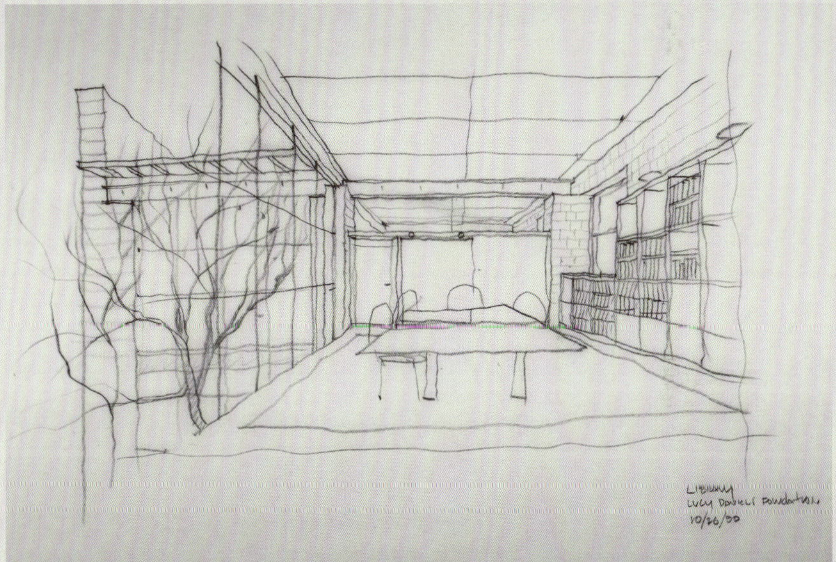

Design sketch perspective of library, Lucy Daniels Foundation.

In summary, Clark's lessons regarding "thinking and making" and "how to design" center around learning from the site, context, and land; learning from local building and craft culture; and learning from the discipline of architecture. Clark suggests that his students remember that design is not linear, rather it is most effective when it is constantly moving back and forth from the largest to the smallest scales. He suggests that students learn to simultaneously see their project through four "lenses": designing the building as part of a much larger context and place; designing the building as a composition in its immediate landscape, asking if the building becomes its landscape; designing within the floor plan, as what Kahn called "a society of spaces"; and designing the section, and how the parts and materials go together, how they are structured, and how these determine the experience of the inhabitant.

For Clark, architectural design begins and ends in the room and its materials, fittings, and furnishings that integrate architecture and its use through its being inhabited. Kahn believed that "the room is the beginning of architecture," and, similar to Kahn, Clark believes that each room should be articulated so to have its own structure, independent of the other rooms, as if it were a separate building, and the plan is the ordering of these room-buildings into a larger composition. As a primary illustration of the importance of the room at this finest grain of architectural design, which Clark calls "investments in the room," he employs Antonello da Messina's *St. Jerome in his Study.* The painting presents a view of the saint sitting at a wooden desk, set within a raised wooden room, with his books and intimate belongings surrounding him and within easy reach. This double-layered wooden-walled room, small and intimate, warm to the touch and sheltering the body, in turn stands within a larger, taller, massive masonry-walled space, cold, hard, and uninviting to touch, which is itself one bay of a multi-bayed sanctuary structure. The way in which the entire space, from the individual body scale of the built-in furnishings, to the collective public scale of the stone vaulting of the monastery church, to the extended cultivated landscapes seen through the windows, are all precisely scaled by and ordered by the interior experience of the inhabitant—the saint at work in his study—makes this a definitive demonstration of the ideal of the room in architecture. As Clark said of one of the rooms of his design, "It's interesting how place and purpose often conspire to make a room." For 50 years, with a combination of quiet modesty and obstinate rigor, WG Clark has made architecture that realized these ideals of the room, the land, and the place they can make together.

REPLACEMENT

Architecture, whether as a town or a building, is the reconciliation of ourselves with the natural land. At the necessary juncture of culture and place, architecture seeks not only the minimal ruin of landscape, but something more difficult: a replacement of what is lost with something that atones for the loss. In the best architecture this replacement is through an intensification of the place, where it emerges no worse for human intervention, where culture's shaping of the land to specific use results in a heightening of beauty and presence. In these places we seem worthy of existence.

We don't know why we are here on this Earth. We do know, from the most primitive to the most sophisticated among us, that our presence is probably harmful, an imposition. This knowledge makes us want to assuage the fouling aspects of our existence in order to simply be more at ease with our occupation. We want to belong rather than only use. Sick at killing the cow, yet having to eat, we make rules of propriety and economy governing the slaughter: we must eat the whole cow; we may not kill extra cows; we may never take pleasure in the kill. In a bare existence, economy is necessary for survival. But it is also, in any existence, an ethical act that regrets the taking, imposing itself as a respectful, if insufficient, act of atonement.

In settlement, we are only satisfied when we see evidence of the necessity to occupy. We are pleased by a settlement based on cultivation, where at least to our minds we offer the farm as an assuagement of the lost forest. We are also pleased by deference to the natural land, to the places we refuse to change, the places we save from ourselves. We vacation in those places where we have either left the Earth alone or have engaged it in a way that is satisfying, where there are the fewest needless and senseless acts to represent our being. In our towns and our buildings we search for deference and reverence. We want civilization to be a good thing. We want our artifacts and habitats to become part of the place and to substantiate our wish to belong. We want our things, like those of the civilizations we admire, to form an allegiance with the land so strong that our existence becomes an act of adoration, not an act of ruin. We are only happy where this occurs, where we have managed to make something good to replace what we have taken. Always, we must start from that initial, crucial, puzzling recognition: that we are seeking justification through deference – and, failing that, through economy and respectful use. That is why farms, barns, and silos always seem appropriate and beautiful. That is why we like pig-pens and deplore theme parks, because it is not necessary that buildings be beautiful, but it is necessary that they be necessary.

There was a water mill near my hometown. It was a tall timber structure raised on a stone and concrete base that held the water wheel and extended to form the dam. One did not regret it being there because it made more than itself; it made a millpond and a waterfall, creating at once stillness and velocity; it made reflection and sound and mist. There was an unforgettable alliance of woodland to pond to dam to abutment to building. It was not a building simply imposed upon a place; it became the place, and thereby deserved its being – an elegant offering paid for the use of a stream. Its sureness made other buildings appear to be lost and haphazard.

I cannot convince myself that settlement, even the most thoughtful, the most beautiful, is better than wilderness. Even the mill is not better than no mill; but the mill is necessary for our existence, and therefore worthwhile. It is an image that endures – rare proof that use of the Earth need not be ugly or destructive, and that architecture can be the ameliorative act by which, in thoughtfulness and carefulness, we counter the destruction of construction. Nothing else is architecture; all the rest is merely building.

The American landscape is being sacrificed to building. The result is dismal, adding up to nothing satisfying or significant except as an accurate self-portrait of our cultural and ethical dissolution. The condition is one that we all see and feel every day, one that we abhor yet perpetuate. The senseless spread of profit-motivated building has none of the good characteristics of settlement. It looks more like a carnival designed to be moved and put up anywhere. The comparison becomes more apt with the realization that most of the things built are unnecessary. Settlement implies benign and sympathetic occupation, the selection of a favored place, and the engagement of that place to meaningful use: settlement is the establishment of home. Our growth is the opposite of settlement. We have forgotten the rule that the use of a place must not be separate from abiding in it.

And it is not surprising that a culture such as ours, preoccupied with the notion of a Heaven hereafter, would not respect its land. How can Eden be properly cared for if it has been abandoned for a deferred Paradise for which the Earth is a mere staging area? When a land is removed from worship, it is no wonder that conscience regarding the use of it is profoundly deficient. We have no sacred places. We have no Delphi. Where there was once spirit, the Serpent Mound or in the kiva, there is now only curiosity and the haunting relics of Earthbound reverence.

Nor is it surprising that a culture, which has traditionally thought of the rural as good and the urban as bad, would insist on populating the former until it is no longer there. We fail to realize that cities and towns by their conciseness are great acts of conservation and deference, and that they alone offer any hope for protection of the land. We fail to realize that good cities have distinct edges, and the placement of cities, their allegiance to the natural setting, is as important as that of the built form. Towns, like the mill, must engage the land in a way to improve and heighten the natural beauty of its setting; a town must engage its place and make it better.

The sickness of the heart that we all feel when development spreads from every town into the countryside, is recognition that it is not only lost nature, but also lost settlement. What home have we made? Given a new world, we have let the land degenerate into real estate and architecture into style. The implication is frightening, that we don't belong here, that we are no longer of the place, but merely on it: a lost colony in a paradise lost.

Yet that very sickness of heart and its universality is hopeful; it is what has always spurred reassessment. When we build, we ought not to ignore it but let it guide our efforts. We ought to keep before us the images of settlements that have successfully established a reverence for place necessary to the making of a collective home.

I like to read Thoreau's *Walden*, especially the chapter titled "Economy" about his thoughtful struggle with the matter of building. At first he just seems to be carefully building his small house. His considerations seem failed, doomed, artificially precious out there in the woods on that pond. But then I see that what he builds is not just spare and conservative, but stunningly rich, imbued with luxurious and profound images. He is not a dirt-dauber, locked into the immutable pattern of his genes, but a sentient, worried, thoughtful being, determined to be at one with his place and respecting it with his presence, drawing analogies to nature, to the elements, and to his curious earthly existence with every act of building, looking not for a way out of the forest, but for a way to stay there with grace. All of which is easy for the dauber, and not too hard for primitive human mind, but extraordinarily difficult for Thoreau's great intelligence.

I think it will always be difficult to build; it should be difficult. We cannot always succeed and sometimes will not even recognize our own success or failure. But we want to stay with grace, and therefore do what we can, whether we are making a tiny house in the woods or a great city. Our gradual understanding is that we are not true colonists, with our home elsewhere. Our home is here, and what we build will be its parts. It is worth the effort to try to build well.

THREE PLACES

It is not only buildings that interest us: there is something of greater importance, which, through them, we are trying to reach. It has to do with the joining of structure and land, and how this can and should result in a sureness of place that is made all the stronger by the union.

The most important quality of architecture is the way it relates to, signifies and dignifies a place on the earth. This is why most of the architecture we most admire, be it the product of individuals or of civilizations, is that which has been built with a sense of allegiance to the land.

Architecture is a disturbing art; it destroys places. Construction sites always have the scent of sacrifice, barely masked by the exciting and hopeful smell of building. It is our job to assuage the sacrifice and make building an act of respect for and adoration of the place.

In our work, we concentrate on trying to achieve this difficult objective, in the hope that our buildings will become part of their place, rather than just being sited on it, and will gain strength and meaning from the alliance.

We admire the mill and its dam for making a pond, an act which transforms a mere building into an engagement with the land, thereby improving on what was existing. We notice how a bridge abutment can be seen as the shaping of land to specific duty, an intensification of a natural place as it accepts an alien function. We also envy the insubstantial beauty of thin shacks and sheds, which seem so casually, effortlessly, at home along dirt roads. And we worry about how to make places as genuine and as profound as these.

Every site contains three places: the physical place with its earth, sunlight, and rain; a cultural place, the locus of the traditions of human intervention; and a spiritual place, a place of evocation that stirs our imagination and reminds us of far away, ancient images and analogs.

We use these different aspects of a place when we design a building. Using the physical place we try to draw the landscape into the composition, with the architecture, or rather the building, playing a part, but only a part. Sometimes this is achieved by contrasting the building and its setting, but often we merge the two, even trying to blur the distinction between them to make them the same. We use the second, cultural place as a source of patterns of habitation and associated architectural traditions, so that there may be some sympathy of existence between neighbors, as well as times. We look to the spiritual or evocative place for images that strengthen the architecture, making it memorable in the landscape.

LOST COLONY

I can only imagine what it must be like to be an architect in a country where the built form allies itself with and springs from ancient traditions and meanings that are understood and shared by everyone; where the language of the architect and the builder is the same; where buildings are of the place, and not just on it in some obscure and alien reference. Our architecture, like our culture, was transplanted and imposed upon the land. Any colonial architecture is odd, representing traditions of another land, with hybrid adaptations to the conditions of the new place. Ours is particularly rich because of the many cultures represented, but this richness nevertheless lacks a profound sense of belonging. So "traditional" American architecture has never stirred me. It is not that I don't find it interesting or beautiful, nor that I think it is not a legitimate representation of our cultural past. It is just that I am more moved by things that have sprung from this land, forms subjected to an early sense of economy, inventiveness, and questioning. We transcended colonialism. Our independence established a real home and that home was founded on more than just a separation: it was founded on ideals. So, naturally, one looks for a true indigenous expression of these ideals, one rooted in traditions of simplicity and practicality, at home in our beautiful, stolen place.

Modern architecture has always seemed to come close to being this: as if our own Declaration made its way into architecture. Those political ideals of our early country were born of the same spirit of Enlightenment that generated modern architecture, whose concern for plainness, honesty of expression, and modesty appealed to American sensibilities. It's as if we invented it to replace an unnecessary and obnoxious posture, not so unlike learning to shoot from behind trees. While I find this exciting and hopeful, it is disturbing that the imported models of modernism, no matter how based on principles that would seemingly be at home here, are as alien to our land as the traditional models. Modernism's insistence on universality ironically made buildings for nowhere, which seem un-rooted with respect to real place, ungrounded in terms of form, tentative, and ill-at-ease in our land.

It would seem that we are in a hopeless position, that our architecture has not developed a legitimate character as strong and sure as that early ideal that we think of as young America. We have failed to establish a respectful settlement. We have become so intent on development that we have ignored the more serious objective of becoming an inspiring civilization. We are lost.

Of course we are still only beginning. We are still basically an uncivilized nomadic culture, moving about, using the place and its resources, seeking momentary transportable wealth and satisfaction here and there, staying in no one place long enough to develop either an understanding of it or a veneration for it. It will take thousands of years to come to terms with this land and for our architecture to assimilate its character and its ideals. It is hopeful to realize that the real traditions are yet to come, that the ones we have been working with were provisions for the voyage. We need to learn to plant corn. We are still a young country in search of a native form. The confusion and disarray that appear to be lost-ness and misadventure may simply be that initial awkwardness and stridency that always accompanies new things. I prefer to think that maybe we are not bereft of genuine architecture, but merely fumbling around at the beginning of one.

The American architecture that I admire is almost invariably that which has sprung naturally from local conditions and customs. It is remarkable that these buildings are more often generated by poverty than by wealth; thin shacks and sheds with an insubstantial beauty that seems so casually, naturally, and effortlessly at home. It is wonderfully troubling that the more naive and innocent these buildings are of formal architecture, the more profoundly suitable they seem to our land. More troubling still is the recognition that those buildings that seem to be the most beautifully and surely placed were done so with more regard to economy and practicality than to any notion of landscape design. This is because their placement was based on a more profound sense of appropriateness and fit than formal architectural language can address.

Admired too is another kind of American architecture which has a more substantial beauty that is heavy and of the earth itself, blurring the distinction between place and building, between landscape and architecture: the earthen architecture of Mesa Verde and Pueblo Bonito, emplacements and defenses as well as towns. At ancient structures, fortifications and so forth, where the earth has been shaped to specific duty, it is hard to tell where the earth stops and the building begins, and there is nothing separating the place and its occupation. In ruins, where the intended use of the building has departed and the building merges with the land, it is often unclear whether the structure is landscape or architecture. Conditions are reversed and a long departed roof allows sunlight and rain inside. Room becomes garden. These places in their earth-bound, reductive condition are satisfying because they offer us a primitiveness we need, one not found in our transplanted formal models.

We have been asked to comment on our theory and methodology. I am not aware that we have either. I don't believe that either is necessary. We do know that all building involves the use of a place and that all architecture, regardless of program or cost, must become that place. The things that we admire most accomplish this either through an architecture of innocence or through an architecture of emplacement which seeks to make the building and the place one thing. This makes the job quite difficult since it is probably impossible for an architect to achieve innocence, and just as unlikely that one can achieve that profound engagement of building and land, which was so maddeningly easy for primitive man. But I think we all crave an ancientness that we never had and an innocence that we have lost, desperately, if futilely, seeking their realization.

LESSONS OF CONSTRAINTS

Charleston, South Carolina affords two important lessons about architectural design as related to a specific place. One is cultural, the other natural.

Charleston is a place of strongly rooted building traditions, consistent topology of forms, and a determination to preserve its historic appearance. Building design has to relate not only to the established and beloved formal context, but also to a very narrow tolerance of the new. This protection offers a severe constraint on the modernism to which we were both politically and aesthetically devoted. How to add to a beautiful place respectfully and critically. And how to prove that modern did not mean alien. This resulted in intense study regarding how to make new things fit, to belong. It meant that it was necessary to learn the history of the city to know its underlying principles of design: order, proportions, textures, materials, details, responses to climate, and, of course, light. Only then could new work be infused with sympathetic character and sensibilities without simply aping old styles. Our modern buildings sought to explore the characteristics inherent in the place, both natural and cultural, in search of a critical fit. Fit: not stylistic reference, but a reverence for the qualities that distinguish the Low Country as a place. Lesson one involved respecting a place.

Lesson two was related not so much to formal design as it was to construction. Despite a calm, idyllic appearance, Charleston is a very difficult place in which to build. It has poor soil, earthquakes, hurricanes, salt air, harsh sun, and Formosan termites. Almost nothing is built without careful soil analysis (pilings can be a hundred feet long); windstorms destroy buildings; it is the second worst seismic zone in the country. Coastal salt air destroys normal hardware in weeks; the sun eats finishes; and the termites eat the wood. This is not the place for amateur, negligent builders. Nor is it the place for normal modern Minimalist detailing. But it is a place for young architects to learn respect for nature, and for what it means to build.

What valuable lessons: the constraints of both a stubborn Culture and a stubborn Nature, to be learned from in the effort to prove that a modern building could belong to its place.

AFTERTHOUGHTS

In retrospect, the relative sparseness of commissions, as well as the patience of good clients, has allowed us the time to question designs and change them. Multiple studies of projects became the normal process of design, yielding time to reconsider, criticize, and honor afterthoughts. In fact, appraisal and reappraisal became the necessary and constant part of every project. It happened in the day-to-day work in the form of debate and argument regarding everything from a detail to a scheme. It also happened near the completion of the project when, for the first time, enough work was done and details considered to make it possible to judge whether elegance and economy had been achieved. Or, failing that, whether a conceptual flaw had been revealed by the tests of resolution and realization: like details not quite meshing; the plan and section in disagreement; systems in conflict; the design simply doesn't sing. This is the dreaded condition when the parts of the building revolt and conspire to say that they are not pleased with themselves or with one another. This is a good thing; this is a signal, not a failure.

All buildings are difficult to resolve, but there is a difference between normal difficulty and the kind that results from a flaw in thinking, which results in a bad scheme. So much of design is the discernment between the merely difficult and the wrong, and a primary lesson is to not dread, but be curious about and appreciative of those things that won't satisfactorily resolve. These are the canaries of mines that tell you to run. They are critical information.

It takes awhile, maybe years, to fully realize that design does not proceed in a neat linear path from idea to resolution. In truth, it is a much messier democratic operation wherein every part must be considered from the start and constantly consulted throughout the process. So, as frustrating and expensive as it is to rethink a design, few things are as exhilarating as beginning over with the hard-earned sense of the right direction. Design, after all, is not about determination alone, it is about evolution. As valuable as instinct is, determination usually happens in the early, uninformed hours of design. It is often based on past thoughts and successes, and is, therefore, limited. The evolution of these early thoughts, intentions, through many trials is where the real design is, when the shy idea, like a sand crab, can be coaxed and dislodged from its safe hole.

WG Clark is an Architect of beauty so rare in our bloated commercial world today. The beauty of the site, scale, material, and detail all merge in the serene proportions of his architecture.

Is beauty important? Without it what do we have?

I became aware of the work of WG Clark when he won first place in the 1983 New Orleans Museum of Art competition, which I participated in. I remember our hard work on the competition in a hot New York City August when I was sleeping above my door on a lofted plywood shelf. The ease of WG's winning design struck me.

The next inspired encounter came when I saw the publication of his 1985 Middleton Inn. The precision of his design stood out against a time when architecture was littered with post-modern kitsch. WG discovered his own, straightforward language to express materials and shape space.

Later, I learned he has worked for Venturi … so we shared points of rejection. Instead of complexity and contradiction, we both strive for clarity and simplicity.

If I remember correctly, I visited the Clark House with WG in 1996 when I was working on a scheme for the addition to the University of Virginia School of Architecture (which was rejected by the board of visitors). I loved the cubic purity of this house and clean expression of concrete with glass blocks.

Here, as Kenneth Frampton teaches, the tectonic becomes the poetic utterance of a house. Now, looking at WG's body of work. I feel he remains true to the core aim of architecture – a poetic utterance in landscape.

New York, New York
9/18/18

would like to try to thank the people who helped make this book possible. The first would certainly be the author, Robert McCarter, who has written about the most important modern architects. That he would choose to write about my marginal, to say the least, practice is an honor dear, and most likely undeserved.

I would like to thank Kim Tanzer, then dean of the School of Architecture, for promoting this book, and Ila Berman, current dean, for supporting its publication. Charles Menefee, my former partner, with whom I now teach, was a significant contributor to much of the work. Yale Perspecta once asked me to describe my "design methodology," and, hating the term, I replied something to the effect that it was Charlie and me screaming ugly words about our work until it improved so that no bad words were needed. To all of our clients over the years, thank you for your trust. Thank you for your remarkable patience, patience that allowed time for rethinking and, usually, the multiple iterations of schemes. During the course of one's work there are people who make a huge difference. Charles Duell, owner of Middleton Place, is one of those. He had the courage to entrust me with the design of Middleton Inn in the very beginning. He had studied with Vincent Scully at Yale, and was a truly enlightened patron of architecture. I found this trust and courage again in Karen van Lengen, dean of Architecture at UVA when the Campbell Hall Addition was first considered. She reversed long-standing university stricture against hiring faculty for the design of buildings here. This was a brave fight on her part, which allowed for the new review building to be built. Special thanks to Tashana Starks, Silvi Stefi, and Joshua Stastny for their work in transferring images and text to the author.

—WG Clark, Charlottesville, Virginia

I would like to begin, and end, my acknowledgements by thanking WG Clark, whose work has been an inspiration not only for myself, and the architects of my generation, but for many generations of architecture students. Truth be told, this is the second time I have proposed to author a book on WG Clark's work. The first attempt took place at dinner in Charlottesville, following a day spent participating on the retiring Professor Mario Valmarana's last studio jury at the University of Virginia School of Architecture in spring 2000. I had asked WG if just the two of us could have dinner that evening, as I wanted to make a proposal to him. I told him in advance that there were only two responses to my proposal that would be acceptable to me: "Yes" or "There is already one being done." I then proposed that I would author a book on his exceptional work, to which WG replied that, in fact, there was a book about to be published, authored by Richard Jensen and published by Princeton Architectural Press.

I would therefore like to begin by acknowledging the support and kind assistance of Richard Jensen, author of the beautiful book, *Clark and Menefee*, published in 2000. I would also like to thank former University of Virginia Architecture Dean Kim Tanzer, a colleague of many years at the University of Florida before she accepted the deanship at Virginia, who sponsored and supported my work on the book. Her support included but was not limited to sponsoring several critically important trips to Charlottesville, during which I was able to spend long hours talking with WG, visiting his nearby buildings, as well as participating in design juries and giving lectures at the school. I would also like to thank Joshua Stastny for redrawing the plans and sections of the recent projects, Silvi Stefi for assembling the catalog of project materials for my use, and to Tashana Starks, whose assistance in the last few months of work on the book has been of critical importance. I would also like to thank University of Virginia School of Architecture Dean Ila Berman for her support of this publication. I would also like to thank Gordon Goff and Jake Anderson of ORO Editions and AR+D Publishing, who have made it possible for this "labor of love" to become a reality. I would also like to thank the architects and landscape architects who, because of their admiration and respect for the architecture of WG Clark, have generously supported the publication of this book.

Finally, I would like to again acknowledge WG Clark for making some of the most tectonically resolved, spatially articulated and experientially enriching works of architecture it has ever been my privilege to visit and to inhabit. During my 16 years as Director and Professor at the University of Florida's School of Architecture I had the pleasure of participating in the annual field trip by the almost 100 third-year architecture students to Charleston, where the highlight of the trip for the students was always the visit to WG Clark's Middleton Inn. The inspiring lessons learned by the students, and aspirations kindled in them by this great building, make these annual visits some of the most meaningful events in my entire 32-year teaching career. In ways similar to the students, but also as a practicing architect, I was profoundly moved and inspired by my first visit to Middleton Inn, which took place in late 1991. I would like to close by quoting from the letter I wrote to WG Clark, which was written on Middleton Inn stationery and dated 28 December 1991:

"I am writing to tell you how very impressed I am with your Middleton Inn. I stayed a night at the Inn both going and coming during my travels over the winter holidays, and I feel compelled to tell you that I believe it is the best piece of architecture built in the US in the last 15 years – since the death of Louis Kahn. Indeed, it reminds me in its massing and its detailing of Kahn's work, and it also recalls the Usonian houses of Wright. I can think of no higher compliments I might be able to pay you and your work.

"I have never felt moved to write to another architect before, which is perhaps an indication of how hard it is for us to compliment the work of others, but this profession is so very difficult that we should acknowledge the successes of our fellows when we are able. But it is also true that I have rarely been inspired by a building designed by a living architect to the degree that I was by your Middleton Inn. Well done!"

—Robert McCarter, St. Louis, Missouri

All illustrations and drawings furnished by the offices of WG Clark,
with specific photography credits noted below:

Front cover photograph, Scott Smith
Back cover photograph, Back cover photograph, Richard Jensen

Jack Alterman: 21, 28 top
Bill Clark: 55, 57
Tom Crane: 19, 29, 31, 32, 33, 34, 35 top
Richard Jensen: 9 left, 30, 35, 74 bottom right, 77 bottom left, 86 bottom, 87 bottom,
101, 106 bottom, 107 lower, 111 left, 115, 117, 118 lower, 119
Mick Hales: 43, 45, 46, 48, 49
Timothy Hursley / The Arkansas Office: 65, 66, 67, 69, 73, 74 left and top right, 75, 76,
77 top left and right, 82, 83, 84, 85, 86 top, 87 top, 88-89, 90 top, 91
John Moore: 118 top
Undine Pröhl: 93, 95, 97, 98, 99
Francis Humphreys Roosevelt: 39, 41
Jim Rounsevell: 64
Scott Smith: 105, 106 top, 107 top, 108, 109, 110, 111 right, 149, 154 top, 155, 156, 157,
158, 159, 174, 177, 179, 180, 181, 182, 183, 185, 188, 189, 190-191, 192, 193, 194, 195,
197, 206-207, 208, 209, 210, 211, 213, 223, 224, 225, 226, 227, 228-229
Virginia State Archives: 9 right

Place Matters

1　WG Clark, "Three Places."
2　WG Clark, "Replacement."
3　 WG Clark, from correspondence with the author, spring 2018.
4　William Curtis, *Modern Architecture Since 1900* (London: Phaidon Press, 1982), 237.
5　WG Clark, from correspondence with the author, spring 2018.
6　WG Clark, from correspondence with the author, spring 2018.
7　WG Clark, from correspondence with the author, spring 2018.
8　WG Clark, from correspondence with the author, spring 2018.
9　WG Clark, from correspondence with the author, spring 2018.
10　WG Clark, from correspondence with the author, spring 2018.
11　WG Clark, from correspondence with the author, spring 2018.
12　WG Clark, "Lessons of Constraints."
13　WG Clark, "Lessons of Constraints."
14　WG Clark, "Lessons of Constraints."
15　WG Clark, from correspondence with the author, spring 2018.
16　WG Clark, "Lessons of Constraints."
17　The term "critical regionalism" was coined by Liane Lefaivre and Alexander Tzonis in 1981, "The Grid and the Pathway," in *Architecture in Greece*, no. 5, 1981. The concept was expanded and deepened in the writings of Kenneth Frampton, beginning in 1983, "Prospects for a Critical Regionalism," *Perspecta* 20, 1983.
18　Lewis Mumford, *The South in Architecture* (New York: Harcourt, Brace and Co., 1941), 17.
19　Mumford, *The South in Architecture*, 13, 16.
20　Mumford, *The South in Architecture*, 22, 26.
21　Mumford, *The South in Architecture*, 30–32.
22　Clark, "9 Price's Alley, Charleston, SC," office text.
23　Clark, "The Charleston Museum Competition," office text.

Middleton Inn

1　WG Clark, "Three Places."
2　Louis Kahn, "On Philosophical Horizons," Alessandra Latour, ed., *Louis I. Kahn: Writings, Lectures, Interviews* (New York: Rizzoli, 1991), 101.
3　Louis Kahn, "Form and Design," 1961, Latour, op. cit., 116.
4　WG Clark, "Middleton Inn," office text.
5　WG Clark, "Middleton Inn," office text.
6　WG Clark, "Middleton Inn," office text.
7　WG Clark, "Middleton Inn," office text.
8　WG Clark, "Middleton Inn," office text.
9　Clark and Menefee, "On Rigour," R. Burdett and W. Wang, eds., *9H, On Rigour* (Cambridge: MIT Press, 1989), 105.
10　WG Clark, lecture on 4 March 2014, University of Virginia.

New Orleans Museum of Art

1　WG Clark, "Competitions," in R. Jensen, *Clark and Menefee* (New York: Princeton Architectural Press, 2000), 35.
2　WG Clark, "The New Orleans Museum of Art Competition," office text.
3　WG Clark, "The New Orleans Museum of Art Competition," office text.
4　WG Clark, lecture at University of Virginia, 2011.
5　Competition jury, quoted in "The New Orleans Museum of Art Competition" (Clark and Menefee office document).
6　WG Clark, "Competitions," in R. Jensen, *Clark and Menefee*, op. cit., 35.

Reid House

1　Clark and Menefee, "On Rigour," R. Burdett and W. Wang, eds., *9H, On Rigour* (Cambridge: MIT Press, 1989), 105.
2　Kahn, "Toward a Plan for Midtown Philadelphia," 1953, Latour, *Louis. I. Kahn: Writings, Lectures, Interviews*, op. cit., 45–46.

Arizona History Museum

1　WG Clark, "Arizona History Museum," in R. Jensen, *Clark and Menefee* (New York: Princeton Architectural Press, 2000), 51.
2　WG Clark, "The Arizona Museum Competition," office text.

Charleston Bus Stop

1　WG Clark, "Charleston Bus Stop," in R. Jensen, *Clark and Menefee* (New York: Princeton Architectural Press, 2000), 165.
2　The term coined by Kenneth Frampton, *Studies in Tectonic Culture: The Poetics of Construction in Nineteenth and Twentieth Century Architecture* (Cambridge: MIT Press, 1996).

South Carolina Aquarium

1　WG Clark, "South Carolina Marine Science Museum Competition," office text.
2　WG Clark, "The South Carolina Aquarium," office text.

Croffead House

1　It is worth noting that the cubic dimension of 32 feet, a bit less than 10 meters, was a favored dimension for interior spaces for both Frank Lloyd Wright in Unity Temple (1908) and Louis Kahn in Exeter Library (1972).
2　Wilfried Wang, "Places Transcending Time," Richard Jensen, *Clark and Menefee* (New York: Princeton Architectural Press, 2000), 22.

Lucy Daniels Foundation and Preschool

1   Kahn, "On Form and Design," Latour, op. cit., p. 105.

Menefee Mountain House

1   Clark and Menefee, "Mountain House," office text.
2   Again, as in the Croffead House, this detail was likely inspired by Kahn's Esherick House.

Clark House

1   This term has been used by Wendell Burnette to describe the degree to which the dimensions of construction materials in the US are determined by the 4 x 8-foot plywood sheet.
2   WG Clark, "Clark House," Jensen, ed., *Clark and Menefee,* op. cit., 123.

National Association of Realtors Headquarters Competition

1   WG Clark, "National Association of Realtors Competition" presentation boards.

South Eastern Center for Contemporary Art

1   WG Clark, "SECCA Habitat for Humanity Competition," office text.
2   Louis Kahn, "The Room, the Street, and Human Agreement" (1971), Robert McCarter, *Louis I. Kahn* (London: Phaidon Press, 2005), 480–482.

Sheldon Retreat

1   WG Clark, lecture at the University of Virginia, 2011.
2   WG Clark, letter to the client for the Sheldon Retreat, 29 July 2004.

Mepkin Abbey

1   Father Stan Gumula, quoted in Stephen Hiltner, "Hearts Are Willing, but Their Numbers Are Dwindling," *The New York Times,* 21 March 2018, A11.
2   Ibid.

Campbell Hall East Addition

1   WG Clark, from correspondence with the author, spring 2018.
2   WG Clark, in a lecture given at University of Virginia in 2011; the American Folk Art Museum opened in 2001, and, in arguably the most appalling act of cultural savagery of recent times, the building was purchased and then demolished by the Museum of Modern Art in 2014.
3   WG Clark, in a lecture given at University of Virginia in 2011.
4   WG Clark, from correspondence with the author, spring 2018.
5   WG Clark, in a lecture given at University of Virginia in 2011.
6   Louis I. Kahn, *What Will Be Has Always Been: The Words of Louis I. Kahn,* ed. Richard Saul Wurman (New York: Rizzoli, 1986), 111.

Thinking and Making

1   WG Clark, "Lost Colony," reprinted in this book.
2   These and all later quotes regarding the seminar on "how to design" are from WG Clark's syllabus outlines and notes, "Thinking and Making," 2014–2018.
3   Eugene-Emmanuel Viollet-le-Duc, *Entretiens sur l'architecture* (1872), English translation, Lectures on Architecture, Volume 1 (New York: Dover, 1987), 187.
4   Alvaro Siza, quoted in Kenneth Frampton, "Poesis and transformation: the architecture of *Alvaro Siza, in Alvaro Siza: Poetic Profession* (New York: Rizzoli, 1986), 12.
5   Gianni Vattimo, quoted in Kenneth Frampton, *Studies in Tectonic Culture* (Cambridge: MIT, 1995), 299.
6   Igor Stravinsky, *Poetics of Music* (Cambridge: Harvard University Press, 1942), 63.
7   Wright, *The Future of Architecture* (New York: Horizon, 1953), 62.
8   WG Clark, "Lessons of Constraints," essay republished in this volume.
9   Kahn, quoted in "Kahn on Beaux-Arts Training," ed. William Jordy, *Architectural Review* 155 (June 1974), 332.
10 Viollet-le-Duc, *Entretiens,* op. cit., 189.

COMPLETE LIST OF PROJECTS

1974   Charleston Museum Competition: Second Prize
        Charleston, SC

1975   9 Price's Alley House
        Charleston, SC

1976   Middleton Place Visitors' Orientation Building (Project)
        Berkeley County, SC

1980   Slotchiver House
        Isle of Palms, SC

1981   Schreck House
        Mt. Pleasant, SC

1977–   Middleton Inn
1985   Berkeley County, SC

1983   New Orleans Museum of Art Competition: First Prize
        New Orleans, LA

1985–   Reid House
1987   John's Island, SC

1986   Miniature Portrait Gallery Gibbes Art Museum
        Charleston, SC

1986   Orvin House Addition/Renovation
        Charleston, SC

1986   Arizona Historical Museum Competition
        Phoenix, AZ

1987–   Charleston Bus Stops
1992   Charleston, SC

1987–   South Carolina Aquarium Competition: First Prize
2000   Charleston, SC

1987   "Chapel" Installation American Craft Museum
        New York, NY

1988   Mulberry Plantation House Renovation
        Berkeley County, SC

1986– Croffead House
1989   Charleston, SC

1988   Simonds House Renovation/Addition
        Charleston, SC

1990– Lucy Daniels Foundation and Preschool
1992   Cary, NC

1990– Mountain House
1993   Zirconia, NC

1991   Adams House Renovation /Addition
        Charleston, SC

1992   Maybank House Addition
        Charleston, SC

1994   Rawle Beach House Renovation
        Isle of Palms, SC

1994– Clark House
1996   Charlottesville, VA

1994– 8 Bedon's Alley Renovation/Addition
1999   Charleston, SC

1998   Taylor/Andrews House Renovation
        Charleston, SC

1998   Fort/Magee House Renovation
        Charlottesville, VA

2000   Colorado House (Project)
        Telluride, CO

2002   National Association of Realtors Competition
        Washington, DC

2003   SECCA Home House Competition: Shared Prize.
        Winston Salem, NC

2003   Palisades Glacier Mountain Hut Competition
        Sierra Nevada, CA

2004   Sheldon Farm Retreat (Project)
        Wadmalaw, SC

2005   Clemson Architecture Center Competition: First Prize.
        Charleston, SC

2001– Beckerdite/Scholley House
2005   James City County, VA

2003– Hillman House
2005   Schuyler, VA

2006   62 Tradd St Renovation (Project)
        Charleston, SC

2005– Cameron Lane Addition
2007   Charlottesville, VA

2004– Campbell Hall Addition
2008   Charlottesville, VA

2008   Bleam House Renovation
        Charlottesville, VA

2007– Les Yeux du Monde Art Gallery
2009   Charlottesville, VA

2009   Boys & Girls Club
        Charlottesville, VA

2005– Mepkin Abbey Entrance Gates
2009   Berkeley County, SC

2009– Mepkin Abbey Guest House and Father Francis Kline
2013   Memorial Chapel
        Berkeley County, SC
        (With Joshua Stastny Architect)

CONSULTANTS AND ASSOCIATES

Dian Boone Interior Design
Gregg Bleam Landscape Architect
John Moore, 4SE INC. Structural Engineers
Charles Yeager, Metal Fabrications
SMBW Architects
John Ireland, Fox + Associates Structural Engineers
Steve Barber, DMWPV Structural Engineers
2RW Consulting Engineers
Mark Schuyler, Lighting Engineer
Shoolbred Engineers Incorporated
Shelia Wertimer, Landscape Architect
Rosser White Hobbs Davison McClellan & Kelly
Soil Consultants, Incorporated
Charleston Architectural Group
Engineering Technology Incorporated
Judith Morrill Hanes, Artist
Eskew Vogt Salvato & Filson Architects
Blum Engineering
Lyons/Zaremba
Coe Lee Robinson Roesch Exhibit Designer
Frank Harmon, Architect
William Riesberg, Architect
Dennis Hoyle & Associates
Engineering, Surveying, & Planning, Incorporated
Dennis Moller
Nelson-Bryd Landscape Architects

OFFICE PERSONNEL

Azadeh Rashidi
Joshua Stastny
John Quale
Wendy Redfield
Nathan Petty
Maynard Ball
Daniel Stuver
Annaliese Altenbach
William Vukovich
Frances Humphreys Roosevelt
Robert Amerman
Jeffrey Greene
Dabney Staub
Francisco Gomes
Allison Wierman
James Rounsevell
James Duxbury
Joan Baxter
Terry Buckman
Schaeffer Somers
Joann Im

BUILDERS

Peter Johnson Builders
Hightower Construction
Rob Collins
William Doggett
Donley's Construction
Stier, Kent + Canady
W.R. Hunt Construction Company
Clancy + Theys Construction
Barry Tetrault
Daly + Sawyer
Alloy
Richard Marks Restoration
Ace Contracting

Croffead House:
National Honor Award, American Institute of Architects, 1992.
Record Houses, *Architectural Record,* 1990.

Reid House:
National Honor Award, American Institute of Architects, 1989.
Record Houses, *Architectural Record*, 1988.

Middleton Inn:
National Honor Award, American Institute of Architects, 1987.
"Emerging Generation in the USA," Exhibit, GA Gallery, Tokyo, 1987.
"Design: The Best of 1986," *Time*, 1987.
"40 Under 40," Architectural League of New York, 1986.

Competitions:
First Prize, Clemson Architecture Center in Charleston, 2005.
Palisade Glacier Mountain Hut Competition, 2003.
First Prize (shared), SECCA Home House Competition, 2003.
National Association of Realtors Competition, 2002.
First Prize, South Carolina Marine Science Museum Competition, 1987.
Arizona Historical Museum Competition, 1985.
First Prize, New Orleans Museum of Art Competition, 1983.
First Prize (shared), Savannah Housing Competition, 1982.
Second Prize, Charleston South Carolina Museum Competition, 1975.

"Savannah Housing Competition," *Architectural Record*, March 1982.

"New Orleans Museum of Art," *Progressive Architecture*, April 1984.

"Ten Architects: New York," *Perspecta* 21 Yale Architectural Journal, 1984.

"Landscape Strategies: The New Orleans Museum of Art," *Princeton Journal: Thematic Studies in Architecture, Vol 1 Landscape*, 1985.

"Middleton Inn," *Progressive Architecture*, May 1986.

"Middleton Inn," *Art Papers*. Architectural Society of Atlanta, July 1986.

"40 Under 40," *Interiors*, September 1986.

"Design: an 'A' List," *Time*, November 10, 1986.

"Art Museum", *Progressive Architecture*, September 1986.

"Design: The Best of 1986," *Time*, January 5, 1987.

"South Carolina Marine Science Museum," *Progressive Architecture*, March 1987.

"Tenth Review of American Architecture," *Architecture Journal of the American Institute of Architects*, May 1987.

"Middleton Inn," *Architectural Digest*, September 1987.

"Case a misura di natura/ Houses that relate to nature," *Abitare*, Milan, Italy, December 1987.

"International Annual Review of Architecture," *Architecture Contemporaire*, Paris, France, 187/1988.

"The Emerging Generation in U.S.A," *GA- Global Architecture*, Tokyo, Japan, Fall 1987.

"Projects of Clark & Menefee Architects," *Werk, Bauen + Wohnen*, Zurich, Switzerland, Spring 1988.

"Reid House," *Architectural Record*, Record Houses 1988, Mid–April 1988.

"USA: Ein klassische Scheune war Vorbild," *Hauser*, Hamburg, Germany, April 1988.

"Beyond Postmodern," *American Craft*, August/ September 1988.

"Reid House," *Nikkei Architecture*, Tokyo, Japan, October 1988.

"Projects of Clark & Menefee," *A+U: Architecture + Urbanism*, Tokyo, Japan, February 1989.

"1989 AIA Honor Awards," *Architecture: Journal of the American Institute of Architects*, May 1989.

WG Clark, "On Rigour," ("Three Places"), 9H No. 8 1989 *On Rigour*, London, England.

The Experimental Tradition, Helen Lipstadt, Ed., *The Architectural League of New York*, Princeton Architectural Press, 1989.

"Croffead House," *Architectural Record*, Record Houses, Mid–April 1990.

"Croffead House," *Metropolitan Home*, July 1990.

"Croffead House," *Hauser*, Hamburg, Germany, January 1991.

WG Clark, "Replacement," *Modulus* 20 University of Virginia, 1991.

18 Houses, Princeton Architectural Press, 1992.

"Critique: The Art of Accommodation, Middleton Inn," *Progressive Architecture*, April 1994.

"Lucy Daniels Foundation and Preschool," *Architecture: Journal of the American Institute of Architects*, July 1994.

"Projektiesittelyjå Clark & Menefee," *Arkkitehti: Finish Architectural Review*, 2/3 1994.

"Ten Who Make a Difference," *Inform*: Journal of the VSAIA, Number 3 1994.

"Greatness by Design," *New York Times Magazine*, March 12, 1995.

"Grau, Aber Keine Graue Maus," *Hauser*, Hamburg, Germany 3/1995.

"Tough as the Wilderness," *Architecture: Journal of the American Institute of Architects*, June 1995.

"Make Way for the Sky," *Inform*: Journal of the VSAIA, Number 1 1996.

Architecture in North America: Since 1960, Little Brown, New York 1996.

"Nei Boschi Del North Carolina," *Case Da Abitare Estate*, Milan, Italy, 1996.

"Domestic Rigour: Three Houses," *The Architectural Review*, London, England, November 1997.

WG Clark, "Lost Colony," *Perspecta 28 – Architects Process Inspiration*, MIT Press, 1997.

American House Now: Contemporary Architectural Directions, Universe, New York, 1997.

"Aree di Rigore," *Capital*, February 1998.

A Field Guide to Contemporary American Architecture, Dutton, New York, 1999.

The New American Cottage: Innovation in Small Scale Residential Architecture, Watson-Guptill, New York, 1999.

Clark & Menefee, Richard Jensen, *Princeton Architectural Press*, New York, 2000.

"Preservation Has a Modern Moment," *The New York Times*, April 2000.

"Architecture With Impact," *The News & Observer*, Raleigh, North Carolina, August 2000.

"On the Boards," *Architecture*, August 2003.

The Home House Project, David J. Brown, The MIT Press, 2004.

"35 Visionaries that Shaped Our City," *Charleston Magazine*, 2010.

Artillery Magazine, Sarah Sargent, Los Angeles, March 2011.

Wunderkammer, Tod Williams and Billie Tsien, Yale University Press, 2013

ACKNOWLEDGEMENT OF SUPPORT FOR BOOK

The author and publisher would like to acknowledge and
thank the following persons and institutions for their support
of the publication of this book:

The University of Virginia School of Architecture
Steve Dumez, Eskew Dumez Ripple Architects
Mark MacInturff, MacInturff Architects
Richard Jensen